HISTORY OF ICELANDIC POETS: 1800-1940

ISLANDICA

AN ANNUAL RELATING TO ICELAND AND THE

FISKE ICELANDIC COLLECTION

IN CORNELL UNIVERSITY LIBRARY

EDITED BY KRISTJÁN KARLSSON

*

VOLUME XXXIV

HISTORY OF ICELANDIC POETS
1800-1940

BY RICHARD BECK

ITHACA, NEW YORK

CORNELL UNIVERSITY PRESS

LONDON: GEOFFREY CUMBERLEGE

OXFORD UNIVERSITY PRESS

COPENHAGEN: EJNAR MUNKSGAARD

REYKJAVÍK: BÓKAVERZLUN SIGFÚSAR EYMUNDSSONAR

1950

History of Icelandic Poets

1800-1940

RICHARD BECK

Professor of Scandinavian Languages and Literatures
University of North Dakota

Cornell University Press

ITHACA, NEW YORK * 1950

PRINTED IN THE UNITED STATES OF AMERICA
BY THE CAYUGA PRESS, ITHACA, NEW YORK

Preface

IN his preface to his *History of Icelandic Prose Writers: 1800–1940*, Dr. Stefán Einarsson has told how I readily undertook to write a parallel survey of the Icelandic poets, feeling as keenly as did he the need of a history of modern Icelandic literature. During our summer at Cornell in 1928, I drafted a preliminary account of the earlier nineteenth-century poets. Later, from time to time, I spent several summer vacations in the Fiske Icelandic Collection at Cornell carrying on my research in the field and I have devoted much other spare time to it in the course of the past twenty years. A number of studies and articles on individual Icelandic poets published in American and Icelandic periodicals, notably *Scandinavian Studies* and *Tímarit Þjóðræknisfélags Íslendinga,* were the by-products of that extensive preparation. Because of pressure of teaching duties and other commitments, the final draft of the manuscript was not, however, completed until the winter and spring of 1949; it was revised and typed during the following summer months.

Books and other special studies bearing on the subject, from J. C. Poestion's *Isländische Dichter der Neuzeit* (1897) to Kristinn E. Andrésson's *Íslenzkar nútímabókmenntir 1918–1948* (1949), were, of course, diligently consulted, although the latter came to hand after the manuscript had virtually all been drafted in its original form. Material was also collected from articles in periodicals and newspapers. The most important sources are referred to either in the text itself in connection with editions of the works of the poets or in the footnotes. The latter bibliographical references are, however, selective and limited to books or articles in periodicals for reasons of space.

To avoid duplication, the poetry of those writers whose work is primarily in prose has been dealt with in Stefán Einarsson's parallel volume, unless some special reason justified its mention here. In common with him, I have also ended my survey with the year 1940, similarly making an exception of poets since deceased, whose careers have been surveyed in full. Bibliographical references have been included up to the date of the completion of the manuscript, as, in almost all cases, they cover works written within the time limits of the volume. The inclusion of individual poets has generally been limited to those whose works had appeared in book form before 1940; in the interest fo fairness and completeness, an exception has been made in the case of a few older Icelandic-American poets.

It would indeed have added interest and value to the book if translations from the works of the poets could have been included, but space did not permit this. Selections from their poetry are to be found in Watson Kirkconnell's *The North American Book of Icelandic Verse* (1930) and *Canadian Overtones* (1935), as well as in the author's *Icelandic Lyrics* (1930) and *Icelandic Poems and Stories* (1943).

Specific acknowledgment of indebtedness is due many scholars and friends. I have found Dr. Sigurður Nordal's studies and articles on the poets especially valuable and stimulating; and I further owe him and his successor, Dr. Steingrímur J. Þorsteinsson, both of the University of Iceland, thanks for helpful suggestions, in particular with respect to the general classification of the poets included. I also wish to thank my friend Dr. Einarsson for his co-operation; the groundwork which he has laid in his parallel volume, not least in the matter of background, is amply recognized by frequent references.

I am indebted to Mr. Kristján Karlsson, Curator of the Fiske Icelandic Collection, for reading my manuscript and making various profitable suggestions, as well as for helpfulness in other ways. I also desire to record my indebtedness to Mrs. Mary Hanson Deason for assistance in preparing the copy for the printer.

I further express my gratitude to the many poets who have sent me books and biographical material, to the Icelandic Althing for making a generous grant toward the publication of the book, and to the publishers concerned for permission to use the quotations included in the text.

Especially do I desire to express my thanks to my old teacher and longtime friend, Dr. Halldór Hermannsson, for his unfailing aid and advice in the preparation of the volume, and to him and the Cornell University Press for publishing it in the *Islandica* series. I also take this opportunity to acknowledge my great indebtedness to his bibliographical and other work in the Icelandic field generally.

Last though by no means least I owe my wife, Bertha Beck, an inestimable debt for her constant encouragement in an undertaking that often must have taxed her patience.

R.B.

University of North Dakota
February, 1950

Contents

HISTORY OF ICELANDIC POETS: 1800-1940

I

The Icelandic Poetical Tradition

VIGOROUS and unbroken to this day, the Icelandic poetical tradition is as old as the nation itself, its roots buried deep in the ancient Germanic and Scandinavian soil. Not only did the Norsemen who settled the country (874–930) bring with them a tradition of heroic poetry; there were several gifted poets among them.

The Eddic poems and the Skaldic or court poetry, together with the Sagas, form the remarkable body of Old Icelandic literature, the finest flower of the heroic spirit and the epic tradition of the Scandinavian north. Known collectively as the *Elder*, or *Poetic*, *Edda*, the Eddic poems are preserved in the priceless thirteenth-century manuscript *Codex Regius* (Konungsbók) in the Royal Library at Copenhagen. The twenty-nine lays making up the collection cover a wide range. They open dramatically with the "Vǫ́luspá" (The Sibyl's Vision), on the origin and ultimate destiny of man and the world; grandeur, sweeping imagination, and masterful form go hand in hand. The "Hávamál" (The Sayings of the High One) tersely expresses the Norse view of life, embodies the distilled and dearly bought wisdom of the race. "Þrymskviða" (The Lay of Thrym), a rollicking ballad on Thor's recovery of his stolen hammer, is notable for its racy humor, narrative excellence, and vivid characterization. Particularly significant is the cycle of heroic poems preserving an older Northern version of the *Nibelungenlied*, remarkable for its descriptive quality, penetrating insight, and vigorous expression of the heroic ideal.

The Eddic poems are composed in an alliterative meter, simple but elevated and impressive, with theme and form generally blending harmoniously. While they appear, broadly speaking, to have been composed between 800 and 1100, they were not written down until later; probably most of them were recorded between 1150 and 1250. Whatever their original home, they have been preserved only in Iceland. They are anonymous, although ingenious conjectures have been made concerning the authorship of some of them.

Side by side with the Eddic poems, from the tenth to the thirteenth century, there flourished in Iceland the Skaldic or court poetry (*dróttkvæði*), a vast literature composed by poets attached to the courts of kings and earls in many lands, lauding their victories, heroic deeds, and magnanimity. The names of a great many of these court poets have been preserved with their complete or fragmentary poems. These men were the masters of a highly developed, difficult poetic technique that involved an intricate, alliterated verse form and a specific poetic diction abounding in metaphorical descriptive terms (*kennings*), presupposing an intimate knowledge of Norse mythology and legends.

Although Eddic and Skaldic poetry sprang from the same soil, the contrast between them is fundamental and striking both in subject matter and metrical form. The Eddic is characterized by a great variety of themes, rich imagination, and freedom in verse form, while the Skaldic is restricted in subject matter, is more prosaic, and places the main emphasis on strict adherence to a rigid and involved metrical system. In view of its very origin as a professional production, it is not surprising that the Skaldic poetry, although impressive in its sonorousness and metrical excellence, suffers from a certain sameness of theme and recurrent phraseology, as well as from a general lack of personal feeling. It has, as a rule, much greater historical and cultural than literary value. The remarkable thing, however, is the fact that several of the skalds triumphed over uninspiring, ordinary themes, and great metrical obstacles to produce poetry of lasting interest and literary merit.

While the first skalds were Norwegian, the Icelanders later monopolized and elaborated the art of Skaldic poetry. The greatest of these Icelandic skalds was Egill Skallagrímsson (900–983), the hero of the famous saga bearing his name, which also preserves his three major poems. All of them, and especially his "Sonatorrek" (Sons' Lament), an elegy commemorating his two sons, reveal his forceful personality and defiant spirit, his robust intellect and poetic genius. He was followed by a long line of highly gifted Icelandic skalds who flourished in the tenth, eleventh, and twelfth centuries, together with a number of lesser lights.

For various reasons, including the impact of new cultural currents flowing in the wake of the Christianization of Iceland and the growing influence of the clergy, the court poetry began to decline in the thirteenth century. Snorri Sturluson (1178–1241), the great Icelandic historian, attempted to stem the tide with his famous *Prose*, or *Younger*, *Edda*. In this *ars poetica*, he brilliantly summarizes and interprets Old Norse mythology and legends, knowledge of which was basic for an understanding of the Skaldic vocabulary. He discusses in detail poetic diction and the principles of Skaldic verse, illustrating his discourse with numerous examples from the works of earlier poets or his own. His *Edda* became for the court poetry "a stronghold and an arsenal, which safeguarded its dominance in Icelandic poetry for centuries to come, in fact, to this day."[1]

The court poems went out of favor at the close of the thirteenth century, as the kings no longer understood or appreciated them. Icelandic poets began assiduously to devote themselves to the writing of poetry on religious themes, in the dignified Eddic meters or more often in the sonorous verse forms of the Skaldic poems, testifying to the vigor and vitality of the time-honored poetic tradition. It was clearly a case of pouring new wine in old bottles, and they served the purpose excellently. Previously, religious poems in that form had been minor, although two merit special mention: the earliest poem remaining of that type, "Geisli" (The Sunbeam), by the priest Einarr Skúlason, the leading court poet of the twelfth century; and, by all odds the most significant, "Sólarljóð" (The Lay of the Sun), by an unknown author, dating about 1200. A vision poem in a resonant alliterative meter, didactic in theme and spirit, it possesses such descriptive power and imaginative quality that it has been referred to as "An Icelandic *Divine Comedy*."

[1] Sigurður Nordal, Introduction to *Íslenzk lestrarbók 1400–1900* (Reykjavík, 1924), p. xvii.

It is indicative of the prominence of religious poetry that the sacred poem "Lilja" (The Lily) by the monk Eysteinn Ásgrímsson (d. 1361) was the most important literary production of the fourteenth century and enthroned him as the outstanding poet of his time. Composed in the sonorous *hrynhenda*, a variety of meter developed from the intricate verse form of the court poetry, this poem of one hundred stanzas, on a Biblical theme, is an eloquent and masterfully constructed intepretation of the prevailing medieval religious teachings. That it is an acknowledged masterpiece is evinced by the Icelandic saying: "All poets wished they had written "Lilja." Poetry of a similar nature continued to flourish abundantly far into the sixteenth century, both in the old verse forms and in new meters of foreign origin.

The second main branch of medieval Icelandic poetry is the dance-songs, southern in origin and common in the twelfth and thirteenth centuries but now lost, except for insignificant fragments. This type was, however, superseded by the *rímur*, which arose in the fourteenth century and remained extremely popular down to the latter part of the nineteenth century. Even to this day they have their admirers. The origin, nature, and purpose of this remarkable phase of Icelandic literature, destined to play such an important part in the cultural life of the nation for centuries, is well described in the following passage:

About 1300 Scandinavian ballads began to find their way to Iceland; they were roughly translated into Icelandic and sung at festival gatherings. The themes of most of those which gained popularity were love and disappointment in love. To Icelandic taste, however, they were too slipshod in form and gradually changed into a new kind of poetry, the *rímur*. Every *ríma* began with a *man-söngur*, or maid-song, the theme being similar to that of the old ditties (dance-songs); then followed the narrative, most frequently based on heroic tales or chivalric romances. The metres gradually became very elaborate and diversified, and the old poetical phraseology, the figurative terms or circumlocution and synonyms, were extensively used. In both these respects they were related to the *dróttkvæði* (poems in court-meter). The *rímur* soon became too long to be sung and danced to, but instead they became the chief evening entertainment in the homes of rich and poor alike. They united most of what amused the popular classes, the historical themes were juicy, bloody battles, deeds of prowess and adventure. The maid-songs, as the name implies, were most frequently love ditties, where the poet with mock sentimentality describes his afflictions and longings. The elaborate metres awakened admiration for the art of the authors, but the listeners themselves had also to show their skill in understanding the figurative terms and what was designedly obscure in these poetical compositions. The *rímur* were most frequently chanted to melodies which at the time were considered beautiful, whatever modern man may think of them. . . . But the popularity of the *rímur* may be partly gathered from the fact that from the period 1350–1600 about 80 *rímur* cycles have been preserved, though some have doubtless been lost.[2]

The basic meter of the *rímur* is the alliterative four-line stanza. The rhyme schemes, however, are so numerous that over two thousand varieties have been recorded, eloquently bespeaking the ingenuity and the metrical preoccupations of the authors. On the other hand, the *rímur* are generally lacking in genuine poetic quality; their significance is primarily cultural and linguistic. Sir William A. Craigie observes: "They had the great value of preserving, throughout all classes of the population, a feeling for language and rhythm, a knowledge of the past, an interest in myth and legend, which helped as much as anything to maintain the continuity of Icelandic literature."[3] Moreover, the *rímur* contributed to Icelandic literature a verse form (*ferskeytt*) corresponding to the modern epigram and flourishing in a highly varied and elaborate form to this day. It has been a favorite and effective vehicle of expression for Icelandic poets, learned and unschooled alike.

The vitality of the native Icelandic literary tradition and continued interest in the court poetry is strikingly revealed in the poem "Háttalykill" (Key to Meters) by Loftur Guttormsson (d. 1432), a series of ninety love songs in as many meters, addressed to his mistress Kristín Oddsdóttir. A leading chieftain and the greatest Icelandic poet of his generation, the author here directly emulated Snorri Sturluson's *Prose Edda* and vigorously championed the national poetical tradition. Others followed in his footsteps and wrote similar cycles traditional in meter and language.

[2] Sigurður Nordal, Introduction to *Bishop Guðbrand's Vísnabók* ("Monumenta. Typographica Islandica" [Copenhagen, 1937]), V, 10–11.

[3] *The Art of Poetry in Iceland* (Oxford, 1937), p. 21.

A very significant poem from the fifteenth century, although vastly different in spirit and form, is the eloquent and deeply felt social satire "Heimsósómi" (A Deplorable World)) by a man known only as Skáld-Sveinn (Sveinn the Poet). Here he bitterly attacks the worldliness, greed, and lawlessness of the upper classes of his day. With it he also set a literary fashion that many poets were to follow in times to come.

The leading poet of the first half of the sixteenth century was the great patriot Jón Arason (1484–1550), the last Catholic bishop of Iceland. Important as his religious poems are, marked by genuine feeling and mastery of form, his secular poems on contemporary themes are even more significant and unusual. A fearless leader who touched the life of his nation at many points, he has a secure place in the cultural and literary history of his country for having brought it its first printing press about 1530.

Of the numerous conventional ballads of foreign origin that circulated widely in Iceland from 1400 to 1600, "Tristrams kvæði" (The Tristram Poem) is an outstanding example because of its gripping theme and haunting, rhythmic beauty. It has elicited admiration and praise from non-Icelandic specialists in medieval literature.

After the Reformation reached Iceland in the sixteenth century, the old Catholic religious poetry began to die out. It was gradually replaced by Lutheran hymns, especially through the vigorous and far-reaching efforts of Bishop Guðbrandur Þorláksson (1542–1627), an untiring champion of Lutheranism and a man of great learning, energy, and wide interests. The preface to his new hymnal (1589), in which he pleaded eloquently for greater poetic excellence in hymn writing, was not only a most timely admonition but a literary document of first importance. His *Vísnabók* (1612), a very significant collection of older and contemporary poetry, religious and edifying in theme, was published to compete with and uproot the secular poetry of the day, not least the popular *rímur* and the dance-songs; it aimed also at improving the prevailing literary taste. The principal contributor was the Reverend Einar Sigurðsson (1539–1626), the leading poet of the Reformation period in Iceland. His poems, often akin in flavor and style to the ballads and other folk poetry, are characterized by mastery of form and fluent language, with an undercurrent of sincere feeling. Despite Bishop Þorláksson's heroic efforts, the *rímur* retained their popularity undiminished, side by side with other secular and sacred poetry and a new type of dance-song (*vikivaki*), which arose early in the sixteenth century and continued in favor down to the end of the eighteenth. The chief literary value of those songs is in their refrains, often both lyrical and beautiful.

The seventeenth century in particular was characterized by a new and rising interest in historical and antiquarian studies, which later were to bear fruit in a general revival of Scandinavian literature. It is not surprising that both the leading poets of the era were men well versed in ancient and historic lore, in whose works the time-honored tradition of Icelandic poetry runs strong. With his inspired *Passíusálmar* (Passion Hymns), which have appeared in over fifty editions and have been cherished by generation after generation of Icelanders down to the present time, the Reverend Hallgrímur Pétursson (1614–1674) established himself not only as the outstanding Icelandic writer of sacred poetry in his day, but also as one of the great Lutheran hymn writers of all time. His equally masterful funeral hymn, "Alt eins og blómstrið eina" (Even As a Little Flower), is still generally sung at Icelandic funerals. His secular poetry also possesses high literary merit and is marked by graphic realism and rare metrical skill. In that field he was, however, equaled and in some respects surpassed by his gifted contemporary the Reverend Stefán Ólafsson (1620–1688), a very prolific and popular poet, who wrote notable religious poems, but excelled in highly realistic descriptions of everyday life, especially in his satires and humorous pieces. Some of his songs have remained popular and a selection from his poems was published in 1948.

Learning and antiquarian interest characterized Páll Vídalín (1667–1727) and the Reverend Gunnar Pálsson (1714–1791), both of whom were poets of note in their day. The former was a master of the quatrain, with a number of pithy and fluent verses to his credit; the latter wrote effectively in the spirit of the Eddic poems—another instance of the strength and vitality of the native poetic tradition.

The most important writer and cultural figure during the middle of the eighteenth century was Eggert Ólafsson (1726–1768), an able poet no less than a distinguished scientist. Deeply influenced by the utilitarianism and the optimism of the Enlightenment, he wrote edifying and inspirational poems, the most notable of which is his *Búnaðarbálkur* (Poems on Farming), eulogizing the blessings of rural life. Although immersed in the history and ancient classical literature of his country, he occupied a still more significant place as the leader in a nationalistic movement of lasting and far-reaching influence. His patriotic poems reveal his deep love of country and strike a new note. In his fervent nationalism, his interest in the past, and his genuine concern for the preservation and the purification of his mother tongue, he became the direct forerunner of the Icelandic Romantic poets of the nineteenth century. They recognized their spiritual kinship and debt to him, and Jónas Hallgrímsson acknowledged it in his masterful poem "Hulduljóð" (The Song of the Fairy).

The leading poet of the latter half of the eighteenth century, indeed the greatest and most gifted poet of the entire period, was the Reverend Jón Þorláksson (1744–1819). His work was both extensive and varied, showing on the one hand, as might be expected, influences from the Enlightenment, and on the other, in a still more marked degree, his deep roots in the cultural soil and traditions of his native land. A brilliant satirist and a master of epigrams, he also wrote noteworthy commemorative and obituary poems and highly regarded hymns, some of which are still included in the Icelandic hymn book. While his original poems are significant because of their literary merit and their influence on later poets, they were far surpassed by his numerous verse translations, notably those of Milton's *Paradise Lost* and of Klopstock's *Messias.* Faithfully and fluently rendered into the elevated verse form of many of the Eddic poems, these translations retain in a surprisingly large measure the flavor and the spirit of the originals. And with them, Jón Þorláksson became the great pioneer in the realm of modern Icelandic translations, enriched his native literature vastly, and paved the way for the poets of the next generation.

A contemporary of his, and a poet who enjoyed a great reputation in his day, was Benedikt Gröndal (the Elder, 1762–1825), whose translation of Pope's *Temple of Fame,* in a time-honored Eddic meter, is fluent and faithful.

While Sveinbjörn Egilsson (1791–1852), the great philologist and lexicographer, is more properly considered with the prose writers of the period, he wrote some poems of merit, even if he did not cultivate his poetic gift to any great extent in the field of original verse. He was unmistakably a transition poet, belonging both to the Enlightenment era and the Romantic Movement and thus, in a sense, bridged the gulf between the two. The Romantic tradition is strong, especially in his translations from the *Odyssey* and the *Iliad.* His prose versions of these are justly considered epoch-making in the history of modern Icelandic prose; and, while his verse rendition of the *Odyssey* in an Eddic meter is inferior to the prose one, it is, nevertheless, a noteworthy piece of work. In the interest of accuracy, it should be added that Sveinbjörn Egilsson did not live to translate into verse more than about three-fourths of the *Odyssey*; his son Benedikt Gröndal the poet completed the translation, which was published by the Icelandic Literature Society in 1853–1854. Sveinbjörn Egilsson's great significance is, however, that he was both the teacher and the forerunner of many of the Romantic poets, the champions of that movement in Iceland all having been his admiring pupils. In them he aroused a greater appreciation of their mother tongue and their literary heritage.

In concluding this brief view of Icelandic poetry from its beginning down to the nineteenth century, let it be emphasized that both the great translators, Jón Þorláksson and Sveinbjörn Egilsson, resorted to the elevated, tested, and time-honored verse form of the Eddic poems when they came to render the works of foreign masters into their native tongue. The unbroken continuity of the Icelandic poetical tradition is here amply revealed. This tradition, as we shall come to see later, is an equally fundamental and unique characteristic of Icelandic poetry down to the present day, in spite of the waves of foreign literary currents that from time to time and in varying strength have reached the shores of Iceland.

II

Romantic Poets

THE nineteenth century, especially after 1830, is a remarkable period in the history of Icelandic literature. It was an era of national awakening generally. That awakening is not least reflected in a richer and more varied literary production than Iceland had possessed for centuries. Without minimizing the fructifying influence of the native literary tradition, in which continued interest now was renewed and strengthened, it is no exaggeration to assert that vitalizing foreign influences also played an important part.

The Romantic Movement is here of first importance. And its influence on Icelandic literature, where its excesses are rarely in evidence, was by and large very wholesome. Its love of beauty developed in the Icelandic poets of the day a greater appreciation of the scenic grandeur of their native land. Similarly, its interest in things old and remote gave to these poets a deeper understanding and a resultant greater love of their national heritage—their language, history, and ancient literature.

This nationalism, the most fundamental characteristic of nineteenth-century Iceland, also stemmed and drew strength from the liberal and progressive political currents flowing from the French Revolution of 1830. This phase of the national awakening, appealing to the spirit of freedom inherent in the national character and stimulated by the proud memories of the Icelandic commonwealth of old, found expression in a continued and increasingly vigorous demand for Icelandic political independence.[1]

[1] The beginnings of Icelandic Romanticism, with all its ramifications, are

1. The pioneer Romantic poet in Iceland and the first great writer of the new and flourishing era in Icelandic letters, which began during the earlier part of the nineteenth century, was BJARNI THORARENSEN.

He was born at Brautarholt in southern Iceland on December 30, 1786, and came of an excellent and prominent family, which included both men of literary interest and ability and leaders in national affairs. His early environment doubtless also exerted a profound and lasting influence upon him. From the age of three he grew up in Fljótshlíð, at Hlíðarendi, the historic home of Gunnar of *Njáls saga* fame. The region abounds in hallowed memories that could not but stir the imagination of a precocious, alert youth. And he paid tribute to the surroundings of his youth in poems destined to live long. Fortunate indeed it was for him, and even more so for Icelandic literature, that he spent his formative years in a district where the scenic beauty of his native land and some of its richest traditions mingle to an uncommon degree.

Belonging to a family of means, Thorarensen early enjoyed educational advantages. Having completed his preparatory course under private tutors, he entered the University of Copenhagen in the spring of 1802 at the early age of fifteen. Here he excelled as a student, receiving his law degree with high honors in 1807. The next four years he spent in the Danish govermental service. He was then appointed Deputy Justice of the Superior Court at Reykjavík, attaining the rank of Justice in 1817. With but a few years' interruption he held that office until 1833, when be became Governor of North and East Iceland, occupying that high position until his death in 1841.[2] It is worthy of note that twice during his years on the Superior Court he served temporarily as Governor General of Iceland. His brilliant educational career and comparatively rapid professional advancement eloquently bespeak his unusual ability. Besides his official duties, he also took considerable interest in public

considered in detail in Stefán Einarsson, *History of Icelandic Prose Writers 1800–1940* ("Islandica," Vols. XXXII–XXXIII [Ithaca, N. Y., 1948]).

[2] Concerning his death and funeral, see Sigurður Guðmundsson, "Við fráfall og útför Bjarna Thorarensens," in the author's collected articles and essays *Heiðnar hugvekjur og mannaminni* (Akureyri, 1946), pp. 5–20.

affairs. Thus he interested himself actively in the re-establishment of the Icelandic parliament, the Althing, favoring the idea that it should assemble at its ancient meeting place, Þingvellir. This choice was, of course, dictated by his interest in the past.

It is, however, Thorarensen the poet, not the distinguished and in many respects successful public man, who occupies a permanent place of honor in the history of his country. He was, as already suggested, a trail blazer, the first of a long line of Icelandic poets writing in the spirit of the Romantic Movement. During his student days in Copenhagen he had come under the quickening influence of this new literary tendency, which was bringing about a revival in Danish letters through the epoch-making lectures of Henrik Steffens and even more through the high-toned poetry of Adam Oehlenschläger. These comrades-in-arms had declared war on the matter-of-fact, utilitarian poetry of the Enlightenment, and its defeat was imminent. Love of country, nature worship, love of beauty, interest in the past—these were some of the fundamental tenets of the new literary era; and those ideals were frequently accompanied by a deepened religious faith, the natural reaction to the rationalism of the Enlightenment.

We know that Thorarensen listened to some of Steffens' lectures; and it is clear that the new movement struck deep roots in him. Besides his law studies at the university, he devoted much time to literature. Of foreign poets Oehlenschläger and Schiller were his favorites, his debt to the former being especially great. Their works, together with the Eddic poems, are reported to have been his cherished subjects of discussion in later years. He translated selections from the Romanticists mentioned. Belonging to an era of transition, the product both of the late eighteenth and early nineteenth century, he also rendered into Icelandic poems by ancient classical authors. References in his original poems and other writings, generally speaking, point to the same sources. His verse forms also reveal him as a poet of transition, bearing the earmarks, especially during his less mature years, of eighteenth-century Icelandic poetry.

Thorarensen is, however, overwhelmingly an adherent of the Romantic Movement; all its main elements referred to above are in evidence in his poems. Fruitfully, it directed him to the life-giving fountains of Old Icelandic literature. Spurred on by the Romantic interest in the past, scholars were now giving increased attention to the unearthing of its buried treasures; and leading Danish poets, particularly Oehlenschläger and N. F. S. Grundtvig, worshipped at the same shrine, finding in the classical literature of Iceland both inspiration and themes worthy of their genius.

Under the impact of such impulses during his sojourn in Copenhagen (1802–1811), when he was still at the impressionable age between sixteen and twenty-five, Thorarensen's nationalism was stimulated and fructified, as his patriotic poems from the period clearly show. His interest in the glorious past of his nation, already awakened by the historic environment of his youth, now received increased vigor and a definite goal. During these years abroad he obviously buried himself deep in the study of Old Icelandic literature, especially the Eddic poems, which more than any other one source have left their mark on his poetry. In this respect he was not, however, by any means an exception. His Icelandic predecessors of the previous century, such as Eggert Ólafsson, Benedikt Gröndal (the Elder), and Jón Þorláksson, and his older contemporaries, had found their model in the Eddic poems, not least as far as metrical form was concerned. The works of Gröndal and Þorláksson, his immediate forerunners, Thorarensen had read in youth; and influence from them is traceable in his works.

Upon his return to Iceland in 1811, Thorarensen, as spokesman of the new ideals of Romanticism, naturally found little favor with the champions of the old order, the Enlightenment. Its high priest was Magnús Stephensen, a cosmopolitan rationalist and humanitarian. He was far removed from the ardent young Romanticist, who was profoundly national and therefore had no sympathy with the unnational tendency of the Enlightenment advocates. Nor could he accept their rationalism, as he was a man of deep and firm faith. Not that Stephensen and Thorarensen waged an open war over their fundamentally differing views; these remained in the background while they clashed over policies and public questions. Thorarensen's championship of his Romantic ideals was passive rather than active, confined for the most part to his poetry. His loyalty to his early convictions remained unshaken, however; he supported his more revolutionary and outspoken fellow Romanticists, the "Fjőlnismenn," when they appeared on the scene in 1835 with their important and influential annual *Fjölnir*, although he could not by any means go all the way with them.

Thorarensen was not a productive writer, no doubt in a considerable degree because he was burdened all his life with the cumbersome duties and details of public office. But his artistic temperament and explosive nature and his emotional life had their effects and likewise account for the upsurge of his creative activity at certain periods in his career.[3]

His poems, consisting of one rather slight volume titled *Kvæði* (Poems), were first published in Copenhagen in 1847 by the Icelandic Literature Society and again, with some additions and an introduction by Einar Hjőrleifsson (Kvaran), the novelist, in 1884. A selection from these, *Úrvalsljóð* (Selected Poems), appeared in Reykjavík in 1934 (second ed., 1945), edited with an introductory essay by Kristján Albertsson.[4] A definitive edition of the poet's works, *Ljóðmæli* (Poems), was published in two volumes in Copenhagen in 1935, with a long introduction and detailed notes by Jón Helgason, the editor. Several of his poems in facsimile from his own manuscripts were included in *Digte af Bjarni Thorarensen og Jónas Hallgrímsson* (Copenhagen, 1938), edited with an introduction by Jón Helgason; and the original edition of Bjarni Thorarensen's poems was reproduced and published in photostatic form in 1945. The quality of his poems more than makes up for their limited quantity; many of them are marked by rare originality in thought and style as well as by high literary excellence.[5]

---

[3] The interesting question of the poet's limited productivity was raised and discussed in a notable address by Sigurður Nordal on the occasion of Thorarensen's 150th anniversary (published in *Skírnir*, CXI [1937], 5–14) and later dealt with in detail by Sigurður Guðmundsson in his lecture "Líðan og ljóðagerð Bjarna Thorarensens á Mőðruvőllum" (published in the collection *Samtíð og saga* [Reykjavík, 1946], III, 59–137.)

[4] Unless otherwise specified, the place of publication is Reykjavík.

[5] Concerning Thorarensen's literary career and works, see also Þorsteinn Gíslason, "Bjarni Thorarensen," *Lögrétta*, XXVII (1932), 47–59; Sigurður Skúlason, "Um Bjarna Thorarensen," *Samtíðin*, II (1935), no. 5, 12–18; no. 6, 18–23; Richard Beck, "Bjarni Thorarensen—Iceland's Pioneer Romanticist," *Scandinavian Studies and Notes*, XV (1938), 71–80.

Characteristically, the earlier editions of Thorarensen's poems opened with a patriotic poem, a veritable hymn of praise to Iceland, "Eldgamla Ísafold," written during the author's sojourn in Copenhagen. It struck so responsive a chord in the hearts of Icelanders at home and abroad that it readily became the Icelandic national song. A well-wrought poem, though not one of Thorarensen's greatest, it contains a skillful word picture of Iceland as contrasted with Denmark and breathes throughout that genuine love of country that is one of the strongest undercurrents in Thorarensen's poetry. The poem is also noteworthy for having popularized the personification of Iceland as a woman. The idea had originated with Eggert Ólafsson and has been elaborated upon by later Icelandic poets, but Thorarensen in this poem was the first to apply to Iceland the cherished designation "Fjallkonan" (The Maid of the Mountain).

His other popular poem on Iceland, "Þú nafnkunna landið" (Land of Renown), is, however, superior to the national song in grandeur, elevation, and boldness of thought. Here occurs one of the most striking and most frequently quoted descriptions of Iceland, concisely and effectively bringing out its contrasts of ice and fire. Here the poet also sounds a ringing challenge to action, reflecting his truly heroic spirit.

A closer look at Thorarensen's nature poems is highly revealing. The ones written about his beloved Fljótshlíð, the historic district where he spent his youth, are excellent illustrations of his approach to such themes and of his poetic tendency generally. Charming and graphic descriptive passages reveal his appreciation of the beauty and uniqueness of external nature. Invariably, however, his interest in the past is so strong that references to the heroes of old, whom he constantly presents as worthy ideals for his countrymen, crowd out the description. Whenever, for instance, he calls to mind the haunts of his happy youth, he recalls them even more vividly as the home of the heroic Gunnar of Hlíðarendi (Lithend) and the scene of his great deeds.

Considering Thorarensen's heroic temperament and his interest in men of heroic mould, it is not surprising that he was most attracted to the sterner side of the Icelandic landscape and climate, to the elemental grandeur of his native land. His pen picture of a volcanic eruption, in a poem otherwise traditional in theme, is an impressive descriptive passage. In a strikingly beautiful poem "Vetur" (Winter), one of his best, he paints a memorable portrait of winter in Iceland, personifying it as an ancient hero in full armor, dashing onward astride his snow-white steed.

Thus Thorarensen's nationalism generally expresses itself in love of the Old Icelandic valor and virtues, which he is untiring in extolling as a challenge to his people, sorely in need of encouragement and renewed self-confidence after centuries of oppression. His kinship to the heroic spirit of his ancestors is further seen in his two martial songs, a rare phenomenon indeed in later Icelandic literature. By far the more notable of these is "Herganga" (Military March), inspired by the famed Old Norse war song "Bjarkamál en fornu," from which whole lines are incorporated almost unchanged. Here the author succeeds admirably in harmonizing subject matter and form. The verse lines are resonant with the measured footbeats of marching men. In short, the poem is a masterpiece of metrical precision no less than a brilliant expression of the heroic spirit.

Although Thorarensen primarily strikes a serious and elevated note in his poetry, it is by no means devoid of humor. This quality, which not infrequently takes the form of biting sarcasm, is found especially in his epigrams. At other times it appears as good-natured banter, as in his whimsical poem "Freyjukettir" (Freyja's Cats), describing the dangers lurking in the paths of those who submit too readily to the lure of the fair sex. This poem may, however, have deeper significance under the surface and be the direct result of a personal experience.

Thorarensen's serious love poems are in an entirely different vein and unquestionably belong among his most unusual and most beautiful productions. They are the very acme of purity and spirituality, ethereal to the extent that the earthly element in human love is virtually absent. Nevertheless, they are not, as might be thought, merely vague sentiment, boneless and bloodless; on the contrary, they vibrate with deep though restrained feeling and fairly glow with rare imagery. This is particularily true of the one most admired, "Sigrúnarljóð" (The Song of Sigrún), in which the poet's spiritual conception of love between man and woman is most forcefully expressed. This unique poem recalls in some respects the famous lay "Vǫ́lsungakviða en forna" of the *Poetic Edda*, a poem also on the theme of love and death, telling of Sigrún's visit to Helgi's burial mound. It may to some extent have served Thorarensen as a starting point, the name of the heroines being especially suggestive; but his poem is not in any considerable degree imitative of the ancient lay.

Down through the centuries obituary poetry has been popular in Iceland and has formed an important branch of Icelandic literature. In Thorarensen's hands this form of expression reached a level that has not been surpassed and very rarely equalled. Such poems of his, at their best, never suffer from the triteness common to that type of verse; they are original and personal; the characterizations are clear-cut and individualized. His intellectual vigor, wealth of imagination, and penetrating psychological insight appear nowhere to better advantage than in his memorial poems. A remarkable one is that on his friend Oddur Hjaltalín, masterfully constructed and fraught with deep thought, both graphic and epigrammatic in its rich imagery and concentration, and universal in theme. The author excels in portraying and interpreting noble-minded and unusual men who refused to follow the beaten path, whose ability was frustrated by hostile social enviornment, but who, nevertheless, unflinchingly faced their tragic fate. His sympathy for these stepchildren of fortune and his keen understanding of their inner lives were rooted in his own bitter experience with misunderstanding and abuse and his own sense of frustration. He was recording the tragedy of his own life, writing his own obituary. Hence, he succeeds so admirably in identifying himself with the subjects of these poems; they are flesh of his flesh and blood of his blood. For example, he knows, whereof he speaks when, in his great obituary poem on Sæmundur Magnússon Hólm, he writes a scathing indictment of a world infested with greed, in which might is right.

In another notable memorial poem, one of his best, he strikingly characterizes and warmly eulogizes Sveinn Pálsson, a man of true greatness and heroic stature but also a tragic figure, especially moving because of his fearlessness and magnanimity in the face of adversity. For manliness, the heroic spirit, is the keynote of Thorarensen's poetry, as it was of his philosophy of life. He repeatedly stresses the ennobling influence of sorrow and misfortune when faced bravely; and, as his poems eloquently reveal, adversity had provided him with a fertile source of inspiration. The following penetrating characterization of his Norse ancestors is equally applicable to him: "Disaster is the ultimate test of human character. Now we may understand why the Teutonic peoples enshrine only failure and defeat; they realized that defeat well met magnifies a man more than any success."[6] Emphasizing the inner life and moral development, Thorarensen was not primarily concerned about the material progress of the Icelandic nation, although he took some interest in such problems and had at heart the material welfare of the people of his gubernatorial district. He knew that his people had nothing to fear from the future if the national character remained sound and strong.[7]

Generally speaking, he was far more interested in the contents of his poetry than in the form, though examples of great technical skill are to be found among his poems. Frequently, however, his verse lacks smoothness and polish, not seldom betraying the fact that he is to some extent still the product of the Enlightenment in Icelandic letters. Fortunately, he wrote many of his poems in the simple, unrhymed verse forms of the *Poetic Edda,* which proved particularily well adapted to his favorite themes. In that way, as in many others, Old Icelandic literature was for him a fountain of living water; nor is it difficult to detect his spiritual kinship with the Eddic poems. His language, in his greatest and noblest poems, such as the elegy on Oddur Hjaltalín, is pure and vigorous, rich in similes and metaphors often taken directly out of the life of the people.

Although some of Thorarensen's contemporaries, especially among the learned and educated men of the day, recognized his greatness as a poet, it remained for later generations to accord him the high place to which he is entitled especially because of the striking origin-

---

[6] Bertha Phillpotts, *Edda and Saga* (London, 1931), p. 137.

[7] His obituary poems, especially the ones on Oddur Hjaltalín and Sveinn Pálsson, are discussed and interpreted in detail and with skill and insight in Sigurður Guðmundsson, "Læknakviður Bjarna Thorarensens," in the collection *Samtíð og saga* (1946), III, 9–58.

ality and vigor, the depth and sweep, of his obituary poems. Even if he did not form a school, he is of first importance in the history of Icelandic letters, as he charted the course that a number of Icelandic poets were to follow, more or less, for years to come. Happily, for him as well as for those who came in his wake, his Romanticism led him chiefly to an increased devotion to the classical literature of his native land and was characterized by restraint of style and a sound admixture of idealism and realism. Thereby he and nearly all of his Icelandic successors were saved from the aberrations and excesses of Romanticism elsewhere.

2. Tradition has it that shortly before his death Bjarni Thorarensen hailed a younger contemporary as his successor with the words: "When I die, you will be our only national poet." The prophetic statement is said to have been directed to Jónas Hallgrímsson; and even if it is merely a legend, it both reflects the public attitude toward the two poets and is indicative of their fine relationship. During his early years Jónas Hallgrímsson was inspired and influenced by Thorarensen's poems; and he mourned his friend's death in one of his most excellent elegies, an eloquent tribute to his fellow poet and a deeply felt expression of his personal grief.

Jónas Hallgrímsson was born at Hraun in Őxnadalur in the north of Iceland, November 16, 1807. Here he also spent his youth, in scenically unique surroundings which awakened his love of nature and his interest in natural phenomena. Many of his poems hark back to the scenes of his childhood, where the charm of the Icelandic countryside was indelibly impressed upon him.

Uncommon ability and poetic gifts characterized his forebears. On his father's side he was related to Hallgrímur Pétursson, Iceland's great hymn writer of the seventeenth century, author of the famed *Passíusálmar* (Passion Hymns). Furthermore, Jónas Hallgrímsson's associations during his formative years were highly favorable to the development of his poetic talents. His father, Hallgrímur Þorsteinsson, was assistant pastor to Jón Þorláksson, the leading Icelandic poet of his generation, remembered especially as the translator of *Paradise Lost* and other masterpieces.[8] The stimulating influence of

[8] See Richard Beck, "Jón Þorláksson—Icelandic Translator of Pope and

the older poet on the young Jónas Hallgrímsson can be readily understood. One of his earlier efforts, "Vorkvæði" (Spring Song), is in fact consciously or unconsciously imitative, both in mood and metrical form, of a well-known poem by Jón Þorláksson.

Other less pleasant circumstances helped to mould Jónas Hallgrímsson. When the poet was nine years of age, his father was drowned. The son was deeply moved and later expressed his grief in his beautiful poem "Saknaðarljóð" (Lament) and elsewhere. No doubt this tragedy to some extent accounts for the note of sadness and sorrow running like an undercurrent through his poetry.

In spite of his father's untimely death, his mother managed to provide for his schooling by having him tutored by a prominent clergyman who was a relative of his. After two years of preparatory training, he entered the Latin School at Bessastaðir, where he spent six years, graduating in the spring of 1829. Here he came under the influence of acknowledged masters of the Icelandic language, notably Sveinbjörn Egilsson, who revealed to him the beauty and the richness of his native tongue and intensified his interest in the sagas and the Eddas. Jónas Hallgrímsson studied these diligently, together with Greek and Roman classical literature; he read and translated Ossian; and he began to show his preference for the natural sciences. While at the Latin School, he also formed lasting friendships with those progressive contemporaries of his, who a few years later in Copenhagen were to be associated with him in the publication of *Fjölnir*.

After holding a secretarial position for three years in Reykjavík, Jónas Hallgrímsson entered upon his university career, arriving in Copenhagen in the fall of 1832. He planned to study law, but was soon attracted, partly through the influence of his friends, to the natural sciences and literature. Through his closest associate, Konráð Gíslason, the noted philologist, he was introduced to German literature, reading Schiller, Tieck, and especially Heine, who later came to mean much to him.

New ideas and stimulating currents of thought burst upon Jónas Hallgrímsson from other directions. Romanticism was in full flower

Milton," *Journal of English and Germanic Philology*, XXXIII (1933), 572–585; XXXV (1935), 74–100.

in Denmark. Politically also these were stirring years in Scandinavia and elsewhere in Europe. Echoes of the July Revolution in France had reverberated through the northern countries, rousing the slumbering national feeling and putting a spark to the latent love of liberty. In Denmark this movement brought about the establishment of consultative assemblies. Iceland alone, of the sister nations of the north, lagged behind. This was forcefully brought home to alert and forward-looking Icelandic students in Copenhagen, who were face to face with the new developments. Responsive to the challenge of the hour and closely associated with the most active of his fellow students from Iceland, Jónas Hallgrímsson readily joined them in their progressive endeavors on behalf of their nation.

He was one of the group of four such students who established the important annual *Fjölnir* (1835–47), the others being Konráð Gíslason, Brynjólfur Pétursson, and Tómas Sæmundsson. Inspired by the wave of nationalism and liberalism sweeping Europe and doubtless also stimulated by the example of the Icelandic poet and patriot Eggert Ólafsson, whose poems appeared in 1832, these ardent young progressives made their publication the avowed vehicle for awakening their countrymen from their centuries-old lethargy. It was on the one hand to remind them of their proud past, their classical literature, and their venerable language: and on the other to hold up before them the example of foreign nations where the spirit of freedom and progress was bearing fruit in greater general well-being and richer national life. The results of their efforts were epoch-making. As has been repeatedly emphasized the appearance of *Fjölnir* marked the beginning of a new and flourishing era in Icelandic literature.[9]

To those fruitful and far-reaching results none of the sponsors of the publication contributed more than did Jónas Hallgrímsson. With his poems he sang the new ideals and aspirations into the hearts of his countrymen. His beautiful and challenging poem "Ísland" (Iceland), printed in the first volume of the annual, was deservedly given the place of honor, because its clarion call vigorously and artistically contrasted the difference between the past and the present.

---

[9] See H. Hermannsson, *The Periodical Literature of Iceland Down to the Year 1874* ("Islandica," Vol. XI [Ithaca, N. Y., 1918]), pp. 42–48. See also Einarsson, *Prose Writers*, pp. 20–24.

Other important writings of his, in poetry and prose, also appeared in *Fjölnir*, including his famous review of Sigurður Breiðfjörð's *Rímur af Tistrani og Indíönu*, which will be considered below. However timely and important his criticism, it was the constructive side of Jónas Hallgrímsson's literary work and the high standard that he set for future poets that more than anything else inaugurated a new era in Icelandic letters.

His work as a scientist was also noteworthy. He spent the summer of 1837 in exploration and scientific research in Iceland, traveling through the southern part of the country. With the help of a governmental stipend, he continued his travels during the summers of 1839–1842, covering the major part of the inhabited area of the country. Although hampered by ill health, limited means, and other difficulties, he gathered much information about Iceland and made some important observations and investigations in the field of the natural sciences. He was, in more than one respect, a pioneer in the study of the geology of Iceland. Besides, he wrote popular articles on scientific subjects, still notable for their stylistic excellence, and made a masterful translation of G. F. Ursin's book on astronomy, in which he coined a number of scientific terms that have become an integral part of the Icelandic language.[10]

On his return to Copenhagen in the fall of 1842, Jónas Hallgrímsson devoted his time to arranging the scientific material he had gathered and began writing a geographical description of Iceland, having for that purpose received financial aid from the Icelandic Literature Society, which planned to publish the book. He made but little progress, however; continued ill health, lack of funds, and growing melancholy (stemming from an early disappointment in love) sapped his energies. Most profitable and pleasant was the period from the summer of 1843 to the spring of 1844, spent at Sorö as the guest of his friend Japhetus Steenstrup, the Danish naturalist, who had been a traveling companion of his in Iceland. While at Sorö, Jónas Hallgrímsson also made the acquaintance of the Danish poets B. S. Ingemann and Carsten Hauch, which was naturally a genuine source of pleasure. When Steenstrup had to leave on an extended journey in the spring

[10] See Bjarni Vilhjálmsson, "Nýyrði í Stjörnufræði Ursins," *Skírnir*, CXVIII (1944), 99–130.

of 1844, Jónas Hallgrímsson returned to Copenhagen. He died there on May 26, 1845, having remained to the last actively interested in various progressive measures concerning his beloved Iceland.

As already mentioned, many of Jónas Hallgrímsson's literary productions, including a large number of his poems, appeared in *Fjölnir*, the last volume of the publication (1847) being devoted almost exclusively to his unpublished writings. The same year saw the first edition of his poems, *Ljóðmæli*, edited by his comrades Brynjólfur Pétursson and Konráð Gíslason and published in Copenhagen by the Icelandic Literature Society. Selections from his prose were included in the second and enlarged edition, *Ljóðmæli og önnur rit* (Copenhagen, 1883), with a biographical introduction by the poet Hannes Hafstein. A third and annotated edition of the poems was prepared by Jón Ólafsson and Jón Sigurðsson and appeared in 1913. A definitive edition of all the poet's works, *Rit*, including his letters and a detailed biography, was published in five volumes (1929–1936), edited by Matthías Þórðarson. A fifth edition of the poems, edited by Freysteinn Gunnarsson, was published in 1944. A special memorial edition of the poems, together with an extensive selection from the prose writings, edited with an appreciative introduction by the poet Tómas Guðmundsson, appeared the next year to commemorate the centenary of Jónas Hallgrímsson's death. This edition was reprinted in 1947. Selections from the poet's works have been published at various times, including *Ljóð og sögur* (Poems and Stories), edited with an introduction by Jónas Jónsson in 1941; a photostatic reproduction of the original edition of the poems appeared in 1945.[11]

Jónas Hallgrímsson was fundamentally a nature poet who de-

[11] For further information about his literary work, see Þorsteinn Gíslason, *Jónas Hallgrímsson, fyrirlestur*, (Seyðisfirði, 1903); Guðmundur Finnbogason, "Jónas Hallgrímsson (Ræða 16. Nóvember 1907)," *Skírnir*, LXXXI (1907), 15–25; Halldór Kiljan Laxness, "Um Jónas Hallgrímsson," in the author's collected articles and essays *Alþýðubókin* (1929), pp. 79–98; Einar Ól. Sveinsson, "Um kveðskap Jónasar Hallgrímssonar," *Lesbók Morgunblaðsins*, IV (1929,) 345–349, and "Jónas Hallgrímsson," *Skírnir*, CXIX (1945), 5–22; Fr. de Fontanay, "Um ljóð Jónasar Hallgrímssonar," *Jörð*, II (1941), 195–214; Pálmi Hannesson, "Íslandslýsing Jónasar Hallgrímssonar," *Helgafell*, IV (1945), 7–17; Kristján Albertsson, "Vorskáld Íslands: Minningaræða," *ibid.*, IV (1945), 81–86.

delighted in singing the praises of the scenic beauty of his native Iceland—"the land of the mild countenance, the blue mountain peaks, swan song, trout streams, waterfalls, clear lakes, and broad glacial domes," to paraphrase a popular poem of his on Iceland. Such is frequently the warp and woof of his poems, and his similes are generally drawn from the same source. In an exquisite lyric, "Dalvísur" (Valley Verse), in which lilting music and graphic word pictures go hand in hand, he has immortalized rural Iceland. In another poem, "Fjallið Skjaldbreiður" (Mount Skjaldbreiður), perhaps the most powerful to come from his pen, he has written a magnificent description of a volcanic eruption, highly poetic to be sure but, according to the testimony of competent natural scientists, equally remarkable for its geological correctness. His descriptive poems, uniformly characterized by rare charm, reveal the observing scientist who has a keen eye for the peculiar beauties of his homeland no less than the richly gifted poet.

Some of Jónas Hallgrímsson's most notable and best-loved nature poems are at the same time and in a special sense patriotic poems, such as "Ísland" and "Gunnarshólmi." Here his love of the country—the scenery and the Icelandic language, life, and traditions—largely finds expression in his admiration of the past. Here speaks Jónas Hallgrímsson the Romanticist. Expressing not only his individual point of view, but also that of his co-workers, the poet effectively contrasts the present and the past, reminding his countrymen of the fact that they have deteriorated and not the country, which is still as beautiful as of old. His was a backward look with an eye to the future, for Jónas Hallgrímsson had a strong and abiding faith in his nation. Here, as in so many of his poems, he sounds a clarion call to action, a challenge to his countrymen. The challenge did not fall on deaf ears.

Love of liberty is at the heart of the patriotic confession of faith expressed in "Ísland." The poet deliberately dwells on the glorious days of the Icelandic Commonwealth, when the country enjoyed complete independence. Naturally his attention is focused on the Althing, the center of the political and cultural life of Iceland of old. Re-establishment of the Althing and the restoration of political freedom for their nation were the fond hopes of Jónas Hallgrímsson and his associates and the principal goals of their endeavors. In their romantic attachment to the past, they demanded, moreover, that the reborn national assembly should meet at Þingvellir, its ancient site. This idea recurs in Hallgrímsson's poetry. When the Althing was re-established (in 1840), although not at Þingvellir, he greeted it with a splendid poem, in which his concern for the freedom of his country is again forcefully expressed.

In "Gunnarshólmi" (Gunnar's Island), unquestionably one of his most beautiful and impressive poems, Jónas Hallgrímsson glorifies the patriotism of the most renowned hero of ancient Iceland, Gunnar of Hlíðarendi (Lithend). He had been exiled from his native land and with his brother Kolskegg had set out on his journey abroad; a short distance from his home, according to the saga, he stopped his horse and, surveying the beautiful district, said: "Fair is the mountain side, fairer than I have ever seen it: the fields are golden, the home meadow mown; I shall return home and not go away at all." The scene of the poem is, of course, southern Iceland where Gunnar's home was located. Shortly before writing it, the poet had traveled through that historic region, which once upon a time had been a fertile land, but was now laid waste by floods. Only a small patch of land, grown with grass, remained. Tradition held this to be the spot from which Gunnar turned toward home; hence the title of the poem.

The outstanding element in this justly admired poem is not, however, the portrayal of the ancient hero, but the marvelous nature description, a graphic word picture on a large scale, so characteristic of the author. In this respect he differs greatly from Bjarni Thorarensen, in whose poems of a similar sort the past and the great men of old overshadow the description. The latter would undoubtedly have stressed the hero's courage and defiance in the face of certain death, not his love for his surroundings, as Jónas Hallgrímsson does. These two great pioneers of modern Icelandic literature present a contrast in other ways as well; whereas Bjarni Thorarensen was the poet of winter, of snow and ice and northern lights, Jónas Hallgrímsson was the poet of spring and summer, of verdant hillsides and meadows, sunshine and soft breezes. The former exclaims: "Shall we give more attention to the rose than the northern lights?" The latter hails as his special friends the spring flowers, the blue wave, and the sunlit sky.

Because of Eggert Ólafsson's idealism, his forward-looking patriotism, his love of everything Icelandic, language, literature and scenery, Jónas Hallgrímsson especially admired and loved him and paid him tribute in one of his masterpieces, "Hulduljóð" (Song of the Fairy), elevated in tone, fraught with deep feeling for nature, and exquisitely constructed.[12] Here, as in many of his other great poems, the poet and the idealist are one, his love of beauty blending harmoniously with the progressive spirit.

Among Jónas Hallgrímsson's descriptive poems there is a group of special interest. These have their roots in his fondness for nature, but deal particularly with the life of the people and its relationship to the soil, the sea, and the animal kingdom. Some of these are among his most charming verses, such as "Sláttuvísur" (Song of Haymaking), which is particularily effective metrically, and "Formannsvísur" (Fisherman's Song), in which a fishing trip is graphically portrayed with suitable variation of meter and with strikingly faithful realism.

Nowhere does his love of the sun and of the joy and life-giving power of light, one of his most fundamental characteristics, express itself more beautifully than in his "Sólseturslјóð" (Song of Sunset). His love of nature is both deep and all-embracing. In a description of a summer night he says: "the pretty dandelion in the pasture was already asleep, the mouse under the moss, the sea gull on the wave." His sympathy extends to all living things.

Small wonder that adversity left deep scars on Jónas Hallgrímsson's sensitive character. A disappointment in love during his youthful years colored both his outlook on life and his poetry, especially, as might be expected, his love poems. These are not numerous, but they are instinct with a charm all their own, a touching note of sadness delicately phrased. "Ferðalok" (Journey's End), addressed to his old sweetheart, is a poem of rare perfection; and "Söknuður" (Lament), similar in theme, was suggested by Goethe's "Nähe des

[12] For further information about Ólafsson, see H. Hermannsson, *Eggert Ólafsson* ("Islandica," Vol. XVI [Ithaca, N. Y., 1925]) and Vilhjálmur Þ. Gíslason, *Eggert Ólafsson* (1926).

Geliebten," but grew directly out of the author's own bitter experience.

A different side of Jónas Hallgrímsson's character is seen in his mocking and jocular poems, like the inimitable "Borðsálmur" (Table Skit), a subtle satire on his countrymen, delightful in its quiet irony. These and other verses, many of them parodies, and some of his prose sketches show his keen sense of humor, which is generally good-natured.

Jónas Hallgrímsson is Icelandic to the core; even his poems written abroad are thoroughly Icelandic in theme and spirit. Nevertheless, national as he was, his genius was fructified by foreign influences. He was especially indebted to Heine. The German's mastery of form, rare lyricism, irony, and not least the duality of his nature appealed to him. Heine's ability to laugh out loud when his heart was bleeding, to hide his real feelings behind a mask of mirth, found a counterpart in Jónas Hallgrímsson, whose sorrows are usually more implied than expressed in his poems. In the first year of *Fjölnir* (1835) Jónas Hallgrímsson and Konráð Gíslason had introduced Heine into Icelandic literature with a short article about him and a selection from his "Die Reisebilder." He remained a favorite with Jónas Hallgrímsson, who not only translated, or rather rewrote in Icelandic, a score of his poems, but who also reveals in a number of original poems a definite influence from him in mood and form. This is especially notable in the cycle of descriptive poems "Á sjó og landi" (On Land and Sea; also called "Annes og eyjar," Capes and Islands), although they also bear the unmistakable stamp of the author's individuality.[13]

Jónas Hallgrímsson also translated in his free fashion a number of poems or fragments from other sources, including some by Addison, Ossian, Schiller, Oehlenschläger, and Horace. Of these Ossian appears to be the only one who influenced him to any extent during his early years. The main stream of foreign influences in Jónas Hallgrímsson's poetry therefore comes from the Romantic poets. There is, however, a classical restraint and clarity that can perhaps be traced to his classical training and the influence of his school years at Bessastaðir. His faithfulness to reality is probably to some extent accounted for by his scientific spirit, as well as by the realistic character of the

[13] For a detailed treatment of this phase of his poetry, see Einar Ól. Sveinsson, "Jónas Hallgrímsson og Heinrich Heine," *Skírnir*, CXVIII (1944), 51–74.

native literature that was bred in him. Jónas Hallgrímsson's translations further reveal emphatically how Icelandic he was. He lets literalness go by the board, recasting the thought in an Icelandic mould; and as a rule he succeeds in reproducing faithfully the spirit of the original. As a result, many of his versions of foreign poems have become an integral part of Icelandic literature, favorite songs of the people.

Love of beauty in its various visible manifestations, not least in literary expression, is the chief characteristic of Jónas Hallgrímsson. He loved beautiful and simple language and flowing rhythm, and therefore he excelled in exquisite lyric form, in both original poems and translations. His sensitive ear was attuned to the rich nuances of his native tongue, which was to him "the most beautiful of all melodies." This love of beautiful form made him abhor ugliness and prevented him from falling into unnaturalness and excesses. He masterfully harmonized language, thought, and metrical form. Here once more he is a contrast to Bjarni Thorarensen, whose main concern was thought and poetic imagination rather than form, although he produced some notable exceptions. Jónas Hallgrímsson is superior to his immediate forerunner and master not only in polish and literary artistry, but even more in the much greater variety of his verse forms. Deeply indebted to the Icelandic classical literature, he used the Eddic and Skaldic meters with great skill, not infrequently embellishing the former and adding to their rhythmical beauty. With equal mastery he introduced foreign forms such as the sonnet, the *terza rima*, the strophe, and the meter of Heine. He is modern Iceland's first great master of poetic form and, as such, one of its greatest men of letters of all time.

Further, it was doubtless primarily Jónas Hallgrímsson's sure and refined literary taste and his love of beauty that caused him to write in *Fjölnir* his celebrated review of Breiðfjörð's *rímur*, already referred to. A contributory cause may have been the fact that the latter had written derogatory verses about *Fjölnir*. He criticized not only Breiðfjörð, but the *rímur* poetry as a whole, directing his attack against its violations of good literary taste in metrical form and language and against its stereotyped ideas and phaseology, its lack of poetic imagination and originality. As he attacked a literary form that for centuries had been a favorite entertainment of the people and simultaneously condemned the most popular contemporary author of the type, he naturally reaped opposition and abuse. Nor can it be denied that he was somewhat one-sided in his condemnation. Time, however, has proved him right in his major contentions, although the *rímur* poetry still has its devotees and Breiðfjörð has received his just recognition. Jónas Hallgrímsson's review, nevertheless, in reality marked the beginning of literary criticism in Iceland. He was also a master of prose and a pioneer in the field of Icelandic fiction, but his prose works have been discussed in the account of Icelandic prose writers.[14]

Jónas Hallgrímsson wrote once these memorable words: "What is longevity? Fruitful living, the fullest development of the spirit, and useful activity."[15] A more fitting epitaph could not have been written for him. Although he died at the age of 37, he left behind such achievements as are vouchsafed to only a chosen few of human kind. He had contributed immeasurably to the new era in the national life and the literature of his country. He had sung into the hearts of the Icelandic people a greater love of their country and a new faith in their future. With his unusually pure and idiomatic diction he had been and continued to be a powerful force in the movement for the purification of the Icelandic language. He greatly enriched Icelandic poetry with new metrical forms and lifted it to a higher artistic level with his exquisite lyrics. Finally, he has had such great influence on succeeding Icelandic writers that he may be said to have formed a school. In short, his poems have been for the Icelandic nation a rich source of inspiration in its struggle for freedom and higher culture.

3. Although Jón Thoroddsen (1818–1868) occupies a place of honor in Icelandic literature primarily as "The Father of the Modern Icelandic Novel" and has therefore been discussed extensively among the prose writers of the period,[16] he also wrote lyric poems of merit.

[14] For a discussion of the prose works of Jónas Hallgrímsson, see Einarsson, *Prose Writers*, pp. 35–37, and his article "Gamanbréf Jónasar Hallgrímssonar," *Skírnir*, CIX (1935), 147–156.

[15] From his memorial poem "Séra Stefán Pálsson," included in all the editions of his poems listed in text.

[16] See Einarsson, *Prose Writers*, pp. 41–48. For an account of Jón Thoroddsen's

Although they are far less important than his fiction, they were very popular in their day and several of them still retain their popularity.

Thoroddsen began writing poetry at an early age; only two quatrains of his youthful efforts have been preserved, however, one dating from his thirteenth year well written and pointing forward to his fluency in versemaking. He received some encouragement in that direction from Bjarni Thorarensen, a cousin of his. But it was not until his student days in Copenhagen (1841–1847) that he seriously interested himself in the writing of poetry. He then cultivated it from then on fairly steadily until his comparatively early death in 1868. His collected poems, *Kvæði* (Poems), were first published in Copenhagen in 1871; a second edition, including some additional poems, appeared in 1919, also published in Copenhagen. A selection from his poems, *Úrvalsljóð* (Selected Poems), edited by the poetess Hulda (Unnur B. Bjarklind), appeared in 1944. Many are also included in the collection *Snót*, which he published in collaboration with Gísli Magnússon in 1850, and which has run through several editions, the fourth (including the first edition and later additions) appearing in two volumes in 1945, edited by the Reverend Einar Thorlacius, with introductions by Snæbjőrn Jónsson.

Doubtless spurred on by his adventurous spirit and ardent love of liberty, Thoroddsen enlisted as a volunteer in the Danish army during the war between Denmark and Germany in 1848 and participated in several battles; this experience furnished him with material for some of his poems. As might be expected, he took an active part in the movement for Icelandic independence and progress. He wrote numerous patriotic poems and exhortations to his countrymen, including the ever-popular "Ó, főgur er vor fósturjőrð" (Our Native Land, How Beautiful), which appears destined to outlive most of his other productions. Nor is that at all surprising. It is a graceful poem, musical and mellow, sincere and warm, deeply patriotic

novels, see also Sigurður Guðmundsson, "Jón Thoroddsen," *Skírnir*, XCIII (1919), 209–233 (reprinted in his collection of articles and essays *Heiðnar hugvekjur og mannaminni* [1946], pp. 22–45); and especially Steingrímur J. Þorsteinsson, *Jón Thoroddsen og skáldsögur hans* (1943). Concerning Jón Thoroddsen's poetry, see Sigurður Guðmundsson, "Af ljóðagerð Jóns Thoroddsens," *Skírnir*, XCIV (1920), 207–214 (reprinted in his *Heiðnar hugvekjur og mannaminni* [1946], pp. 47–55).

without being extreme. The first two stanzas, describing Iceland in winter and summer garb, are especially effective and accurate, while the elves dancing on the ice are quite in keeping with time-honored Icelandic folk belief.

This very ability to describe truthfully and fluently the beauty of Iceland with her markedly changing seasons and the attractive side of her rural life is the principal characteristic of Thoroddsen's serious poems and probably also the main reason for their popularity. Excellent illustrations are his "Rokkvísa" (Spinning Song) and his spring poem "Vorið er komið" (Spring Has Arrived). The latter is a charming description of the delights of an Icelandic spring—the streams rushing down the mountain side, the swans on the tarn, the throstles in the field, frolicking lambs, and children playing with their sea shells (a typically Icelandic feature) near their farm homes. The picture is graphic, entirely true to life, and remarkably concise.

The other noteworthy and equally characteristic group of Thoroddsen's poems is his humorous verses and satires, ranging from gay mockery and irony to spiteful invective. Not infrequently these poems are clever parodies, resembling his prose style in that respect, but they are often too restricted in theme and lacking in universality. A different and more attractive side of his character, as reflected in his poetry, is seen in his tender poems about children, such as "Vőggukvæði" (Cradlesong), appropriately inserted in his novel *Piltur og Stúlka* (Lad and Lass).

All things considered, Thoroddsen is not, however, a great lyric poet. His lightness of touch, his national spirit, his refreshing humor, and his descriptive ability have, to be sure, endeared him to his countrymen; but his poems lack depth, flight of imagination, and originality. To be more specific, they are often imitative, in meter as well as in subject matter, of his great forerunners Bjarni Thorarensen and Jónas Hallgrímsson. Thoroddsen also employs verse forms from the Swedish poet Bellman, but whether or not he knew the latter's works at first hand is a matter of conjecture. It is, however, reasonable to assume that he became familiar with them during his student days.

4. Ranging from an influential position in the Danish Department of Foreign Affairs and Diplomatic Service to the life of a gentleman

farmer in his native land, the career of GRÍMUR ÞORGRÍMSSON THOMSEN was a most unusual one. He was born at Bessastaðir in southern Iceland on May 15, 1820. His father, Þorgrímur Tómasson, a jeweller by trade, was business manager of the Latin School at Bessastaðir, at that time a center of learning. He was a man of means and more than ordinary ability, who had served as a member of the Althing. Thomsen's mother, Ingibjörg Jónsdóttir, who belonged to a prominent family, was also a person of uncommon gifts and strength of character. The poet is reported to have said that he had inherited his wordly wisdom and practical sense from his father, his literary and scholarly interest and his native intelligence from his mother. But her letters to her brother, Governor Grímur Jónsson, written during the forty-year period, 1809–1849, and published under the title *Húsfreyjan á Bessastöðum* (The Mistress at Bessastaðir) in 1946, reveal that her son could indeed have received his worldly and practical sense from her side of the family also. Much light is thrown on his character and the earlier part of his career (1838–1858) in the companion volume, *Sonur gullsmiðsins á Bessastöðum* (The Son of the Jeweller at Bessastaðir, 1947), which contains letters written to him and about him by his parents and others. Both volumes are edited with introductions and notes by Finnur Sigmundsson, and they constitute an important contribution to an understanding of the poet, his background, and his works. Also of interest is Thora Friðriksson, *Merkir menn, sem ég hef þekkt: Dr. Grímur Thomsen (1944)*.

Instead of attending the Latin School, Thomsen received his preparatory education privately from Bishop Árni Helgason. He matriculated at the University of Copenhagen in 1837, when he was only seventeen years of age, specializing in aesthetics and philosophy and also interesting himself in foreign languages and literature. He was no mere bookworm, however, for he actively identified himself with the Danish Student Society, where he made the acquaintance of many of Denmark's leading men of letters, including Oehlenschläger. These years were the heyday of the Pan-Scandinavian movement; and Thomsen, alone among his countrymen of the day, joined the Scandinavian Society whose aim was a closer association between the northern nations, intellectually, commercially, and politically. At the same time his continued interest in things Icelandic is indicated by his lecture on Iceland before the Scandinavian Society (1846) and his articles on Icelandic literature that appeared during this period in various Danish publications. He formed lasting friendships with many of his fellow countrymen in Copenhagen, and his admiration for the *Fjölnir* group is unmistakably seen in his splendid and genuinely felt memorial poems about three of those four remarkable patriots.

Thomsen's study of aesthetics and philosophy also bore fruit in a number of essays and more ambitious productions in Danish, the most notable of which were his prize-winning essay on French literature *Om den nyfranske Poesi* (On Contemporary French Poetry; Copenhagen, 1843), and his book, *Om Lord Byron* (About Lord Byron; Copenhagen, 1845), for which he received his M.A. degree from the University of Copenhagen (later made the equivalent of a Ph.D. degree) by a royal decree.[17] This book was both a noteworthy interpretation and a pioneer work in the realm of Byron study; it introduced Byron not only to Denmark but virtually to Scandinavia as a whole. Although rather heavy in style and bearing the earmarks of the Hegelian philosophy in vogue at the time, the book still makes interesting reading. Thomsen, the scholar and literary critic, can there be seen to good advantage.[18] His most memorable achievement in the field of literary criticism was, however, his review of Hans Christian Andersen's works (1855). The first appreciative evaluation in Danish of that great genius, it opened the eyes of Andersen's countrymen to the greatness of their "Master of the Fairy Tale." With other writings Thomsen aroused the interest of Danish readers in contemporary Norwegian poetry and introduced to them such a poet as the Swedish-Finnish Runeberg. As far as Icelandic literature is concerned, Thomsen's most important critical essay was his interpretation of Bjarni Thorarensen's poetic genius (originally

[17] See Sigurður Nordal, "Frá meistaraprófi Gríms Thomsens," in *Afmæliskveðja til Halldórs Hermannssonar 6. janúar 1948* (1948), pp. 93–98 (reprinted in *Landsbókasafn Íslands, Árbók 1946–47* [1948], pp. 151–156).

[18] See Richard Beck, "Grímur Thomsen—A Pioneer Byron Student," *Journal of English and Germanic Philology*, XXVII (1928), 170–182; also in Icelandic as "Grímur Thomsen og Byron," *Skírnir*, CXI (1937), 129–143. Concerning his life and literary career, see also Þorsteinn Gíslason, "Grímur Thomsen," *Lögrétta*, XXVIII (1933), 171–184.

published in the Danish magazine *Gæa*, 1845, and lately in an Icelandic translation by Sigurjón Jónsson in *Andvari*, 1948), still of first importance in any study of the poet.

A year after the appearance of his book on Byron, Thomsen was granted a governmental stipend for travel in Europe, primarily for language study; he visited France, England, and Italy, sojourning the greater part of the time in Paris and London. Upon his return to Copenhagen in 1847 he was for many years in the service of the Danish Department of Foreign Affairs, first as secretary of legations in various European countries, later as deputy and division-chief in the Department, wielding for a time some influence in Danish politics. When, in 1866, a shift took place the Department as a result of a change in policy, he obtained his release.

The next year Thomsen returned to Iceland, settling down to the life of a gentleman-farmer at Bessastaðir, where he resided until his death. He soon became active in Icelandic politics, as a member of the Althing (1869–1891), and as an editor of the important *Ísafold* (1878–1881). Much of his time, however, he devoted to literary pursuits, writing many of his best poems and studying and translating classical poetry during his later years. He died on November 27, 1896. The following year the Althing recognized the importance of his work by voting his widow a special pension in his honor.

Grímur Thomsen is one of those literary figures whose permanent place among the leading poets of his nation has become more secure with the passing years. Many readers still fail to recognize his literary greatness, however, and will doubtless continue to do so, as his appeal is first and foremost intellectual and literary. The comparatively late flowering of his genius and correspondingly late publication of his poems has also resulted in a slower recognition of his worth than would otherwise have been the case. The poems did not appear until a new literary tendency (Realism) was gaining ground and, therefore, since they were somewhat out of tune with the times, did not at once achieve deserved recognition. Although a number had previously appeared in Icelandic periodicals (his first original poem in *Fjölnir* in 1844), the first collection, a slender volume titled *Ljóðmæli* (Poems), was not published until 1880, when he was sixty years of age. A second edition, greatly enlarged, appeared in Copenhagen in

1895, when he was seventy-five, and a third edition, again including a number of new poems, in 1906, ten years after his death. A collected edition in two volumes appeared in 1934, edited by Snæbjőrn Jónsson, with a biography by Jón Þorkelsson and an essay by Sigurður Nordal. A selection from his poems, edited with an introduction by Andrés Bjőrnsson, was published in 1946.

Thomsen was uncommonly widely read in modern and ancient literatures. He translated or paraphrased, more or less successfully, poems by Ossian, Milton, Byron, Runeberg, Oehlenschläger, La Fontaine, Schiller, and Goethe. The number of Romantics in this group clearly indicated the translator's sympathy with their literary creed and their choice of themes. Among English poets Shelley and Byron were Thomsen's favorites. He wrote a sympathetic elegy on Shelley; and the poems, especially those written about the time he was working on his book on Byron (1844–1846), definitely show the influence of Byronism. With a translation from Goethe ("Ný Félagsrit," The Fisherman, 1844), Thomsen introduced him into Icelandic literature. Uhland must have seemed to him a kindred spirit and may have stimulated his interest in the Middle Ages. Often, as in his popular "Landslag" (Landscape), modeled on a Finnish folksong, Thomsen succeeds admirably in producing a version thoroughly Icelandic in mood and pictorial quality.

Thomsen's numerous translations from the ancient Greek lyric poets and tragedians are, however, his most important productions in that field. A labor of love, they were the fruit of his later years. The rigid mental discipline of wrestling with them no doubt greatly developed his poetic ability, especially his mastery of form. Numbering over fifty, these translations are from the works of no less than twenty poets, including all the greatest Greek masters of antiquity. As may be expected, these translations vary in excellence, but generally they are very well done, some exceptionally so. Among his translations from classical literature, none, however, surpasses his adaptation of Horace's famed "Integer vitae," which brilliantly reproduces the mood as well as the thought of the original, cast in a strikingly Icelandic mould.

Significant as Thomsen's translations undeniably are, his own poems are of course his principal contribution to Icelandic literature.

Of these, his historical and narrative poems are in turn the most characteristic. Clearly, the poet felt at home with the mighty and unusual men and women of the saga period, whose strong individuality set them apart from their fellow men. Their characteristics, and his own kinship with them, drew him to such personalities. Romanticism, under whose influence he had come early in life, also directed his thought to the past, to folklore, to the mysterious and awe-inspiring in nature. Like Bjarni Thorarensen he is the poet of winter, of the sterner side of the Icelandic landscape, the glaciers, the rushing rivers, and the surging sea. His much admired and much sung poem "Á Sprengisandi" is alive with the spirit of the wasteland and the haunting fear of the traveler on the desert trail.

Thomsen's Old Norse temperament and his intimate knowledge of Old Icelandic literature and medieval ballads more than anything else made him succeed well in treating historical subjects and in interpreting heroic men and women of bygone days. His poem on Halldór Snorrason is a notable illustration, a vivid and concentrated narrative and an equally graphic and vigorous delineation of the whole-souled and strong-willed hero, who defies his king rather than suffer injustice at his hand. Here was a man after the poet's own heart; and his attraction, no doubt rooted in a feeling of kinship with him and his fate, is further revealed in other historical poems of Thomsen's. He appears in "Hemings flokkur Áslákssonar" (Cycle on Hemingur Áslåksson), one of Thomsen's most ambitious poems on a saga theme, remarkable alike in narrative excellence, insight, and characterization.[19] His series of poems, *Rímur af Búa Andríðarsyni og Fríði Dofradóttur* (originally published separately in an edition by Jón Þorkelsson, 1906), also on a saga theme, not only contains a striking expression of the poet's Romantic confession of faith and some magnificent descriptive passages, but has genuine epic quality in both mood and the treatment of the subject matter.

Thomsen's fondness for ancient and national lore and his spiritual affinity with the past are likewise evident in his successful treatment of ghosts and monstrous creatures. His poem "Glámur," based on the episode in *Grettis saga* describing Grettir's fight with the ghost

[19] For a detailed analysis, see Andrés Björnsson, "Um Hemings flokk Áslákssonar," *Skírnir*, CXX (1946), 57–79.

Glámur, has a demonic and specterlike quality; enveloped in a supernatural atmosphere, the poem makes the reader shudder with cold fear for the fate of the hero.

Besides Thomsen's spiritual kinship with the past and his Romanticism there were other factors which turned his thought backward. There he found a refuge from adverse circumstances; there he could freely associate with men and women of his own mould and to his liking. Sigurður Nordal has rightly emphasized this in his essay on Thomsen: "Much of his poetry is simply a search for better company than life offered him."[20] Fortune had, to be sure, smiled on Thomsen in several respects. He had won high honors and fame abroad, where he became, if but temporarily, a man of considerable influence. At the same time he had also come to know, through bitter experience, the seamy side of political and social life, its emptiness and heartlessness. This he has portrayed, indirectly, in one of his most effective and outstanding poems, "Á Glæsisvőllum," in which the picture of life in the festive hall of the legendary King Goðmundur at Glæsisvellir is both graphic and striking in its symbolism. Thomsen's poems about leaders of men and heroes from days of old were, without doubt, written in part to hold the mirror up to his contemporaries; such poems are intended as a challenge to greater achievements and nobler living.

Although Thomsen was a widely traveled man and a cosmopolitan, he was profoundly Icelandic. His contacts with foreign culture had taught him to understand and appreciate his national cultural heritage all the better. The prolonged sojourn in other lands had linked him more strongly to Iceland; and in his poems he has pictured it in its varied seasonal garb, although in his nature descriptions he favors the more desolate and sterner aspects. Moreover, his Iceland is primarily the saga land, where the voices of the past resound, where the presence of men of old is still felt, and where every farm is the resting place of a hero. Further, when Thomsen wrote about men of his own day, he chose those who were, spiritually speaking, direct descendants of heroic ancestors.

[20] "Grímur Thomsen," introduction to *Ljóðmæli eftir Grím Thomsen* (1934), II, xvii. Also in S. Nordal's collected articles and essays, *Áfangar* (*Svipir*), Vol. II (1944).

Thomsen had interests besides historical narratives and nature descriptions. He was a genuine friend of animals, and this characteristic is expressed in several especially appealing poems, including the well-known "Rakki" (A Dog), a eulogy on the fidelity of a dog that starves beside his dead master rather than go away to search for food. In prose he has written about animals with the same sympathy.

This trait reveals that Thomsen had a warm heart despite his proverbially harsh exterior. He detested lack of manly qualities as much as he admired greatness of soul. He had an idealistic conception of man and his destiny, considering him of divine origin; and, therefore, he looked upon materialism as a cheap view of life. At the same time as he glorified the Old Norse heroic spirit, he was a man of firm and deep Christian faith. He was, however, far from being hidebound by narrow creeds. There is about his religious belief a grandeur and a sweep becoming a great poet. In one of his most remarkable poems, "Stjőrnu-Odda draumur nýrri" (Stjőrnu-Oddi's Newer Dream), his church was a temple where all lovers of truth assemble.

It is clear that Thomsen's poems are weighty in subject matter and abound in stimulating content. On the other hand, they have been criticized for faulty form and lack of smoothness. This cannot be denied for Thomsen was far more concerned with originality of expression and concentrated thought than with polished meter. He possessed, however, in an unusual degree the ability to harmonize words and thoughts. His similes are striking and emphatically Icelandic, his language restrained and meaty. Nor must it be forgotten that he wrote some poems of marked musical quality, such as his melodious elegy on Jónas Hallgrímsson and other poems even more remarkable for their technical excellence.

Thomsen's narrative poems on historical subjects in ballad style are, however, his special contribution to modern Icelandic poetry. There he stands supreme. He succeeds better than anyone else in recapturing the Old Norse spirit, expressing it tersely and vigorously, in poems often rough hewn in form, but always original and bearing the stamp of a strong personality.

5. Although the humorous stories of Benedikt Sveinbjarnarson

Gröndal (1826–1907) are unquestionably his outstanding and most permanent contribution to Icelandic literature,[21] his poetry also entitles him to a place of honor. He was a richly gifted and very productive lyric poet, and during the earlier part of his career he was probably the most popular of contemporary poets, later to be eclipsed by Steingrímur Thorsteinsson and Matthías Jochumsson.

Gröndal's vast reading is reflected in his poetry. He was not only steeped in Old Icelandic, Greek, and Latin literature, but also widely read in the works of Goethe, Schiller, Heine, Tieck, Byron, Shelley, Victor Hugo, and Lamartine, and others less renowned. Goethe appears to have been his favorite poet, with Byron taking second place. A student of the natural sciences, Gröndal also interested himself in the writings of such philosophers as Aristotle, Plato, and Hegel, the last enjoying high favor during the poet's student days in Copenhagen. According to his own testimony, however, the book that made the deepest impression upon him and most influenced his outlook upon life was *Kosmos*, by Alexander Humbolt; its effects can be seen clearly in his philosophical poems.

Gröndal grew up in a cultural atmosphere favorable to the development of his literary genius, which early expressed itself in verse-making. His first printed poems, four in number, appeared in *Fjölnir* (1847) when he was twenty years of age. The first of these is an elegy on Jónas Hallgrímsson, whom Gröndal greatly admired. Under his influence the other three poems were written for they are imitative of Jónas Hallgrímsson's poems written in the spirit of Heine.

Gröndal's first book, *Örvaroddsdrápa*, was published four years later (second ed., 1906). It is a narrative poem in twelve cantos, based on the *Örvarodds saga*, glorifying the struggle of the brave and noble-minded hero against inescapable fate. Written in an incredibly short time, the poem bears all the earmarks of this circumstance and the youthfulness of the author. It is, nevertheless, a very spirited account and especially interesting as the first Icelandic epic of

---

[21] See Einarsson, *Prose Writers*, pp. 37–41, and his article "Benedikt Gröndal and Heljarslóðarorusta," *Journal of English and Germanic Philology*, XXXVI (1937), 307–325, 543–550. Concerning Gröndal's literary career generally and his poetry, see also *Benedikt Gröndal áttræður* (1906), and Hulda, "Gröndals-minning," *Eimreiðin*, XLIV (1938), 145–155.

modern times. In form it is also a new development in Icelandic literature, since it is written in the *ottava rima* of Byron's "Don Juan."

Two small collections of Gröndal's poems (*Kvæði*) followed within a few years (Copenhagen, 1853 and 1856). Many were published from time to time in his annual *Gefn* (1870–1874), in other Icelandic periodicals and papers, and in the anthologies *Svava* (Copenhagen, 1860) and *Snót*. A collected edition, *Kvæðabók*, appeared in 1900, and a small collection, *Dagrún*, in 1906, which included some older poems not printed in the collected edition together with several new ones. A selection from his poems, edited by the poet Þorsteinn Gíslason, appeared in 1946, and the first volume of an extensive edition of his works, edited by Gils Guðmundsson, was published in 1948.

Gröndal's verse production was extensive and varied. He wrote poems on legendary themes, philosophical and historical poems, patriotic and nature poems, and all kinds of occasional poetry.

One outstanding merit generally characterizes his lyric poems—his mastery of his native tongue. Here few Icelandic poets are his peers. The worthy son of a worthy father, he had not in vain drunk deep of the fountain of Old Icelandic literature; he was never at a loss for an expression. Moreover, he wrote with equal facility in Icelandic and foreign verse forms, even if he was at times unduly careless about rhythm. The beauty of his poems consists, as has been correctly observed, largely in the inherent beauty and majesty of the Icelandic language itself.[22] It is not surprising, therefore, that one of his best poems is an eloquent tribute to his mother tongue. His love of his native land was equally genuine, and this he expressed in a number of poems, of which "Vorvísa 1859" (Spring Song, 1859) is probably the most effective, deep-felt, and sonorous.

Gröndal was a full-blooded Romanticist, the most thoroughgoing Romanticist among the Icelandic poets. Herein lies his weakness as a lyric poet. His fertile imagination carried him so far afield that his poems frequently became a veritable jungle of imagery, vague and obscure. He delighted in spurring his Pegasus through space, midst flashing lightning, comets, or surging northern lights. Or he reposed

[22] Guðmundur Finnbogason, "Skáldskapur Gröndals," in *Benedikt Gröndal áttræður*, p. 43.

on the purple clouds of the sunset, viewing the heavenly bodies sailing their set course and listening to the music of the spheres. His lofty style, fluent and idiomatic as it is, tended to become excessively flowery. These extremes of imagination and style are especially noticeable in his poems on philosophical and legendary themes. Undeniably, however, these poems are conceived on a grand scale and contain some splendid descriptive passages, as for instance the opening lines of "Prometheus," in which subject matter and form blend beautifully.

Gröndal's historical poems are not numerous, but some of them, such as "Balthazar," "Mahomet II," and "Flosi," are among his very best. All show the central figures at fateful moments in their lives. "Balthazar," on the immortal theme of the handwriting on the wall, is particularly impressive and to some extent truly balladic in mood. "Flosi" was suggested by an episode in the *Njáls saga.*

In some of his shorter poems Gröndal also has the true lyric touch, that clarity of expression so often lacking in his more ambitious productions. Lovely in its simplicity is his autumn song "Hret" (Wintry Blast), and the same simple feeling and expression characterize the poems reminiscent of his youth.

His humorous poems are, however, his most characteristic verses. There, as in the inimitable tour de force "Gaman og alvara" (Gay and Grave), is the strangest commingling of bubbling mirth, nonsense, and seriousness. The same is true of the mock-heroic "Þingvallaferð," in which an ordinary pleasure trip is described in the elevated style of the epic. Here, as elsewhere, it is easy to see how adept Gröndal was at burlesque. Such poems with their exaggerations and eccentricities are characterized by the same exuberance of spirit and unbridled flight of the imagination as his humorous stories.

Thoroughgoing Romanticist and idealist that Gröndal was, it was natural that he should react violently against Realism. His reaction is expressed in a number of newspaper articles, but most forcefully in his lecture, "Um skáldskap" (On Poetry), delivered in Reykjavík, February 4, 1888. It was a reply to a lecture delivered on January 14 by the poet, Hannes Hafstein, who, as spokesman of the realistic tendency, had vigorously criticized what he considered the grave defects of Icelandic poetry of the day, particularly directing his thrusts at the Romanticists. The result was a celebrated controversy in which several writers took part. Gröndal's lecture is interesting for the light it throws on his philosophy of life and as a significant literary document.[23]

Gröndal's most notable verse translations are his completion of some four books of the *Odyssey* (1854), which his father, Sveinbjörn Egilsson, had not lived to finish, and his own translation of the *Iliad* (1856), only the first half of which has been published. He also successfully translated shorter poems by Goethe, Schiller, and others.

Benedikt Gröndal had in his day considerable influence on Icelandic literature. The younger poets were fascinated by his bold imagination, his eloquent and flowery style, and imitated these qualities. One of them was Kristján Jónsson, although we are told by one of his biographers that he attempted to avoid Gröndal's excesses.[24]

6. Gísli Brynjúlfsson played quite an important part in the political history of Iceland during the latter half of the nineteenth century and for a time also occupied a place of prominence among his fellow poets. In later years, however, his poetry has very largely fallen into oblivion, not altogether deservedly for he was in some respects an unusual and an individualistic writer.

He was born at Ketilstaðir in eastern Iceland on September 3, 1827. His father Gísli Brynjúlfsson, who was drowned shortly before the poet's birth, was a clergyman and a promising scholar; his mother, Guðrún Stefánsdóttir, belonged to one of the most distinguished and influential families in the land. After graduating from the Latin School at Bessastaðir in 1845, Gísli Brynjúlfsson studied law and later Old Norse philology at the University of Copenhagen; from 1848 to 1874 he was a stipendiary of the Arna-Magnean Foundation. He then became lecturer in Icelandic history and literature at the University, holding that position until his death on May 29, 1888.

A man of cosmopolitan interests and wide learning and skilled in many languages, Gísli Brynjúlfsson wrote a number of articles on political and philological subjects and throughout his life devoted

[23] "Um skáldskap" was published in *Lögrétta*, XXVII (1932), 356–380, 443–469.

[24] Jón Ólafsson in his introductory biographical sketch to *Ljóðmæli eftir Kristján Jónsson* (1911), pp. xx–xxi.

much attention to the writing of poetry. A collected edition of his original poems and translations, *Ljóðmæli,* was published in Copenhagen in 1891. Previously several of these had appeared in Icelandic periodicals, including the annual *Norðurfari* (1848–1849), which he published together with Jón Thoroddsen, and in the collection *Svava,* published with Benedikt Gröndal and Steingrímur Thorsteinsson.[25]

Passionately interested in the cause of freedom and the liberation of oppressed nations, Gísli Brynjúlfsson early threw himself into the struggle for Icelandic independence. Quite naturally he reaped hostility and abuse from his countrymen for opposing their great and beloved political leader, Jón Sigurðsson. But there was no lack of patriotism on Gísli Brynjúlfsson's part, however unfortunate the circumstances, for love of his native land and interest in its progress are clear undercurrents in many of his poems.

Still more characteristic of him and unusual among his contemporaries was his pronounced interest in foreign affairs, especially of Europe and even of America. The two volumes of *Norðurfari,* of which he was the moving spirit, are largely devoted to enthusiastic accounts of the revolutionary movements throughout Europe about the middle of the nineteenth century. They are also favored subjects in his poems. He wrote a large group entitled "Frelsiskvæði íslenzk og almenn" (Songs of Liberty, Icelandic and General), in which he dealt with the February Revolution in France, 1848, and the Irish rebellion of the same year. He was especially interested in the struggle of the Magyars for independence and warmly eulogized Kossuth, their great national hero. All these poems are permeated with ardent love of freedom, the poet unfailingly aligning himself with the oppressed. Of special interest is his forceful poem on the uprising of the laboring class in Paris, June 23–26, 1848, where he sides strongly with the working men. He is clearly sympathetic toward socialism, and its views appear here for the first time in Icelandic poetry.

Gísli Brynjúlfsson's numerous love poems form the other major

---

[25] See also Þorsteinn Gíslason, "Gísli Brynjúlfsson," *Lögrétta,* XXIX (1934), 157–168; and Gils Guðmundsson, "Gísli Brynjúlfsson og febrúarbyltingin 1948," *Tímarit Máls og Menningar* (1945), pp. 241–255.

group of his verse and are also among his most interesting productions. Many of them were inspired by an unsnccessful love affair, including his touching and once popular "Grâtur Jakobs yfir Rakel" (Jacob's Lament for Rachel), which is undeniably well written and fraught with genuine feeling.

His familiarity with world literature is apparent in his translations from classical, German, Italian, Swedish, Norwegian, Danish, and English authors. From the works of Byron, who was his favorite poet and deeply influenced him, he translated no less than ten selections. Deliberately imitating Byron, notably in "Faraldr" (The Traveler), Gísli Brynjúlfsson may be considered the most thoroughgoing representative of Byronism in Icelandic literature.[26] His translations, though not without literary merit, generally lack smoothness and therefore have not worn well.

This is equally true of the majority of his own poems, which frequently are also lacking in originality. Moreover, as they were often on passing political themes and in antiquated language, they were doomed to shortlived popularity. The scholar and the propagandist too often overshadow the poet. As his style reveals, Gísli Brynjúlfsson was steeped in Old Icelandic writings and draws upon them freely in verse forms (not least in his memorial poems) as well as in quotations and illustrations. The ancient Norse heroic spirit appealed to him, and one of his best poems, often sung and quoted to this day, is a striking expression of unflinching manliness. But his classical learning is also much in evidence, and he used foreign verse forms such as the sonnet. Thus, in his poetry currents from abroad blend interestingly with the native Icelandic tradition.

7. STEINGRÍMUR THORSTEINSSON was born at Arnarstapi in Snæfellsnessýsla in western Iceland on May 19, 1831, and came of a prominent family. His father, Governor Bjarni Thorsteinsson, was one of the founders of the Icelandic Literature Society (Hið Íslenzka Bókmenntafélag, 1816); his mother, Þórunn, was the daughter of the learned Bishop Hannes Finnsson, from whom the Danish (Finsen)

[26] See Richard Beck, "Gísli Brynjúlfsson—An Icelandic Imitator of *Childe Harold's Pilgrimage*," *Journal of English and Germanic Philology*, XXVIII (1929), 220–237; also published in Icelandic as "Gísli Brynjúlfsson og Byron," *Skírnir*, CXIII (1939), 136–160.

branch of the family is also descended. Young Thorsteinsson, therefore, was reared in an atmosphere of culture and literary interest. The impressive scenic environment of his youth, which he has portrayed graphically and affectionately in one of his most notable poems, "Snæfellsjökull" (Snæfell's Glacier), was equally stimulating to a budding poet. He was unusually precocious and at an early age interested himself in literature, having at his disposal a good library. In 1846, when he was fifteen, he entered the State College at Reykjavík. Here, like many other Icelandic poets of the period, he came under the beneficial influence of Sveinbjörn Egilsson, who taught him the appreciation of idiomatic and beautiful style and inspired in him an abiding love for his native tongue. In his college days Thorsteinsson likewise began the study of more recent foreign literature; he mastered German and acquired the works of Goethe and Schiller in the original. During these years he began to attract attention by his poetic efforts, which were largely humorous and foreshadowed his later poems and epigrams in that vein. An interesting, though youthful, work from this period is his *Redd-Hannesar ríma* (first published in 1924). A mock epic in Homeric style, it is based on an episode from the poet's youth and is in spots very cleverly done, often hitting the mark and having a certain cultural-historical significance. Prominent in student activities, Thorsteinsson was one of the leaders in a historic uprising (1850) against the college authorities, which came near causing his expulsion. He was, however, graduated in due course in 1851, with high honors in many subjects.

The same summer he matriculated at the University of Copenhagen, first studying law, but soon turning his attention to classical philology. At the same time he devoted himself assiduously to the study of philosophy and aesthetics, reading extensively not only Scandinavian literature, but also the works of leading German, English, and French authors. This wide reading before long bore fruit in his numerous and significant translations into Icelandic.

After receiving his degree in 1863, he remained for a number of years in Copenhagen, where he engaged in teaching and writing; from 1868 to 1872 he was a stipendiary of the Arna-Magnean Foundation. He was never more productive than during his Copenhagen years; many of his most important translations and original poems date from that period. Several factors contributed to this: the metropolitan atmosphere and life, his association with scholars and poets kindred in spirit, and not least the currents of thought then prevalent, the liberal and progressive tendencies following in the wake of the French Revolution of 1848. The movement for Icelandic independence, under the inspired leadership of Jón Sigurðsson, was at its height; and the liberty-loving young poet, upon his arrival in Copenhagen, soon became one of his most ardent followers; Jón Sigurðsson in turn valued highly his gifted fellow countryman, whose interests also were uncommonly many-sided.

In 1872 Thorsteinsson returned to Iceland to become teacher of classical and modern languages in the State College at Reykjavík, serving in that capacity until his death over forty years later. The last nine years he also officiated as rector of the institution. Though burdened with teaching and executive duties, he continued writing poetry and translating foreign masterpieces into his native tongue. He died on August 21, 1913. The Icelandic nation mourned him as a beloved poet, teacher, and patriot, who for over half a century had been one of the brightest stars in its literary firmament and an elevating force in its cultural and spiritual life.

His first printed poems, five in number, appeared in 1854 in the annual *Ný félagsrit*, where many more were printed in the following years. In a short time, they were making the author a national literary figure. From 1858 until 1872, with but brief interruptions, he served on the editorial board of this significant publication. He edited and, for the most part, wrote the annual *Ný sumargjöf* (1859–1862 and 1865). In 1860, as one of the editors, he contributed a number of poems to the collection *Svava*. With Matthías Jochumsson, another leading poet of the day, he published *Svanhvít* (1877), an anthology of translations into Icelandic. Both of these anthologies became very popular and later appeared in further editions. Thorsteinsson was also one of the editors of the periodical *Iðunn* (1884–1889), contributing translations of both stories and poems.

His original poems, *Ljóðmæli* (Poems), were first collected and published in book form in 1881; a second enlarged edition appeared in 1893; a third, again considerably enlarged, in 1910; and a fourth in 1925. Clearly, his poems have enjoyed rare popularity. A selection from them, *Úrvalsljóð* (Selected Poems), edited by the poet's son, Axel Thorsteinsson, was published in 1939 and a second edition appeared in 1946. A biography of the poet, together with an evaluation of his work and a number of translations from his poems, is found in J. C. Poestion's *Steingrímur Thorsteinsson, ein isländischer Dichter und Kulturbringer* (München and Leipzig, 1912).[27]

Nor are the reasons for Thorsteinsson's popularity far to seek. A man of a highly cultivated and sure literary taste, he was the master of the lyric, and he wrote on themes having the widest appeal: patriotism, nature (particularly in her lighter and brighter mood), and love.

His patriotic poems, many of which were written during his sojourn in Copenhagen and under the impact of the determined movement for regaining Icelandic independence, bear unmistakable marks of their origin. They vibrate with profound love of country, but in a still more marked degree with a fervent love of liberty. Hence, they are ringing exhortations to his countrymen, challenging them to action in the interests of their political freedom. Beautifully and vigorously phrased, sonorous, and rich in practical wisdom, these poems did not fall on deaf ears. The response to them was ready and general; the old and especially the young memorized them, quoted them, and sang them. They were the author's contribution to the Icelandic struggle for independence, and by no means an insignificant one, for with them he sang greater love of liberty into the hearts of his countrymen and interpreted for them the ideals of their great leaders. An example of this is his stirring "Vorhvőt" (Challenge of Spring), in which the description of the varied and impressive Icelandic scenery blends harmoniously with the poet's burning love of freedom. Romanticist that he was, he often turned to the historic past for inspiration.

---

[27] See also Guðmundur Finnbogason, "Steingrímur Thorsteinsson," *Skírnir*, LXXXVIII (1914), 1–10; Haraldur Níelsson, "Steingrímur Thorsteinsson," *Andvari*, XXXIX (1914), 1–16; Þorsteinn Gíslason, "Steingrímur Thorsteinsson, aldarminning," *Lesbók Morgunblaðsins*, VI (1931), 153–156; Sigfús Blőndal, "Steingrímur Thorsteinsson 1831–1931," *Nordisk tidskrift* (Stockholm), VII (1931), 585–597; Sigurður Guðmundsson, "Steingrímur Thorsteinsson," in *Heiðnar hugvekjur og mannaminni*, (Akureyri, 1946), pp. 56–61; Richard Beck, "Steingrímur Thorsteinsson—Lyric Poet and Master Translator," *Scandinavian Studies*, XX (1948), 82–91.

His nature poems formed a very important part of his original production, especially after his return to Iceland in 1872. He loved fervently the scenery of his native land and was tireless in singing its praises in graceful, deeply emotional lyrics. Its springs and summers particularly appealed to him, and his descriptions of Iceland in these seasons are among the most beautiful of their kind. He also had an eye for the peculiar beauty of the Icelandic autumn and for the grandeur of Iceland, although its rural charm was more to his liking. He delighted in making summer excursions to the countryside, even into the uplands, and these journeys inspired some of his most notable descriptive poems.

The sea clearly cast a lasting spell upon him, as he wrote about it in its various moods: slumbering sun-kissed in the summer calm, sighing heavily along the coast, or rushing on, storm-driven, in white-crested breakers. A notable example of such poems is the one entitled "Við hafið" (By the Sea), in which the tender and melancholy mood, often characteristic of the poet, merges effectively with the theme and the verse form.

His love poems are frequently in the same key, delicate and touching, mirroring the longing and the sadness of the human heart. He was, however, equally capable of pouring out his disappointment in love in caustic lines trembling with bitterness and piercing like sharp daggers, as in "Kveðja" (A Farewell), with its unmistakable undercurrent of genuine sorrow.

In one of his most ambitious poems, the historical "Gilsbakkaljóð" (Glenside Lay), he successfully weaves together nature description and a love theme. Here he retells, in bold strokes, the tragic tale of Helga and Gunnlaugr of the *Gunnlaugs saga Ormstungu*, against the impressive scenic background of Borgarfjőrður.

Especially noteworthy and perhaps most original of Thorsteinsson's poetry are his epigrams. Here his mastery of terse and striking phrases appears to full advantage, making him one of the most quotable of Icelandic poets. As he was endowed with a keen sense of humor, which inclined toward irony, his verses of this type are often characterized by biting satire, brilliantly expressed.

Significant as was Thorsteinsson's original production, his translations are not only far more extensive, but also of equally great and lasting importance. More than most Icelandic writers, past and present, he has enriched the literature of his country with prose and verse renditions of foreign masterpieces, such as *The Arabian Nights*, Shakespeare's *King Lear*, Defoe's *Robinson Crusoe*, Tegnér's *Axel*, and Andersen's *Fairy Tales*. Besides, he has rendered into Icelandic the choicest gems of lyric poetry from classical and modern literature, poems representing some sixty poets from fifteen nations, including many of the finest works of Ossian, Oehlenschläger, Wergeland, Bjőrnson, Topelius, Tennyson, Byron, Burns, Petőfi, Chamisso, Heine, Goethe, and Schiller. These translations, the majority of which had been published previously in newspapers, periodicals, and elsewhere, together with some of his prose translations, were published by his son, Axel Thorsteinsson, in two volumes, *Ritsafn*, 1924 and 1926.

Steingrímur Thorsteinsson's translations are, however, not notable primarily for their unusual quantity, but rather for their general high level of excellence. Of the prose, the translation of *The Arabian Nights* is particularly successful throughout, whereas in poetry, the renditions of *King Lear* and of Byron's work (for instance, "The Prisoner of Chillon") are nothing short of masterful. The same is true of many of the shorter verse translations.

Thorsteinsson was essentially a Romanticist and at the same time a good deal of a Classicist. To the end of his days he remained devoted to the literary tendency that had fostered him and inspired him. Therefore, as might be expected, Realism did not appeal to him; stark reality, ugly or unpleasant, jarred his sensitivity. It conflicted with his love of purity and beauty, a trait as fundamental to his temperament as it was characteristic of his translations. He was neither particularly original nor profound, but he possessed a wholesome outlook upon life, a genuine sympathy for the less fortunate, and an equally wholehearted dislike for the oppressor; and, free from the artificiality and the narrow-mindedness of small souls, he vehemently detested snobbery of every kind.

But if it cannot be said that Thorsteinsson broke any new trails in the realm of letters, he will, nevertheless, be long remembered as one of the greatest benefactors of Icelandic literature. He was, as Poestion has said, above all a *Kulturbringer*,[28] one who made vast foreign literary treasures the lasting possession of his people and thus gave new depth and color to their cultural life. Just as through his patriotic and nature poems he opened the eyes of many of his countrymen to the beauty of their native land, so through his translations he stimulated their love of beauty generally and their appreciation of beautiful language and style in particular. Through his numerous lyrics for popular tunes he also contributed a great deal to the development of vocal music in Iceland.

8. The life of MATTHÍAS JOCHUMSSON was uncommonly eventful and rich in varied experiences. He has told his own story interestingly and effectively in a series of autobiographical sketches, *Sögukaflar af sjálfum mér* (Akureyri, 1922). His letters, *Bréf Matthíasar Jochumssonar* (Akureyri, 1935), edited with a preface by his son, Steingrímur Matthíasson, also cast a flood of light upon his character and poetic genius and reveal his eloquence, robust imagination, rare mastery of language, and his wide interests and sympathies.

He was born November 11, 1835, at the farm of Skógar in Breiðifjörður in western Iceland. The son of a farmer of small means, he came of sturdy stock. He grew up in impressive and historic surroundings, the scene of *Gull-Þóris saga* (*Þorskfirðinga saga*), which, as he himself emphasizes and his poetry amply testifies, left many marks on his outlook upon life and his literary production. During his early years he tried his hand at many things; he engaged in farm work in the rural district where he grew up, he was a fisherman, and for some years he clerked in a village store. His literary interest awakened early, and he read widely during these years of varied activities. At the age of twenty-two he went to Copenhagen for the purpose of preparing to become a merchant. His literary inclination directed him, however, into more profitable channels culturally. He studied foreign languages and read with avidity and enthusiasm classical, Old Icelandic, and contemporary European literature under the discriminating and capable guidance of Steingrímur Thorsteinsson, the scholar and poet.

---

[28] See his volume published in honor of the poet's 80th birthday, *Steingrímur Thorsteinsson, ein isländischer Dichter und Kulturbringer* (Munich and Leipzig, 1912).

After a profitable year's sojourn in Copenhagen, Matthías Jochumsson returned to Iceland. With the assistance of friends and relatives he began his formal education shortly thereafter and was graduated from the College at Reykjavík in 1863. He studied theology, and in 1865, at the age of thirty, was granted his degree from the Theological School. With the exception of several years spent in journalistic work and travels abroad, he served as pastor in various parts of Iceland until the end of the century. For a six-year period (1881–1887) he was at Oddi in southern Iceland, the historic seat of Sæmund the Learned and his descendants and long an intellectual center.[29] From 1900 until his death Matthías Jochumsson received from the Icelandic government an honorary pension, enabling him to devote himself entirely to literary work. The spirit of adventure was always alive in his heart, however, as was his desire to keep abreast of the spiritual and material progress of the world outside his remote Iceland; therefore he made frequent journeys abroad, eleven in all. He represented Iceland at the Chicago Exposition in 1893 and traveled extensively on the American continent, visiting many of the Icelandic settlements in the United States and Canada. These journeys were a spiritual tonic, opened new worlds of thought, and stimulated his creative urge.

On the occasion of his eighty-fifth birthday, in 1920, the University of Iceland conferred on him the honorary degree of Doctor of Divinity; and the town of Akureyri in northern Iceland, where he had resided over thirty years, made him an honorary citizen. But the aged poet was not long permitted to enjoy these well-earned honors; he died a week later on December 18. The Icelandic people at home and abroad mourned the loss of their leading contemporary poet and profound interpreter of their rich literary and cultural heritage.[30]

Matthías Jochumsson was both a versatile and a prolific writer—a journalist, an essayist, a dramatist, and a lyric poet. The richness and

[29] See H. Hermannsson, *Sæmund Sigfússon and the Oddaverjar* ("Islandica," Vol. XXII [Ithaca, N. Y., 1932]).

[30] See the memorial volume *Matthías Jochumsson 1835–1920; Erfiminning: ræður - erfiljóð - eftirmæli*, ed. Steingrimur Matthíasson (1922), which contains funeral orations, numerous memorial poems, and articles by Einar H. Kvaran and Sigurður Nordal.

variety of his productivity is particularly remarkable when one takes into consideration the conditions under which he labored. He did not complete his professional studies until he was thirty and, until he was sixty-five, cultivated his literary and cultural interests in the time spared from the duties of public office and the support of a large family. During his earlier years he was, moreover, repeatedly weighed down by great personal sorrows. A lesser man would have succumbed to such adverse circumstances, and it cannot be denied that his art and production suffered from the unfavorable conditions under which he was compelled to do his literary work.

For six years (1874–1880) he was editor of the leading Icelandic weekly, *Þjóðólfur*, published at Reykjavík; through it he doubtless exerted considerable influence on public opinion. Later (1889–1891) he edited the semi-monthly *Lýður* (The People) at Akureyri. To the end of his days he contributed frequently to a number of Icelandic papers; his newspaper articles would fill several large volumes.

As an editor Matthías Jochumsson wrote especially on educational and literary subjects, also giving some attention to religion and church affairs. His discussions of the latter in the columns of his own and other papers were characterized by his liberal views and his broad-mindedness. His educational theories were also progressive; he advocated the establishment of rural public schools and wrote in favor of educational institutions similar to Grundtvig's Folk High Schools in Denmark, which he had studied extensively on a grant from the government. In politics his editorial policy was conciliatory. Never an ardent partisan, he steered clear of political quarrels and felt that the interests of his country were best served by middle course. As a journalist he was therefore primarily interested in educating his countrymen and thus furthering their spiritual as well as their material progress.[31] This is clearly stated in his first editorial in which he says that he "wishes to arouse sane and impartial public opinion, a general progressive tendency in the land, based on liberalism, intelligence and justice."[32]

[31] For information about his journalistic career, see Steindór Steindórsson's "Blaðamenska Matthíasar Jochumssonar," *Eimreiðin*, XLII (1936), 167–182; and Richard Beck, "Þjóðmálastefna séra Matthíasar Jochumssonar," *Samtíðin*, II (1935), 7–10.

[32] *Þjóðólfur*, May 4, 1874.

Aside from his numerous essays in papers and periodicals, he wrote three travel books of note: *Chicagó-för mín* (My Journey to Chicago, 1893), *Frá Danmörku* (From Denmark; Copenhagen, 1906), and *Ferð um fornar stöðvar* (Visiting Old Haunts, 1913). The second one is the most substantial, a highly interesting collection of papers on Denmark, Danish history, literature, and culture, and the Danish national character as compared with the Icelandic. Not the least interesting and significant parts of the volume are the poems, about twenty in number, among which are his excellent verses about Roskilde Cathedral ("Í Hróarskeldu dómkirkju") and Grundtvig. *Ferð um fornar stöðvar* is especially interesting for the light it throws on the author's life and character and for the poems included, several of which are notable for their beauty and vigor. Generally speaking, his travel books are written in the lively, poetic style characteristic of all his prose writings.

In literary significance his dramas rank far below his best lyric poetry; nevertheless, they are interesting and of considerable merit and therefore have been discussed in the account of the prose writers of the period.[33] It was, however, in his lyric poetry that his genius flowered most fully, and here *the man*, no less than *the poet*, is seen to the best advantage in all his many-sidedness.

His first book of poems, *Ljóðmæli* (Poems), was published in 1884. Some twenty years later a collected edition in five sizable volumes under the same title appeared (Seyðisfjörður and Reykjavík, 1902–1906), containing both original poems and translations. A third collected edition, much enlarged, *Ljóðmæli*, in one volume edited by his son, Magnús Matthíasson, was published in 1936. Three volumes of selections from his poems have appeared: *Ljóðmæli* (*Úrval*), selected and edited by Guðmundur Finnbogason, 1915; *Úrvalsljóð*, selected by Árni Pálsson, 1935; and *Ljóðmæli* (*Íslenzk úrvalsrit*), edited with an extensive introduction by Jónas Jónsson, 1945. The poet's sustained popularity is clearly reflected in these repeated editions of his works and selections from them.[34]

---

[33] See Einarsson, *Prose Writers*, pp. 57–60.

[34] For additional information on his literary career and works, see the anniversary volume *Matthías Jochumsson* (1905); Sigurður Guðmundsson, "Matthías áttræður," *Skírnir*, XC (1916), 1–16 (reprinted in the author's *Heiðnar hugvekjur*

He also wrote a long narrative poem, *Grettisljóð* (Songs of Grettir; Ísafjörður, 1897), based on the dramatic and tragic *Grettis saga.* Here are several individual poems and passages characterized by genuine poetic feeling, flight of the imagination, and mastery of form. Particularly beautiful are the poems in which Grettir's devoted mother, Ásdís, appears; and very effective also is the much admired description of the coming of the ghost Glámur and his encounter with Grettir.

Matthías Jochumsson's poems deal with a great variety of themes, but many of them are occasional poems. He has written a large number of patriotic poems, festive poems, and obituary pieces, besides others more general. Sometimes, as is only to be expected, his inspiration fails him; but much more frequently he succeeds in producing forceful and original poetry, although uneven in excellence of style. A good example of the beauty and elevation of his poetry, when his inspiration is at its height, is the short poem "Leiðsla" (Ecstasy), a remarkable spiritual autobiography universal in ist appeal.

His nature poems are impressive in their grandeur and contain magnificent passages such as his description of Skagafjörður in northern Iceland, one of the country's most beautiful and historic districts. Here as elsewhere, he weaves the local historical traditions

---

og mannaminni [Akureyri, 1946], pp. 66–81); Árni Pálsson, "Ræða fyrir minni Matthíasar Jochumssonar," *Iðunn,* I (1915–16), 204–209; Sigurður Nordal, "Matthías við Dettifoss," *Eimreiðin,* XXVII (1921), 1–10 (reprinted in his *Áfangar* [*Svipir*] [1944], II, 71–82); Kristján Albertsson, "Matthías Jochumsson, minningarræða, " *Eimreiðin,* XXVII (1921), 303–310; Steingrímur Matthíasson, "Björnstjerne Björnson og faðir minn," *Tímarit Þjóðræknisfélags Íslendinga í Vesturheimi,* XVI (1934), 51–59, and "Steingrímur læknir minnist föður síns," *Lesbók Morgunblaðsins,* X (1935), 370–372; Magnús Jónsson, "Matthías Jochumsson, trúarskáldið," *Kirkjuritið,* I (1935), 369–379; Richard Beck, "Matthías Jochumsson—Icelandic Poet and Translator," *Scandinavian Studies and Notes,* XIII (1934–1935), 111–124; articles by Indriði Einarsson, Einar H. Kvaran, Steingrímur Matthíasson, Árni Pálsson, and Guðmundur Finnbogason, *Skírnir,* CIX (1935), 5–48; Guðmundur Finnbogason, "Matthías Jochumsson, aldarminning," *Eimreiðin,* XLI (1935), 369–373; Benjamín Kristjánsson, "Matthías Jochumsson, aldarminning," *Nýjar Kvöldvökur,* XXIX (1936), 1–11; Stefán Einarsson, "Shakespeare in Iceland: An Historical Survey," *Journal of English Literary History,* VII (1940), 272–285; also published in Icelandic as "Shakespeare á Íslandi," *Tímarit Þjóðræknisfélags Íslendinga í Vesturheimi,* XIX (1937), 24–36; XX (1938), 37–54.

into the nature descriptions, thereby enhancing their general effectiveness and impressiveness. Grim but compelling in its forcefulness and vividness is "Hafísinn" (Drift Ice), describing the arrival of this "ancient foe." Here is an uncommon richness of original and striking similes. Characteristically, the author paints his pictures in large strokes; generally, he writes best on the largest themes.

His poems on subjects from the history of Iceland, of which he possessed both extensive knowledge and penetrating understanding, are particularly noteworthy. He gloried in portraying the great men such as Snorri Sturluson, Bishop Jón Arason, Bishop Guðbrandur Þorláksson, Hallgrímur Pétursson, and Eggert Ólafsson, vividly picturing them at the most decisive moments in their lives. The poem commemorating Eggert Ólafsson's last voyage has deservedly been much admired for its excellent construction, as the mood and the theme blend into an unbroken pattern and the impending doom grips the reader's heart.

Closely related to Matthías Jochumsson's historical poems and equally notable are his elegiac and memorial poems, many of which rank with the greatest productions of their kind in the Icelandic language. No Icelandic poet, past or present, has written so large and varied a group of such poems as he. Frequently, moreover, he succeeded admirably in individualizing his subjects. As has been well observed, his sympathy was so great that his obituary poems are as widely different as were the people he wrote about. Especially impressive in its imaginative and pictorial quality is his memorial poem on Dr. Guðbrandur Vigfússon, the great scholar. He and other such men appealed particularly to Matthías Jochumsson and his historical interest; and, in his graphic portrayals of them, he indirectly describes himself. For he too was Icelandic to the core and steeped in the national cultural and literary tradition. Among his most touching memorial poems, on the other hand, are his lament for his second wife, "Sorg" (Sorrow), and his tribute to his mother, elegies characterized by deep emotion and rich poetic beauty.

Matthías Jochumsson gave much thought to the deepest problems of human existence—life and death, and the hereafter. His religious poems and hymns, often reaching the highest peaks of inspiration, breathe deep faith and strong idealism. His hymn "Ó, Guð vors lands" (Our Country's God), written in 1874 for the millennial celebration of the settlement of Iceland, has deservedly become the Icelandic national anthem.

Equally inspired and profound are other hymns, such as the celebrated New Year's hymn, from which the following verses (in the adaptation of Professor Kemp Malone) are taken:

Fear not, though here be cold today
And worldly joys a feast fordone,
And all thy strength as driven spray,
For God is lord of earth and sun.

He hears the tempest's minstrelsy,
He hears the sleeping babe draw breath,
He hears the very heart of thee
And knows each throb from birth to death.

Ay, God is lord in every age:
He speaks, his creatures but give ear.
His words excite, his words assuage
The mighty deep, the secret tear.[35]

His inspiration, eloquence, and characteristically effective use of contrast are here strikingly illustrated. He has, indeed, written some of the most beautiful hymns in the Icelandic language—hymns in which deep and abiding faith and rare spiritual insight are transmuted into the purest gold of noble poetry. He also translated a number of hymns into Icelandic. Often the raging storms of doubt—for his was an open and inquiring mind—swept his soul, only to make him arrive at deeper and firmer faith. Because of his liberal religious views, many of his best hymns were, however, excluded from the Icelandic hymn book of his day. This injustice has now been rectified, since a large number of his original and translated hymns have have been included in the new Icelandic hymnal (1945). He is unquestionably one of Iceland's two greatest hymn writers of all time, the other being Hallgrímur Pétursson.

The richness and many-sidedness of Matthías Jochumsson's literary genius and his unusual mental stature are further seen in the

[35] Richard Beck, *Icelandic Poems and Stories* (New York, 1943), p. 44.

fact that this great master of the grand style was equally capable of the lighter touch, the humorous and even the hilarious. Surveying his production as a whole, one can readily see that his literary taste sometimes led him astray. At his inspired best, he combined startling imagery, often reckless flight of the imagination, with profound thought. His style is forceful and eloquent. His mastery of his native tongue is astounding; in his hands it becomes a veritable harp of a hundred strings. Small wonder that he wrote its greatest hymn of praise, clothed in its own sonorous garb.

Equally great was his mastery of Icelandic verse forms, old and new alike. He was so steeped in Old Icelandic literature and possessed such kinship with the Icelandic poets of yore that the ancient verse forms were as natural to him as the new. Not uncommonly he successfully harmonized and merged new and old metrical forms, words, and phrases. In his resonant and challenging memorial poem on Bjőrnstjerne Bjőrnson, he dexterously inserted stanzas from "Hákonarmâl" (Lay of Hakon) by Eyvindur Finnsson skâldaspillir of the tenth century. Similarly, the opening lines of his poem to Norway clearly recall Sighvatr Þórðarsons's famous tribute to King Olaf the Holy, from the eleventh century. Thus Matthías Jochumsson bridges the gulf of the centuries, is both ancient and modern. The continuity in Icelandic language and culture down through the ages partly accounts for this. Egill Skallagrímsson, the viking, and Matthías Jochumsson, the clergyman, though separated by centuries, could readily exchange verse lines and understand each other completely.

It was this unusual mastery of his native language and of Icelandic verse forms coupled with his poetic genius and a lifelong desire to share with others his spiritual treasures that enabled Matthías Jochumsson to enrich, in an unsurpassed degree, the literature of his country with translations of a number of major foreign masterpieces. These included Shakespeare's *Hamlet*, *Macbeth*, *Othello*, and *Romeo and Juliet;* Byron's *Manfred*; Ibsen's *Brand;* Tegnér's *Frithjof's saga;* and Topelius's great historical novel, *Fältskärns berättelser* (The Stories of an Army Surgeon); as well as a vast number of shorter poems from Scandinavian, other European, and American literature. Of these may be specially mentioned his masterful renditions of Ibsen's "Terje Viken" and Runeberg's "Fänrik Ståls Sägner." Matthías Jochumsson's translations are memorable not only because of their great extensiveness and variety, but even more because of their uniformly high literary level. He emphasizes faithfulness to the thought and the spirit of the originals rather than to the letter, and for that reason he usually succeeds.

Behind his rich literary production one readily senses the presence of his strong and remarkable personality. His poetry comes from a warm and tender heart and always breathes a love of beauty, a joy in living, and a rejuvenating spirit of optimism. His faith in God and love of his fellow man are the surging undercurrents; the mighty torrents of a great waterfall impress him less than the tears of a child (as in his poem "Dettifoss"). Icelandic to the core, he was nevertheless a true cosmopolitan who interested himself in the material and spiritual progress of mankind generally. High and low, rich and poor, were of equal concern to him. A man of deep faith, he possessed at the same time a mind unusually hospitable to new truths. This rare mental alertness and youthful outlook upon life he retained for his eighty-five years.

The Icelandic nation owes him an inestimable debt. In his own day, in particular during the latter part of his life, his countrymen lavished their esteem and admiration upon him and enshrined him gratefully in their hearts. His reputation and popularity remain undiminished; his literary longevity is assured as long as the Icelandic language is spoken.

9. To few Icelandic poets does the saying "Those whom the gods love, die young" apply more strikingly than to Kristján Jónsson. He was born at Krossdalur in northern Iceland on June 21, 1842. His father, a farmer of very small means but highly gifted, died when the future poet was five years old. An unusually precocious child, he had a hard youth. From the age of fourteen to twenty-two he earned his living as a farm hand. His education at home was most elementary, but he read everything he could lay his hand on, particularly the Icelandic sagas; and through his own efforts he acquired some knowledge of the Danish, Swedish, English, and German languages and literatures. His poems, published in the leading Icelandic papers of the day, attracted attention; and through the

assistance of several generous admirers he entered the college at Reyjavík in 1864. He attended until the spring of 1868, but did not graduate. From then until his untimely death in March, 1869, he was a private tutor in Vopnafjőrður in the northeast.

Kristján Jónsson's poetry and outlook upon life can be fully understood and appreciated only in the light of his early experiences. Uncommonly gifted, he grew up in poverty and under circumstances most adverse to the development of his genius; his desire for learning was thwarted; he was compelled to do work little to his liking and alien to his temperament; and his peculiarities, resulting directly from his dreamy, poetic nature, were the butt of ridicule. Naturally, his sensitive soul was deeply hurt. His spirit was one of melancholy and hopelessness, and a disappointment in love aggravated that state of mind. He became addicted to drink, which both affected his attitude and shortened his life.

As a result, the dominant tone of his poetry is one of brooding melancholy and stark pessimism. Occasionally, however, the other side of his nature, the very opposite, breaks through in an exuberant lightheartedness. In nearly every poem, however, his bitterness and hopelessness appear—even in his beautiful and well-wrought "Vonin" (The Hope), which, after extolling the life-giving powers of hope, closes on this gloomy note: "Hope, nevertheless, is only a delusion." Weary unto death, with no desire to live, the poet welcomed the end, seeing in the grave the only place of lasting rest and solace. This thought he has expressed with characteristic feeling and in polished form in "Grőfin" (The Grave).

This negative view of life, his melancholy and pessimism, doubtless largely accounted for the great vogue that his poems enjoyed for a time. They appealed to the ingrained strain of melancholy in the national temperament, a characteristic accentuated by centuries of oppression and struggle against a hostile environment. In these poems, the common people in particular saw mirrored their broken hopes and sorrows, and they identified themselves with the poet's state of mind and tragic fate.

His poems, *Ljóðmæli* (Poems), were published, with a biographical sketch by the poet Jón Ólafsson, in 1872, 1890, and 1911 and at Akureyri in 1946, edited by Víglundur Mőller. A selected edition appeared, edited with an introduction by the poet's nephew, the Reverend Björn B. Jónsson, in Washington, D.C. in 1907. A smaller selection, *Úrvalsljóð* (Selected Poems), edited by the poetess Hulda (Unnur B. Bjarklind), appeared in 1947. In recent years, however, his poems have generally lost in popularity, although some of them still remain in favor, such as his delicately felt and artistically wrought lyric "Tárið" (The Tear).

Kristján Jónsson also wrote patriotic and descriptive poems of merit. The most notable and successful is "Dettifoss," which is credited with first having drawn public attention to this impressive waterfall. Here the poet's descriptive ability, imagery, and mastery of form are seen to good advantage.

Among his narrative poems, "Veiðimaðurinn" (The Hunter), which enjoyed great popularity, is the most outstanding, both because of the fluent and vivid story and because of the descriptive quality. It strikingly reveals the poet's lively imagination as it tells of a French adventurer who has found a refuge in the primeval forest on the banks of the Mississippi.

When it is borne in mind that Kristján Jónsson died at the age of 26 and when his circumstances are taken into consideration, his production, though at times faulty in workmanship, leaves no doubt as to his great native gift. Of Icelandic poets he was most indebted to Benedikt Gröndal. Of foreign poets, Byron apparently influenced him most, the latter's world-weariness appealing strongly to him and no doubt deepening his melancholy and pessimism. His translations, though not numerous, are generally well done, some even excellently, and show much might have been expected of him in that field.[36] In his death Iceland lost a writer of unusual promise.

---

[36] Concerning his poetry, see also Guðmundur Guðmundsson, *Kristján Jónsson skáld, fyrirlestur* (Ísafjörður, 1908).

III

The Unschooled Poets

AMONG Icelandic writers of note, a considerable number can justly be referred to as "unschooled poets," in contrast to their learned brethren. Highly important and characteristic representatives of that group during the first half of the nineteenth century were Sigurður Breiðfjörð and Hjálmar Jónsson. Their careers were similar in some respects. Abject poverty and a full measure of adversity were the lot of both, partly as a result of hostile social environment, but in no small degree brought on by their own shortcomings. In spite of these limitations, however, their poetry bears ample evidence of their rich native talent and has earned them a secure place in the history of Icelandic literature.

1. SIGURÐUR EIRÍKSSON BREIÐFJÖRÐ was born at the farm of Rifgirðingar in Breiðifjörður in western Iceland on March 4, 1798, and grew up in that vicinity. His father, a farmer of small means, possessed some talent as a versemaker, as did some members of his mother's family. Very early the son showed unusual ability in that direction, writing his first cycle of narrative poems (*rímur*) at the age of eleven, according to his own testimony. After two years of tutoring from a neighboring clergyman, young Breiðfjörð, then only sixteen, was sent to Copenhagen to learn the trade of a cooper. Here he remained from 1814 (or 1815) to 1818. He read much and became well acquainted with contemporary Danish and Norwegian literature, as his poetry reveals. His sojourn in Copenhagen moulded his personality and outlook upon life and influenced his poetry.

Upon his return to Iceland, Breiðfjörð worked intermittently at his trade in the western and southern parts of the country, at the same time writing much verse, particularly of the *rímur* variety. This poetry won him great popularity, as it circulated widely in manuscript and appealed strongly to the popular taste of the day. He led an irregular life, however, having become addicted to strong drink. Financial and domestic troubles harassed him, and his first marriage was a failure.

With the assistance of relatives and friends he again went to Denmark in the fall of 1830 for the purpose of studying law. When, because of his instability and irregular living, the plan failed, his countrymen in Copenhagen secured for him the post of a cooper with the Royal Danish Mercantile Company in Greenland, where he went in the spring of 1831 to remain for more than three years. Although this period was by no means uneventful but was actually rich in new experiences, as he traveled extensively, he suffered from loneliness and homesickness, especially during the winter months. But his poetry, which he now found time to cultivate, offered him a refuge and consolation. Some of his best poetry dates from this period, including his *Númarímur*. His only major prose work, *Frá Grænlandi* (From Greenland; Copenhagen, 1836) was also the fruit of his stay there; it is an interesting description of the country and a lively account of his experiences.

Breiðfjörð returned to Iceland in 1834. The following two years appear to have been the happiest and most successful period of his life; during them he wrote much and prepared many of his best works for publication. Before long, however, misfortune dogged him—in no small measure, as before, the result of his irresponsibility and instability. But the flow of poems from his pen continued unabated. As he married again before having been formally divorced from his first wife, the courts convicted him of bigamy and sentenced him to severe punishment, but from this he was absolved by a royal decree and escaped with a small fine. His happiness in this dearly bought second marriage was, however, short-lived. He spent his last years in Reyjavík, where he died in dire poverty on July 21, 1846.[1]

[1] Jón Jónsson Borgfirðingur, *Stutt æfiminning Sigurðar Breiðfjarðar skálds* (1878); Sighvatur Grímsson Borgfirðingur, *Sigurður Breiðfjörð, fyrirlestur,* (1912); Þorsteinn Gíslason, "Sigurður Breiðfjörð," *Lögrétta,* XXVII (1932),

Breiðfjörð excelled in *rímur* and was one of its most recent major representatives. He is probably the most productive and, in many respects, the most successful. Over twenty-five sets of his *rímur* are in existence, fifteen of which have been published, several of them more than once. His themes are, generally speaking, traditional, although somewhat more varied than those of the average poet in the field; he draws on the sagas of Icelanders, the Romantic sagas, the sagas of the kings of Norway, and the romances, and he appears to have had a special fondness for subject matter from the history of Greece and Rome.

The bulk of this vast production, though in some ways superior to the general run of such poetry, is lacking in literary value, is marred by trite phrasing and poor taste, and does not rise above the pedestrian level of mere versemaking. Jónas Hallgrímsson's celebrated attack on the *rímur* is largely justified, although Breiðfjörð, his principal target, deserved it less than his fellow poets. As might be expected, he retaliated vigorously, both in prose and in verse. He was conscious of the fact that the *rímur* needed improvement, and his efforts in that direction bore some fruit.

To be sure, in his own ballad cycles of that type the prosaic mediocrity is often relieved by masterful and beautiful stanzas. Frequently these are found in his introductory passages. *Núma-rímur*, his most successful work of that type, contains many stanzas, and even passages, genuinely poetic and beautiful, revealing what the poet was capable of doing at his best, his unquestioned high native talent. To a certain degree he, therefore, succeeded in avoiding some of the most glaring pitfalls of the *rímur* poets, although he did not by any means achieve the aims set forth in his preface. The *Númarímur* is a versified paraphrase of J. P. C. Florian's novel *Numa Pompilius*, which Breiðfjörð knew in the Danish version and which he followed quite closely, particularly the first volume. It has been published no less than three times, in 1835, 1903, and 1937. The latest edition, uncommonly well printed, was edited with a preface by Sigurður Nordal and an authoritative introduction by

159–171; *Gísli Konráðsson, Ævisaga Sigurðar Breiðfjörðs skálds*, ed. Jóhann Gunnar Ólafsson (Ísafjörður, 1948); Jóhann Gunnar Ólafsson, "Sigurður Breiðfjörð: 150 ára minning," *Andvari*, LXXIII (1948), 36–56.

Sveinbjörn Sigurjónsson and was dedicated to Sir William A. Craigie on the occasion of his seventieth birthday.

Besides his *rímur*, Breiðfjörð wrote a large number of other poems, the most notable collections of which are *Ljóða Smámunir I–II* (Fugitive Verses; published in Copenhagen in 1836 and at Viðeyjarklaustur in 1839; second ed., 1911–1912), and *Úrvalsrit* (Selected Works, 1894), edited with an introduction by the poet Einar Benediktsson.

Breiðfjörð's poems of a general nature clearly mark him as belonging to a period of transition. One of the common people, he primarily carried on the tradition of the unschooled Icelandic poets. Nevertheless, he was not untouched by currents from abroad; his poems bear the earmarks of the Enlightenment and also of Romanticism. He translated poems from Baggesen, who influenced him considerably, and also translated or paraphrased poems by Oehlenschläger, Ingemann, and Schiller. He rendered freely from Norwegian into Icelandic S. O. Wolff's highly Romantic and one-time popular patriotic poem, "Hvor herligt er mit fődeland" (How Glorious Is My Native Land), localizing it very effectively. Breiðfjörð's original poems also express vigorously his love of country; his appreciation of the Icelandic landscape is seen in excellent nature descriptions, especially in some of his quatrains. Many of these and some epigrams are veritable gems both in verse form and pictorial quality.

There is a cheerfulness and warm humanity in Breiðfjörð's poetry, all the more attractive in view of his troubled life. Roguish humor, which comparatively seldom becomes sarcasm or malice, is characteristic of many of his verses. He is fond of children, sympathizes with the unfortunate, and in a number of poems expresses his love of animals. "Móðuræðurin" (The Eiderduck) is an excellent example and, all in all, one of his best poems, a deep-felt and splendid tribute to mother love.

A master of form and a ready improviser, who wrote on popular themes and carried on a literary tradition dear to the hearts of the common people, Breiðfjörð enjoyed immense popularity in his day and in a lesser degree has continued to do so; the common people identified themselves with him and, despite his many and obvious frailties, enshrined him gratefully in their hearts.

He also influenced later poets. Páll Ólafsson learned from him, as have other recent masters of the Icelandic quatrain. Steingrímur Thorsteinsson, brought up in Breiðfjörð's neighborhood, was very fond of his poetry. Þorsteinn Erlingsson was a still greater admirer of his, steeped in his *rímur* and other verses, and paid him glowing tribute. Einar Benediktsson, who edited his poems, had an equally high regard for him and recognized his great native ability and his contribution.

2. Although Sigurður Breiðfjörð and HJÁLMAR JÓNSSON (BÓLU-HJÁLMAR) had some things in common, they differed in several respects. For an Icelander of his day, Breiðfjörð saw much of the world, whereas Hjálmar Jónsson lived all his life in the north of Iceland, making only one short visit to the western part of the country. His field of observation was, therefore, far more restricted than that of his younger contemporary, whom he outlived by nearly twenty years. Furthermore, Breiðfjörð early became nationally known, all his most important works appearing in print during his lifetime; Hjálmar Jónsson was a man of sixty when his first poem was published (1858), and no collection of his poetry appeared until several years after his death.

Hjálmar Jónsson was born at Halland in Eyjafjörður in northern Iceland in 1796; the day of his birth is in doubt. He was the illegitimate son of a servant woman and a farm hand, but descended on his father's side from forebears of prominence, noted for their ability and learning. As an infant he was adopted by a kindhearted widow in the neighborhood, and later he lived with his father who had married and established a home of his own. Hjálmar Jónsson was a self-willed but promising youth, whose bent toward poetry showed itself unusually early. There is still preserved a quatrain written when he was six years old, testifying to his ready mastery of intricate verse forms. It is also of importance to note that he grew up in the vicinity of the poet Jón Þorláksson, who influenced him considerably, especially in his obituary poems and, perhaps to a lesser degree, in his satirical verse. He was a self-educated man, his instruction having been limited to the mere rudiments of reading and writing; but he read widely and possessed, according to visitors, a large library. He was interested in runology, geneology, and especially Icelandic folk tales. Several accounts from his pen are included in Jón Árnason's monumental collection of Icelandic folk lore. Hjálmar Jónsson's language and verse forms clearly reveal his familiarity with Old Icelandic poetry and the sagas; many of his best poems are written in Eddic meters, and he also uses Skaldic meter successfully. From dependable sources it appears that his mental ability was matched by his physical endowments; he was, for instance, noted for his athletic prowess and for being an excellent artisan and wood carver.

In 1820 Hjálmar Jónsson moved west from Eyjafjörður to Skagafjörður, married two years later, and lived as a cotter on various homesteads in that district until the end of his days. He spent fifteen consecutive years at a small place named "Bóla"; therefore, he is frequently referred to as "Bólu-Hjálmar." His life was a struggle against poverty and other hardships. In 1845 he lost his beloved and devoted wife, whom he mourned deeply in his poems. Her loss increased his melancholy, his sense of loneliness in a hostile world, but his last years, when he was compelled to apply for aid from the commune, were brightened by the rare devotion of his youngest daughter. He died on July 25, 1875.

Hjálmar Jónsson's poetry can be understood and appreciated only in the light of his experiences. He spent his mature years in an environment that was on the whole highly unfavorable to the development of his genius. To be sure, there were those in his neighborhood, especially among the educated class, who appreciated him and with whom he was always on friendly terms. On the other hand, he was the constant victim of scurrilous attacks, insinuations, and contempt from those living around him, especially the ignorant and the materialistic. A man of strong feelings and deep sensitiveness, he naturally struck back and struck hard. Nor is it to be overlooked that his impetuousness, his love of invective, and his sharp tongue also provoked enmity. In addition, there was his continued fight against poverty, even destitution, and the suffering and dissatisfaction brought upon a man of his temperament by the inability to satisfy his mental hunger.

These manifold adverse circumstances were bound to embitter the poet and make him more cynical and ruthless. His poems, as a result, are often scathing denunciations of his age. He was merciless in his satire, whether against individuals or general conditions; and his darts never missed the mark. He vigorously condemned the unequal distribution of wealth and was unsparing in his attacks upon misers and their like. Deservedly bitter in its indictment, as well as pathetic, is his poem "Umkvőrtun" (Complaint). It was written when he was in his seventies and facing starvation; the board of the county, where for half a century he had manfully struggled to eke out an independent if miserable living, had refused him public aid. His invectives, the most defiant and slashing in Icelandic literature, not only are among his most characteristic productions, but frequently rank with the very best because of their striking originality and rugged force.

The conditions under which Hjálmar Jónsson lived also inevitably colored his attitude in other poems, particularly his patriotic works. Not that he is lacking in love of his country. No Icelandic poet has expressed his patriotism more forcefully, one may even say more fanatically, since in his implorations for blessings upon his native land he does not hesitate to defy the Deity outright. But in his descriptions of Iceland, he centers his attention on its harsher features, its barrenness, on its lavas, snow, and ice, on its poverty and hard fate through centuries. Such is the surging undercurrent of his remarkable poem written as a welcome to King Christian IX in 1874, on the historic occasion of the thousandth anniversary of the settlement of Iceland. Nor could the poet, true to his outlook upon life, see Iceland through any other eyes; he is in this respect a direct contrast to Jónas Hallgrímsson, who was no less sincere in his portrayal of his country in its summer garb and its milder and more attractive features. Both were, however, thoroughly national, and Hjálmar Jónsson's concern for the liberty and the progress of Iceland is a strong note in other occasional poems.

There is another side to his character and poetry that should not be overlooked. Numerous poems of his, not least the obituary ones, make it clear that he could be just as grateful and appreciative as he was vindictive and satirical. They reveal him also as a man of deep and humble faith, in full agreement with the traditional religious conceptions of the day, despite his low opinion of certain individual clergymen. This faith, which upheld him in the storms of life, permeates one of his most impressive and most beautiful poems, "Andvaka" (Sleepless Night), a poem vast in its sweep and startling in its imagery, mourning the loss of his wife. Until his death he cherished her memory with a touching affection, and this devotion is one of the most attractive things about him.

Besides the poems considered, Hjálmar Jónsson wrote several *rímur* cycles, in which his mastery of form and knowledge of Old Icelandic literature are evident. He reaches his greatest heights, however, in his shorter poems, in which rugged vigor, incisiveness, and originality of phrase are his outstanding qualities. His racy language is highly idiomatic; his graphic illustrations and similes are drawn directly from the life about him, often from ships and the sea, indicating his experiences as a fisherman. He is especially successful in using objective illustrations to symbolize and make tangible the ideal and the spiritual. It is perhaps the most remarkable thing about him as a poet, an eloquent testimony to the vitality of his genius, that he continued to grow in mental and poetic stature with the years, in spite of hostile conditions, and that he wrote his best poems late in life.

A small volume of Hjálmar Jónsson's poems, *Ljóðmæli* (Poems), was published at Akureyri in 1879. A somewhat fuller selection was *Kvæði og kviðlingar* (Poems and Ditties, 1888), edited with an introduction by the poet Hannes Hafstein. A collected edition of his works, *Ljóðmæli,* appeared, 1915–1919, in two volumes, edited with a biography of the poet by Jón Þorkelsson. A photostatic edition of a few of his poems, *Fáeinir smákveðlingar,* from his original manuscript, was published in 1942, and in the same year a selection of his poems, *Ljóðmæli,* was edited with an introduction by Jónas Jónsson.[2]

Several later Icelandic poets, including Matthías Jochumsson, Einar H. Kvaran, and Davíð Stefánsson, have paid tribute to

[2] For further information about his life and poetry, see Þorsteinn Gíslason, "Bólu-Hjálmar," *Lögrétta,* XXVII (1932), 337–350; "Hæ, hæ, mig ber undan hőrmungastrőndum (Endurminningar Einars Markússonar um Bólu-Hjálmar)," *Lesbók Morgunblaðsins,* XV (1940), 361–362; "Frá Bólu-Hjálmari (Frásőgn Þórarins Þórarinssonar)," *Lesbók Morgunblaðsins,* XVIII (1944), 1–4, 14–15; Bjőrn Sigfússon, "Bólu-Hjálmar og frelsið frá őrbirgð," *Samtíðin,* XII (1945), 15–17.

Hjálmar Jónsson in noteworthy poems indicative of the prominent place he occupies in the opinion of qualified judges.

3. The life of PÁLL ÓLAFSSON was uneventful compared with the careers of many of his contemporary Icelandic poets. He was born at Dvergasteinn in the east of Iceland, March 8, 1827, but grew up at Kolfreyjustaður in the same part of the country, where his father, the Reverend Ólafur Indriðason, a man of learning and poetic ability, was pastor for many years. Páll Ólafsson never attended any school; his education was limited to the instruction received in his home and two or three winters of private tutoring. It is worthy of note, however, that his father possessed an uncommonly good collection of foreign works of literature and books of general interest.

Páll Ólafsson spent most of his mature years as a farmer at Hallfreðarstaðir in eastern Iceland and as superintendent of certain state lands. One of the leading farmers in the district and a man of means at least during his earlier years, he held numerous positions of trust in the community and served for a short period as a member of the Althing. He died in Reykjavík on December 23, 1905.

Páll Ólafsson's versemaking ability came to light very early; several fluent quatrains written before he was ten years of age, survive. Doubtless his father encouraged him, and the writing of poetry remained his major interest until his death. He was in his most formative years when *Fjölnir* spread the seeds of nationalism and progress throughout Iceland. Like many of his fellow poets, he was influenced by Jónas Hallgrímsson, particularly in his patriotic and nature poems. Runeberg, several of whose poems he translated successfully, was his favorite foreign writer. On the one hand, therefore, he belonged with the Romantic poets; on the other, he carried on a different tradition, that of Bólu-Hjálmar, Sigurður Breiðfjörð, and the host of Icelandic peasant-poets preceding them. More specifically, Páll Ólafsson was the leading representative of a popular poetic tendency, characterized by its humor, fluency, and treatment of themes from everyday life, which has flourished in eastern Iceland and appears to be traceable to the Reverend Stefán Ólafsson, whose descendants are numerous in that part of the country. And it was when writing in the traditional vein that Páll Ólafsson produced his most characteristic work.

His poems, *Ljóðmæli* (Poems), did not appear in book form until shortly before his death, when they were edited and published in 1899–1900 in two volumes by his younger brother, the poet Jón Ólafsson. But he had long before become a nationally known and beloved poet, especially among the common people. His verses, especially his light-winged and pertinent epigrams, had been spread orally throughout the country. He had admirers in every Icelandic farmhouse, as the novelist Guðmundur Magnússon (Jón Trausti) put it in his elegy on the poet. A new edition of his poems, also titled *Ljóðmæli*, appeared in 1944, edited with a detailed biographical introduction and evaluation by Gunnar Gunnarsson, the novelist.[3]

Nor was Páll Ólafsson's popularity accidental. He possessed exexceptional lightness of touch and rare skill in versemaking. His poems are easy to memorize and their language is simple and unadorned. Moreover, he wrote on themes dear to the heart of the common man, finding his subject matter in everyday life. His humor and his ability to see the brighter and amusing side of things, despite a strain of melancholy, endeared him to his countrymen.

In a number of poems he sings the praises of the haunts of his youth and of his native land, for he spent his best years in Fljótsdalshérað, a district noted for its scenic beauty. These poems are neither particularly profound nor original, but they are spontaneous like the rest of his works and thoroughly sincere. "Litli fossinn" (The Cataract) is a splendidly wrought nature description, and his popular "Sumarkveðja" (Summer Greeting) is also a very attractive poem. Like Jónas Hallgrímsson he was pleased by the charm of the Icelandic summer, the dew-pearled flowers, the singing birds, the shining sun, and the clear blue sky.

Páll Ólafsson has deservedly been called "the poet of the home," for he lavished his poetry upon his family, relatives, and friends. The loss of his young sons he mourns in appealingly tender verses. Equally genuine in their feeling, as well as artistic in form, are his numerous

---

[3] For further information about him, see also Þorsteinn Gíslason, "Páll Ólafsson," *Lögrétta*, XXIX (1934), 77–88; Valtýr Stefánsson, "Páll Ólafsson skáld (Sonur hans Björn P. Kalman segir frá)," *Lesbók Morgunblaðsins*, XVI (1942), 395–399; Guðmundur Jónsson (frá Húsey), "Um Pál Ólafsson skáld," *Eimreiðin*, L (1944), 140–147.

beautiful love songs addressed to his wife, Ragnhildur. Unceasingly, he idolizes her and expresses his happiness in marriage. His love poems, therefore, differ fundamentally from much similar poetry in Icelandic, in which broken vows and unrequited love are general themes.

Characteristic of Páll Ólafsson are his convivial songs, some of which are strikingly original and have retained their popularity undiminished. In many of these he succeeds excellently in weaving together banter and seriousness. His amusing rhymed letters, addressed to friends and relatives, are a large and significant part of his poetry, and in this field he has few peers among Icelandic poets. Such poems not only reveal his personality and his unusual facility in versemaking, but also present graphic and authentic pictures of Icelandic rural life in his day. No less characteristic and attractive are his poems and ditties in praise of horses. This literary genre (*hestavísur*) is peculiarly Icelandic and has flourished for centuries; the horse, until recently, was the chief means of transportation. Páll Ólafsson owned excellent riding horses, prized them highly, and wrote about them not merely sympathetically but in a very personal manner, identifying his fate with theirs.

Generally speaking, Páll Ólafsson was at his best in his epigrams. His unsurpassed readiness in improvisation made him excel as a master of the Icelandic quatrain, and it became his vehicle for sundry themes, not least for his wit and satire. Often his missiles are innocent and amusing; at other times, on the surface at least, his arrows are tipped with the venom of bitter malice. In any case they seldom miss the mark.

Páll Ólafsson's realm was limited, but he wisely kept within the boundaries of his own experience. Therefore, his poems, which are always spontaneous, are as a rule equally true to life. He was the spokesman of the common people, and his verses are most individual when, as in the poem "Tíminn" (Time), he takes his similes directly from the Icelandic workaday world. Justly it has been said of him that he "represents in perfection the best qualities of the unschooled Icelandic poet."[4] Not a few of his poems still remain popular, and

[4] Sir William A. Craigie, *The Oxford Book of Scandinavian Verse* (Oxford, 1925), p. 339.

his verses will long live on the lips of the Icelandic people. He also influenced later poets; Þorsteinn Erlingsson, for instance, greatly admired him and acknowledged his debt in the matter of metrical form.

4. Besides the three major poets of the unschooled group, who have been dealt with in detail, many of their contemporaries of the same social class but of lesser literary distinction assiduously composed *rímur* and other poems and verses in the national tradition cherished by the common people.

Among such minor poets the most popular in their day were SIGURÐUR BJARNASON and SÍMON BJARNARSON. Sigurður Bjarnason (1841–1865) was a man of more than ordinary promise. His *rímur* cycle, *Hjálmar og Ingibjörg* (or *Hjálmarskviða,* The Lay of Hjálmar), on a favorite theme from the Romantic sagas, has run through four editions (the most recent in 1934).[5] Símon Bjarnarson (Dalaskáld, 1844–1916), was a very prolific writer of *rímur,* many sets of which have been published, and was noted especially for his uncommon ability in extemporaneous versemaking.[6]

5. RECENT RÍMUR WRITERS. Although the chanting and composing of *rímur* has largely gone out of fashion, this time-honored form of entertainment and remarkable branch of Icelandic literature still has its admirers. Three noteworthy cycles of poems of that kind have been written and published since the turn of the century.

In 1902 VALDIMAR ÁSMUNDSSON (1852–1902), a noted newspaperman and editor of popular editions of the Icelandic sagas, published, in collaboration with the poet GUÐMUNDUR GUÐMUNDSSON, *Alþingisrímur,* a well-written and effective satire on the sessions of the Icelandic Althing from 1899 to 1901. A second edition appeared in 1909.

EINAR BENEDIKTSSON, the leading poet of his generation and a genuine admirer of the *rímur* poetry, rendered it his homage with *Ólafs ríma Grænlendings* (1913). Written in the intricate *rímur* meter, *sléttubönd* (palindrome), which can be read backward and

---

[5] Concerning him, see Snæbjörn Jónsson, "Um rímuna og höfund hennar," introduction to the fourth edition of *Hjálmar og Ingibjörg* (*Hjálmarskviða*) (1934).

[6] Concerning him and his writings, see *Sagnakver: Helgað minningu Símonar Dalaskálds,* ed. Snæbjörn Jónsson (1944).

forward without disturbing the thought, diction, or verse form, this cycle of some 160 stanzas is indeed a notable performance.

A more uniformly masterful work among the most recent *rímur* is the cycle *Rímur af Oddi sterka* (1938) by Őrn Arnarson, a poet of great gifts; eloquence, metrical excellence, and vigor of style go hand in hand in this stirring narrative poem.

Others less renowned and less successful have in recent years tried their hand at composing *rímur*, and this ancient form of Icelandic literature has also received increased and deserved attention from Icelandic scholars. The quatrain (*ferskeytlan*), derived from the *rímur* poetry, has continued in high favor.

IV

Philosophical and Religious Poets

PHILOSOPHICAL and religious passages and poems are, of course, to be found in the works of many of the Icelandic poets already considered, such as Bjarni Thorarensen, Jónas Hallgrímsson, Grímur Thomsen, and Benedikt Gröndal. Matthías Jochumsson was no doubt the most inspired and in many ways the greatest Icelandic hymn writer of the period. A consideration of the poets who devoted their attention primarily to philosophical and religious themes is, however, in order.

1. Björn Gunnlaugsson was born September 28, 1788, at Tannstaðir in the north of Iceland, the son of a farmer noted for his craftsmanship and unusually inventive mind. The son's great gifts, especially in the field of mathematics, asserted themselves early. He completed his preparatory studies under private tutors in 1808, but because of the Napoleonic wars did not enter the University of Copenhagen until 1817. Here he studied mathematics, physics, and other natural sciences and twice won the University gold medal for his solutions of mathematical problems. He was a teacher at the Latin School at Bessastaðir and Reykjavík from 1822 to 1862, when he retired. He died on March 17, 1876.[1]

Björn Gunnlaugsson wrote on mathematics, astronomy, and surveying, but his greatest achievement was his map of Iceland (1844), the first detailed and modern one of the country. The fruit

[1] See further Ágúst H. Bjarnason, "Um Björn Gunnlaugsson," *Tímarit Þjóðrœknisfélags Íslendinga í Vesturheimi,* XX (1938), 17–28; Steindór Sigurðsson, "Björn Gunnlaugsson og Uppdráttur Íslands," *Skírnir,* CXII (1938), 166–173.

of his extensive travels and surveying during the summers of 1831–1843, it was indeed a great feat, accomplished under very rigorous circumstances.

He was, however, not only a successful teacher and a consecrated scientist, he was also a deep thinker and, in fact, Iceland's pioneer philosopher. His cycle of poems, *Njóla* (The Night), was the first philosophical work in Icelandic and was widely read in its day. It appeared first at Viðeyjarklaustur in 1842 and later on in enlarged and revised editions in 1853 and 1884.

Consisting of over 500 stanzas written in the popular verse form of the Icelandic quatrain, the cycle is not particularly noteworthy for its literary merit, as the author was not much of a poet. His verses are generally rather stiff and heavy, although smooth-flowing and quotable stanzas can readily be singled out. What the cycle lacks in smoothness and literary excellence, it makes up in rich thought content and sweep of the imagination.

The work, which is definitely didactic, has as its subtitle "A Conception of Universal Teleology" and attempts to interpret not only the Creator's purpose for the universe, but also Man's destiny both in this world and in the hereafter. Naturally, the astronomer, the physicist, and the philosopher are here much in evidence; and the work, as might be expected, reflects the prevailing scientific and philosophical views of the time. In some respects, however, Björn Gunnlaugsson was ahead of his day, particularly in maintaining that energy, not matter is the basic element in the universe, or what he called "The World Force." In the closing part of the poem, the author's ethical and religious views are most pronounced; and while these are in many ways traditional, they reveal his broad-mindedness and humanity, rare in that day, as well as the sincerity and the simplicity of his abiding faith. These attractive qualities of the poet's personality and his views, together with the general appeal inherent in the theme of his *Njóla*, account for the popularity which the work enjoyed; it was not only widely read, but memorized and freely quoted, and thus no doubt had some influence.

2. Brynjólfur Jónsson frá Minnanúpi (1838–1914), a self-educated farmer's son from the south of Iceland, became a prolific folkorist and an archeologist, who traveled extensively throughout

the country for the Icelandic Archeological Society and wrote profusely on archeological and historical subjects. In his philosophical poem, *Skuggsjá og ráðgáta* (Mirror and Enigma, 1875), dealing with his ideas concerning God and the universe, he carries on the tradition of Bjőrn Gunnlaugsson. Other poems of Brynjólfur Jónsson's are also philosophical in theme, and, in general, the penetrating thinking characterizing much of his poetry far surpasses its literary quality. The prose account of his mental development and his views on life, *Saga hugsunar minnar* (The Story of My Thought, 1912), is a notable work, not the least for its intellectual honesty and straightforwardness. The religious element is strong in his poetry, and he has written several hymns, some of which have been included in the official Icelandic hymn book.

3. Besides Matthías Jochumsson, the leading Icelandic hymn writer of the nineteenth century was the Reverend VALDIMAR BRIEM. The richly endowed scion of a distinguished family, he was born February 1, 1848, at the estate of Grund in the north of Iceland; but upon the untimely death of his parents, he was brought up by his uncle, a prominent clergyman in southern Iceland. Valdimar Briem was graduated from the Latin School at Reykjavík in 1869 and three years later from the Theological Seminary. From 1880 until his retirement in 1918 he served as pastor of Stóri-Núpur in the south of Iceland. He was as well a district superintendent during much of that period. From 1909 until his death in 1930, he was vice-bishop of the Skálholt diocese.

Prominently identified with national church and community affairs, Briem made his lasting reputation as the most productive Icelandic hymn writer of the period and one of Iceland's leading hymnologists of all time. His great contribution to the new Icelandic hymnal of 1886 consisted of 102 original hymns and thirty-nine translations. A large number of these deeply felt and beautiful hymns, together with successful translations of hymns from other languages, continue to grace the pages of the Icelandic hymn book. Many, it may be added, are among the most cherished hymns of the nation.

Besides his hymns, he produced a significant work, unique in Icelandic religious literature, in his two-volume collection, *Biblíuljóð* (Bible Songs, 1896–1897), well described as "metrical pictures of biblical events." The poems constituting this extensive work are uneven in inspiration and literary merit, but many of them are characterized by metrical excellence, graphic nature descriptions, and rich imaginative quality. Briem also wrote a collection of songs based on the Book of Job, *Ljóð úr Jobsbók* (Winnipeg, 1908), effective in meter and language and, all things considered, ranking high among his production in the field of religious poetry.[2]

4. Another prolific Icelandic hymn writer during the nineteenth century was the Reverend HELGI HÁLFDÁNARSON (1826–1894), a pastor's son from the north of Iceland, who graduated from the Latin School in Reykjavík in 1848 and received his degree in theology from the University of Copenhagen in 1854. After serving as a pastor for a number of years, he became a teacher at the Theological Seminary in Reykjavík in 1867 and was its president from 1885 until his death.

A successful and beloved teacher, he exerted an even greater influence with his catechism (*Helgakver*), which has appeared in eleven editions, and with his work on the revised Icelandic hymn book of 1886. To it he contributed no less than 211 original and translated hymns, or almost one third of its entire contents. Many of his own hymns have been retained in later editions, and deservedly, for they are generally characterized by genuine religious feeling and fluent form. To an even greater degree he has enriched Icelandic religious literature with his excellent translations of classical hymns from foreign sources.[3]

5. Other hymn writers of note during the period were the Reverend PÁLL JÓNSSON (1813–1889), who wrote a number of splendid original hymns, and the Reverend STEFÁN THORARENSEN (1831–1892), whose contribution consists especially of many excellent translations of significant and widely used hymns. Of more recent hymn writers, the Reverend FRIÐRIK FRIÐRIKSSON (b. 1868), the founder and

[2] For further information about his life and literary career, see Jón Helgason, "Valdimar prófastur Briem," *Óðinn*, III (1907), 29–31; Árni Sigurðsson, "Dr. theol. Valdimar Briem vígslubiskup, aldarminning," *Kirkjuritið*, XIV (1948), 13–51, and "Séra Valdimar Briem vígslubiskup: Minningar séra Ólafs Ólafssonar," *ibid.*, XIV (1948), 52–62.

[3] Concerning him, see Jón Helgason, *Helgi Hálfdánarson lector theol: 1826–1926* (1926).

leader of the Icelandic Y.M.C.A., and VALDIMAR V. SNÆVARR (b. 1883), a former school principal, are the most important, both having written hymns which appear destined to hold their place in the Icelandic hymnal.

V

From Realism to Neo-Romanticism

REALISM, championed by the Danish critic, Georg Brandes, swept the Scandinavian countries in the eighties and with its liberal and revolutionary views profoundly affected both the literature and the national life generally. With a large number of Icelandic students at the University of Copenhagen, personally or indirectly in contact with Brandes and his followers, Realism could not but move to Iceland. And as might be expected, the chief spokesmen were four Icelandic students in Copenhagen, the novelists Gestur Pálsson and Einar Hjőrleifsson (Kvaran) and the poets Hannes Hafstein and Bertel E. O. Þorleifsson (the latter of minor importance), who under the influence of Brandes founded the periodical *Verðandi* (1882) for the purpose of introducing Realism into Icelandic literature. Although they were the principal Icelandic champions of the movement, traces of this new literary tendency can be found in the early writings of Jón Ólafsson, who had come to know it through his associations with leading Norwegian authors and who championed many of its ideas and even wrote a novel in its style.[1]

Only one volume of *Verðandi* appeared; but the publication is, nevertheless, important because of the interest that it aroused in Icelandic literary circles. Its new and challenging ideas are reflected in some heated public discussions of the day. Another annual, *Heimdallur* (1884), also published by a group of Icelandic students in Copenhagen to carry on *Verðandi's* mission, was equally short-lived.

[1] A detailed discussion of Realism and its adherents in Iceland is found in Einarsson, *Prose Writers*, pp. 71–86.

Gestur Pálsson, who remained faithful to the tenets of Realism until his untimely death in 1891, continued to champion it in his various publications; and others, especially among the novelists and the short-story writers of the last decades of the century, took up the torch with renewed vigor. Nevertheless, while leaving its mark upon Icelandic literature, Realism (and Naturalism too, for that matter) did not cause a revolution in Icelandic letters or a break with the national tradition for the simple reason that Icelandic literature, prose and poetry alike, had down through the centuries been rooted deep in the soil of reality.

With the exception of Gestur Pálsson, the pioneer Icelandic champions of Brandesian Realism before long turned their backs upon that literary tendency. Hannes Hafstein became nationalistic and Einar Hjőrleifsson adopted a humanitarian and spiritualistic outlook upon life; they became Neo-Romantic. So in varying degrees did the other Icelandic poets who had for a time been attracted to the Realism of Brandes. This will be pointed out more specifically in the individual discussions. Symbolism, on the other hand, a prominent element in the Neo-Romantic movement in the Scandinavian countries, was only a very minor factor in Icelandic poetry of the period, although discernible in the works of some of the poets.

1. Jón Ólafsson, a brother of the poet Páll Ólafsson, was born at Kolfreyjustaður in the east of Iceland on March 20, 1850. He attended the College of Iceland at Reykjavík, 1863–1868 and during his school years began interesting himself in literary pursuits, journalism, and politics. He published his first book consisting of a story and some poems, in 1867; and a year later, when only eighteen years old, became editor of the paper *Baldur*. An ardent and outspoken lover of freedom and champion of Icelandic independence, he pub-published in his paper in 1870 a revolutionary poem entitled "Íslendingabragur," a scathing attack on the Danish authorities. This brought upon him the wrath of officialdom and compelled him to leave the country. He fled to Norway, where he became associated with liberal leaders and prominent literary figures. Upon his return to Iceland, he founded the paper *Göngu-Hrólfur* (1872) but soon, through his fiery spirit and frank political utterances, clashed with the authorities and again had to flee the country, this time going to

America. In 1874 he was sent to Alaska by the American government to investigate the possibility of establishing an Icelandic colony there, a project which never materialized. Having returned to Iceland in 1875, he engaged in journalism and other literary work during the next fifteen years. Back in America again he edited Icelandic papers in Winnipeg from 1890 to 1894 and from then until 1897 did editorial and library work in Chicago. The remainder of his life he spent in Iceland, where he edited various newspapers, wrote extensively on diverse subjects, and took an active part in public affairs and politics. For many years he was an influential member of the Althing, and the cause of Icelandic independence was always one of his principal concerns. He died on July 11, 1916.[2]

His collected poems, *Söngvar og kvæði* (Songs and Poems), appeared in Eskifjörður in 1877; a second enlarged edition in Winnipeg in 1892; and a third enlarged edition in 1896.

Jón Ólafsson first attracted attention with his vigorous political and patriotic poems, notably his stirring "Íslendingabragur." Fearless in its outspokenness, it was a ringing call to arms that aroused his countrymen and made them generally far more aware of the necessity and the justice of their demands for greater political freedom and self-determination. The same observation applies, if in a lesser degree, to his other poems in similar vein, in which he not only directs his thrusts at the abuses practiced by the Danish authorities in Iceland, but also chastises his countrymen for their half-heartedness, indifference, backwardness, and inability to make full use of the measure of freedom which is theirs. He challenges them to action in resounding exhortations, which not infrequently take the form of outright social satires.

These poems of Jón Ólafsson's are very characteristic and very personal, for they directly reveal the man himself, his fiery and restless temperament, and his ardent patriotism; they also constitute

[2] For information about his early years, see his autobiographical sketches, "Úr endurminningum ævintýramanns," *Iðunn*, I (1915–16), 50–70, 152–176, 280–291, 357–370; *ibid.*, II (1916–17), 78–81. Concerning his life and literary work, see also various articles in *Iðunn*, II (1916–17), including Ágúst H. Bjarnason, "Skáldið Jón Ólafsson," 82–100; Jón Jónsson frá Sleðbrjót, "Um Jón Ólafsson," *ibid.*, III (1917–18), 100–122; Þorsteinn Gíslason, "Jón Ólafsson," *Andvari*, XXXXVI (1921), 5–13.

his most unique contribution to Icelandic poetry of the day. They further clearly show him to be a precursor of the *Verðandi* group of Realists, for in these poems he attacks existing conditions and discusses contemporary problems in the very spirit of Realism. Naturally, poems of that type, closely linked with burning issues of the day—problems that have long since been solved—have lost their immediacy and appeal, but they are still interesting because of the light shed on the political struggle of the time and because of their revelation of the poet's personality and his interests.

Of greater and more lasting literary value are some of his other patriotic poems, such as the ones written during his enforced absence from his country, appealing in their simplicity and sincerity. As a matter of fact, he often succeeds best when he writes in a simple vein and in traditional Icelandic meters. Thus he is related to the unschooled poets and frequently makes effective use of their quatrain.

Many of his nature poems are also attractive and well done, such as his "Smalavísur" (The Shepherd's Verses), graphically portraying his youthful days as a shepherd, and "Niagara," probably the most impressive, in which the poet sees his own turbulent life mirrored in the rushing waters. His sonnet on Alaska, written during his visit there, is particularly well constructed and genuinely felt. Of his love poems, "Skautaferðin" (The Skating Trip) is noteworthy for its truthful and fluent description and sincere feeling.

Circumstances did not permit Jón Ólafsson to cultivate his poetic talent except in a limited degree. Nevertheless, his poems clearly reveal him as a stanch champion of freedom and progress, one of the trail breakers of a new era in the history of his country.

His translations of the poems in Bjőrnstjerne Bjőrnsson's *En glad gut* and *Synnöve Solbakken* are exceptionally well done, as are the translations of the stories themselves.

2. JÓN ÞORKELSSON (FORNÓLFUR) was born at Ásar in Skaptártunga in southern Iceland, April 16, 1859. He was descended on both sides of his family from prominent leaders in church and state; on his father's side he was the great-grandson of the Reverend Jón Þorláksson, leading poet and master translator. Upon his graduation from the College of Iceland in 1882, Jón Þorkelsson specialized

in Icelandic history and literature at the University of Copenhagen, receiving his Ph.D. degree in 1888. His doctoral dissertation, entitled *Om Digtningen paa Island i det 15. og 16. Aarhundrede* (Concerning Poetry in Icelandic during the Fifteenth and Sixteenth Centuries; Copenhagen, 1888), was a pioneer work in the field and of first importance. After further research and editorial work, he returned to Iceland in 1898, where the following year he became director of the National Archives, occupying that position until his death on February 10, 1924. Besides his fundamental work for the National Archives, he was one of the founders of the Icelandic Historical Society in 1902 and its president until his death. He edited and wrote numerous historical, literary, and biographical works, as well as collections of folklore and published a large number of individual articles and studies in the same fields. In short, he was an extremely productive scholar, achieving his greatest eminence as an historian and an archivist. He also contributed extensively to the periodical *Sunnanfari*, which he edited from 1891 to 1897 and 1912 to 1914. This was an important publication, especially during the early years, when many of the coming poets of the day made their literary debuts in its pages. For a number of years Jón Þorkelsson served as a member of the Icelandic Althing and took an active and prominent part in Icelandic politics, vigorously championing the historic rights of his nation in its struggle to regain freedom.[3]

The blood of poets flowed in Jón Þorkelsson's veins, and during his student years he wrote some occasional poems, which showed considerable skill although he himself did not look upon them as worthy of note. When in later years, from time to time, he published his poems, he did so anonymously. The publication of his collection of poems, *Vísnakver Fornólfs* (Fornólf's Booklet of Verses, 1923), revealed a robust and striking poetic gift and came, therefore, as a complete and pleasant surprise to most of his countrymen. He devoted his long and productive scholarly career to research and writing in the field of Icelandic medieval literature and lore, which he had elevated to its proper place; and he found his poetic inspiration and themes in that distant and previously neglected period. This

[3] Concerning his life and work, see Hannes Þorsteinsson, "Fáorð minning dr. Jóns Þorkelssonar þjóðskjalavarðar," *Skírnir*, XCVIII (1924), 1–28.

volume was the harvest of his lifelong labor in the realm of scholarship as well as his literary testament to his nation.

In a notable and self-revealing introductory poem, he reviews his lifework of preserving the cultural values of the past; and he does so with the humility that comes from the sense of proportion acquired only through experience. The bulk of the book, however, consists of poems on historical themes—events and personalities—from medieval Iceland, such as "Bjőrn Guðnason í Őgri og Stefán biskup 1517" and "Őgmundur biskup á Brimara Samson 1541." These and similar poems reveal his vast historical knowledge together with his deep understanding and sympathy for his heroes and heroines. He not only brings the past itself vividly to life, but peoples his stage with flesh-and-blood creatures whose common humanity we cannot fail to recognize.

This is nowhere seen to better advantage than in his beautiful and touching poem "Vísur Kvæða-Őnnu" (Poet-Anna's Verses), probably his greatest poem. Out of a single short paragraph in an Icelandic chronicle, against the illuminating background of a turbulent age, he has recreated the tragedy of the beggerwoman, an outlaw from society, in a penetrating and most sympathetic fashion. The same sympathy is apparent in "Mansaungur Svarts á Hofstőðum um Ólőfu Loptsdóttur" (Svarts at Hofstaðir's Serenade to Ólőf Loptsdóttir). Here the poet reviews the eventful career of his heroine and pays her glowing tribute in a poem not least outstanding for its powerful descriptive passages.

Jón Þorkelsson's rare insight into the history of his nation and its fortunes is memorably expressed in other poems, such as "Yfirlit" (A Survey) and "Hér á landi" (In This Country), aflame with the white heat of emotion aroused by the battle for Icelandic independence and challenging to action. In his fervent nationalism he is clearly akin to the earlier Icelandic Romantic poets, or perhaps we should class him with the Neo-Romanticists. In any event he shares with both the characteristic of turning to history as a main source of inspiration.

Jón Þorkelsson uses with equal skill verse forms from the sacred poetry of Catholic times and meters from the popular *rímur*; the metrical garb is, therefore, in keeping with the themes of his poems, and the language, often deliberately antiquated, also harmonizes splendidly with their spirit and flavor. His style is concentrated and sonorous, rugged and sometimes lacking in fluency, but it always bears the unmistakable stamp of his strong personality.

3. HANNES HAFSTEIN, who combined in a rare degree the statesman and the poet, reminiscent of the chieftain-skalds of old, was born on December 4, 1861, at Mőðruvellir in the north of Iceland. He was the son of Governor Pétur Hafstein. His mother's family was equally prominent. Interest in public affairs and literary and artistic ability characterized both his paternal and maternal forebears. Unusually precocious, Hannes Hafstein graduated from the College at Reykjavík at the age of nineteen, and at twenty-five received his law degree from the University of Copenhagen. Thereafter he held many public offices and became one of the leading and most influential Icelandic statesmen of the day. He served as Secretary of State for a number of years, occupied other important public positions, and was a member of the Althing from the turn of the century. In 1904 he became Prime Minister of Iceland, the first Icelander to fill that office, holding it until 1909 and again from 1912 to 1914. This period, not least the first part of it, has justly been characterized as epoch-making in Icelandic history, for it was not only an era of continued demand for political freedom and of advance in that direction, but also one of notable progress in the social, industrial, and educational life of the nation. Much, without doubt, was the direct result of Hafstein's farsighted and energetic leadership. His personal magnetism, great gifts, and idealism readily inspired confidence; although, as a fearless champion in a period of strife, he also reaped his share of opposition and abuse. He died on December 13, 1922, after a prolonged illness.[4]

---

[4] Concerning his life and literary work, see Ágúst H. Bjarnason, "Skáldið Hannes Hafstein," *Iðunn*, II (1916–17), 258–272; Alexander Jóhannesson, "Um skáldskap Hannesar Hafsteins," *Óðinn*, XII (1916), 81–86; Þorsteinn Gíslason, "Hannes Hafstein," *Andvari*, XXXXVIII (1923), 5–49; Jakobína Johnson, "An Icelandic Statesman and Skald," *American Scandinavian Review*, XI (1923), 364–365; Guðmundur Friðjónsson, "Lífsgleði og karlmennska Hannesar Hafstein," *Tímarit Þjóðræknisfélags Íslendinga í Vesturheimi*, XIII (1931), 89–100; Einar H. Kvaran, "Hannes Hafstein á stúdentsárunum," *Eimreiðin*, XXXVIII (1932), 17–24; "Hannes Hafstein, endurminningar og ræðukaflar,"

Hafstein's literary precociousness is amply attested by the fact that at the age of twenty he wrote excellent poems, which, with their vigor and youthful enthusiasm, progressive and patriotic spirit, found a ready and general audience among his countrymen. Previously published in various Icelandic papers and periodicals, his poems, under the title of *Ýmisleg ljóðmæli* (Various Poems), first appeared in book form in 1893; a collected edition was published in 1916, and again, much enlarged, in 1925. Selections from his poems have twice been published: *Ljóðmæli* (1944), edited with an introduction by Vilhjálmur Þ. Gíslason, and *Úrvalsljóð* (1946), selected by Þorsteinn Gíslason.

Hafstein was one of the four Icelandic students in Copenhagen who founded the periodical *Verðandi* for the purpose of introducing Realism to Iceland. In fact, of the four, he was the most vigorous personality and equally enthusiastic in his support of the new literary and social gospel. This is clearly seen in the poems that he contributed to the periodical. They immediately attracted wide attention and marked him as a poet of uncommon gifts. He was also one of the principal supporters of the monthly *Heimdallur* (1884), which the Icelandic students in Copenhagen founded to carry on the work of *Verðandi.* To this new periodical he contributed, among other things, a biographical sketch of Georg Brandes and a translation of poems by Henrik Ibsen.

Upon his return to Iceland, Hafstein continued his championship of Realism, notably with a critical lecture delivered on January 14, 1888, on nineteenth-century Icelandic poetry, which he considered to be in a state of decline. He attacked its use of antiquated themes, such as one-sided and narrow nationalism, in a day of growing individualism and technical progress. The poverty and the isolation of the country, he maintained, also thwarted the development of poetry; and he emphasized that its revival was dependent upon attention to new and more timely themes. While many applauded these views, others were violently opposed, and Benedikt Gröndal took up the gauntlet for the Romantic and national poets in a vigorous and characteristic lecture. This literary quarrel aroused

---

Lesbók Morgunblaðsins, XVI (1941), 401–414; Arngrímur Fr. Bjarnason, "Um Hannes Hafstein á Ísafirði," *Lesbók Morgunblaðsins*, XVII (1943), 65–69.

wide interest and is a noteworthy episode in the history of Icelandic letters.

Most of Hafstein's poems were written during the first part of his career, for his later years, when he was engaged in politics and public activities, gave him but little time for literary work. He always retained his interest in poetry, however, and produced some of his most notable poems late in life.

His poems published in *Verðandi* (1882) reveal an unusual maturity for his years as well as his vigorous championship of Realism and its social teachings. His poem "Stormur" (The Storm), which holds the place of honor in the publication, forcefully expresses the attitude and the purpose of the author and his colaborers. The keynote of the national awakening and literary revival that they sought to bring about is there struck resoundingly and with youthful ardor. The same is true of several of his other poems included in the publication, in which his vigor, freshness, and manly spirit—qualities that have endeared him as a poet to his countrymen—are the outstanding characteristics. These can be seen to a good advantage in his much-quoted poem "Undir Kaldadal" (Nearing Cold Dale), in which asks for "the lash of an ice wind's wrath, of manly courage a fitting test." He wrote a number of other spirited exhortations in realistic and satirical vein, calculated to awaken his people to greater progressive activity; and the same note is sounded in many of his nature and patriotic poems.

The exuberance of his spirit and his joy in living animate his popular convivial songs and his love poems. Many of his love poems dating from his younger days are, however, written in a jocular vein, the fruit of a short-lived, if impassioned, infatuation; a deep-rooted and genuine love came later and found expression in poems notable for their sincerity and depth of emotion.

Hafstein's nature poems are both vivid and powerful; he has described the varied scenery of Iceland, its waterfalls, rivers, mountains, and rural regions, graphically and with the enthusiasm that stems from true appreciation. Such poems are often in reality striking travelogues in verse, painted in bold strokes. His description of Skagafjőrður, abounding in places of historic interest and in scenic magnificence, is particularly successful. While traces of

Romanticism are not difficult to find, there is frequently a definite strain of Realism. Realism sometimes dominates, as in the impressive descriptive poem "Niðaróður" (Song of the River), with its love theme and a succession of truthful pictures from life, reflected in the surging river.

His many patriotic poems are particularly noteworthy and strike a sober note. Love of country was ever a strong undercurrent in his poetry, blending effectively with his urgent demand for national awakening and, during the earlier part of his career when he was most directly under the influence of Realism, for social reform. During that period he wrote "Ástarjátning" (A Confession of Love), which is indeed a fervent confession of his love for his country, expressing his readiness to sacrifice all for its welfare; and as fate would have it, it was vouchsafed to him to devote his life, in a large measure, to its regained political freedom and progress. With the years the national note became increasingly strong and prominent in his works. His progressive spirit and his patriotism found a harmonious and an eloquent expression in "Aldamótin" (The Turn of the Century), probably his best known poem and also one of his most excellent efforts, containing both a challenge to his countrymen and a program of action for the future. The extreme and exuberant realism of his younger years has been replaced by a calmer and more mature view, a deeper understanding. Moreover, from then on he devoted himself primarily to political and public activity, with correspondingly lessened attention to poetry.

Nevertheless, during his later years he wrote three of his most notable poems, "Í hafísnum" (In the Drift Ice), "Landsýn" (Land Sighting), and a memorial poem on Jón Sigurðsson, Iceland's national hero. They bear unmistakable evidence of the vicissitudes of his political life, but also reveal greater penetration, breadth of view, and sympathy. The first named in particular paints a striking and symbolic picture of his career as a public man and political leader.

During his last years, after the death of his beloved wife, he found release for his great sorrow in deep-felt and noble memorial poems, touching and penetrating alike. And in spite of a lingering illness, which led to his untimely death, he continued from time to time to write poetry, among other things working on a historical poem that he left incomplete.

Hafstein's verse forms show considerable variety, skill, and fluency; and he introduced some new meters into Icelandic poetry, usually characterized by that vigor and straightforwardness that generally marked his style. When he so desired, he could handle elaborate meters with ease and grace, as seen in his sonorous poem "Skarphéðinn í brennunni" (Skarphéðinn among the Flames), a memorable portrayal of the heroic spirit in the face of inexorable fate.

Many of his translations are excellently done, especially those from Heine's works and in an even greater degree those from Holger Drachmann's poems; these two foreign poets attracted him most strongly and left some mark on his poetry.

4. Þorsteinn Erlingsson was born at Stóramörk in Rangárvallasýsla in southern Iceland on September 27, 1858. He grew up at Hlíðarendakot in the district of Fljótshlíð, known alike for its scenic beauty and its rich historic traditions, for it was the scene of *Njáls saga*, renowned in song and story. It is not surprising that the poet deeply cherished the memories of the haunts of his youth and immortalized them in his poems. He came of a good farm family, and poetic talent had been in evidence on his father's side.

Thanks to the encouragement of the poets Steingrímur Thorsteinsson and Matthías Jochumsson, Þorsteinn Erlingsson came to Reykjavík in the fall of 1876 and began preparing himself to enter the College there, having as his private tutors these two and Benedikt Gröndal, the third leading poet of the day. The budding poet became most closely attached, however, to Steingrímur Thorsteinsson and was most attracted to his literary style, as the early poems in particular reveal; he retained both his affection and admiration for Steingrímur Thorsteinsson throughout his life, and eulogized him in a beautiful poem.[5]

[5] Concerning Þorsteinn Erlingsson's life and literary career, see further the introductory material to the third edition of *Þyrnar* (1918), which includes excerpts from various articles about the poet; Guðmundur Magnússon, "Þorsteinn Erlingsson," *Skírnir*, LXXXIX (1915), 1–16; Valtýr Stefánsson, "Skáldið og heimilisfaðirinn Þorsteinn Erlingsson: Frásögn frú Guðrúnar J. Erlings," *Lesbók Morgunblaðsins*, XIV (1939), 400–403, 408; Sigurður Guðmundsson, "Þor-

After six years in college, Þorsteinn Erlingsson graduated in the spring of 1883. He had begun writing verses at the age of five, and it was his early ability in this field that had attracted attention to him and caused the older poets and other friends to make it possible for him to go to school. Little has been preserved of what he wrote before he entered college; but a number of poems written during his school years are in existence, either in manuscript or in print. A representative selection from his work during those early years is included in the fourth edition of his collected poems (1943).

Those were eventful years in Icelandic letters. First collections by several of the leading poets of the day appeared. *Verðandi* burst upon the scene in 1882, the harbinger of a new literary tendency and social teaching; and four new poets, most of them already showing great promise, took the field. In view of these developments, it was not to be expected that Þorsteinn Erlingsson's youthful efforts would attract much general attention. Although he was older than two of the *Verðandi* group, they had entered upon their educational careers ahead of him. His first poems reveal the influence of Steingrímur Thorsteinsson in their Romantic themes, but, at the same time, they point forward and anticipate many of the principal characteristics of his later and more mature work. Here, as has been pointed out by others, are the dreamy nature, the melancholy sensitiveness, the nostalgic longing for youth and its joys, which form such a prominent strain in his mature poems. His profound interest in animals, particularly birds, is much in evidence in his early poems, as are his fervent and active love of country and his attachment to friends and home surroundings, always fundamental in his nature. Strange as it may seem, in view of his later eminence in the field, satire is entirely absent from his early poems. "The beautiful, soft and mellow appeared more in harmony with his natural disposition."[6] Several of his youthful poems readily gained public favor and have retained their popularity because of their inherent lyric quality and the fact that they were written to popular tunes.

Þorsteinn Erlingsson matriculated at the University of Copen-

---

steinn Erlingsson og Eiðurinn," in *Heiðnar hugvekjur og mannaminni* (Akureyri, 1946).

[6] Sigurður Nordal, introduction to *Þyrnar* (4th ed.; 1943), p. xxvii.

hagen in 1883 and studied law for some time, but later he interested himself in studies in philology and literature, especially Old Norse. Soon thereafter he turned his back upon an academic career and devoted himself to literary pursuits; his life in Copenhagen became a struggle with poverty and ill health. Having returned to Iceland permanently in 1896, he was engaged for eight years in journalism in eastern and western Iceland. Thereafter, until his death on September 28, 1914, he resided in Reykjavík. During the latter part of his life he received an annual stipend from the government for literary work, but he had to supplement this with time-consuming and wearying private tutoring in order to eke out a living.

His sojourn in Copenhagen was particularly important in his poetic development. Here he came under the influence of Georg Brandes and his Realism in literature and became an avowed socialist in politics. These were turbulent days in Denmark, with the Social-Democrats vigorously and increasingly opposing the reactionary and arbitrary government and championing radical social changes, some involving the established church and religion. It was in this social environment and under the impact of these new literary and political currents that Þorsteinn Erlingsson lived from 1883 to 1896.

The new and radical note in his poetry was resoundingly struck with his stirring memorial poem on the centenary of the great Danish philologist Rasmus Christian Rask. In addition to the well-merited eulogy of the devoted friend of Iceland, it contains a forceful and fearless attack on Danish misgovernment in Iceland, past and present. The poem, which created a celebrated incident, brought a rebuke from University authorities and probably played a part in making him give up the study of law. The wide attention the poem received, especially the praise from some quarters, probably encouraged him to devote himself more than before to the writing of poetry and other literary pursuits. This meant, however, that, in order to earn a meager livelihood, he had to work so hard that he impaired his health permanently. Small wonder, considering the conditions of his precarious existence, that Þorsteinn Erlingsson should side with those who demanded greater social justice and equality. This pronounced and fearless social criticism was from then on one of the main currents of his poetry; it can be seen in many poems, a number of which appeared in the periodical *Sunnanfari*, 1891–1895, and later in the magazine *Eimreiðin*. These poems, whether in a social satirical or a lyric vein, clearly showed that the poet had fully found himself, and the response on the part of his countrymen was commensurate.

This was still more evident after his first collection of poems, *Þyrnar* (Thorns), appeared in Copenhagen in 1897; second, third, and fourth enlarged editions under the same title were published in 1905, 1918, and 1943. The third edition contained excerpts from various tributes and articles written about the poet at the time of his death, and the fourth edition an extensive and penetrating introduction by Sigurður Nordal, who edited both. In 1913 Erlingsson's notable cycle of narrative poems, *Eiðurinn* (The Oath), appeared; a second edition was published in 1925 and a third in 1937.

The first edition of *Þyrnar* contained many of Þorsteinn Erlingsson's most important and characteristic poems and admirably represents the two main streams in his poetry, the lyrical and traditional and the satirical and revolutionary; the content of the volume is about evenly divided between the two types. Here are, on the one hand, some of his most exquisite patriotic, nature, and love poems, such as "Lágnætti" (Midnight), "Sólskríkjan" (The Snow Bunting), "Vorkvæði" (Spring Song), and "Mansaungvar" (Love Songs), and, on the other hand, revolutionary poems outlining his ideals and arguments, together with bitter social and political satires, such as "Őrlőg guðanna" (The Fate of the Gods), "Arfurinn" (The Heritage), "Skilmálarnir" (The Terms), "Őrbirgð og auður" (Destitution and Wealth), "Vestmenn" (Men of the West), and "Á Spítalanum" (In the Hospital), in which the author fiercely denounces religious bigotry and social injustice. A radical in religion no less than in politics, he attacked that traditional conception of the Deity that portrayed Him as an all-powerful, merciless ruler, permitting oppression and injustice to flourish and favoring the rich above the poor. Love of beauty, love of mercy, love of justice, love of charity, and, above all else, love of truth—these, as one writer[7] has correctly summed it up, were the main strands in Erlingsson's confession of faith; and he, therefore, possessed a deep and abiding admiration

[7] Einar H. Kvaran, quoted in introduction to *Þyrnar* (3rd ed.; 1918), p. xvi.

for Jesus of Nazareth and His teachings. In other words, Þorsteinn Erlingsson attacked creeds, not Christianity itself. He abhorred falsehood and hypocrisy and equally whole-heartedly loved sincerity and genuineness; nor can anyone doubt that his revolutionary poems, his political and social satires were sincere and genuine, rooted deep in his thought and his conditions.

Naturally, however, his attacks on established institutions and traditional views, not least in the realm of religion, met with strong opposition and brought him his full share of misunderstanding and abuse. But with the passing of time, his poems have been evaluated with greater calm and more detachment. From the very first Erlingsson also had his enthusiastic admirers, and in large numbers, for here was much to admire: the fervor and eloquence with which he expressed his views and his tender sympathy for all living things, the poor and the weak and the suffering, a sympathy that extended not only to all the stepchildren of life, but to the animals as well. Rightly it has been emphasized that his socialism and his political and social satire generally had their roots in his all-embracing sympathy and his ingrained sense of justice; out of that soil grew his assault on kingship and royal power, capitalism and the established church, the social structure in its entirety, all that kept man in oppression and hampered his free and full development. Therefore, it was not difficult to detect the warm heart behind his revolutionary poems. And even those whom he had enraged with his radicalism could not but be touched by his rich human sympathy, his genuine love of country, and not least his literary artistry, for here was a master craftsman at work. The fact of the matter is that his light touch and his perfection of form won general admiration; the appeal of his poems was also increased through his constant stress on clarity of thought and simplicity of expression.

Among the most notable poems in Þorsteinn Erlingsson's first collection (and in his whole literary production) is his historical narrative poem "Jőrundur," in which his social satire is seen to excellent advantage. The whimsical quality of the satire clearly shows the author's relationship and indebtedness to Lord Byron, whose work he greatly admired (particularly his "Don Juan"). His influence on Þorsteinn Erlingsson, especially with regard to poetic style, is most thoroughgoing in the cycle of poems "Eiðurinn" (The Oath), and is also in evidence in the poem "Eden."

The first edition of *Þyrnar* undeniably contained many of the author's finest, most popular and influential poems, but it must not be overlooked that the later editions include many new poems of high literary excellence, such as "Við fossinn" (By the Waterfall), "Jól" (Christmas), "Aldaslagur" (Ode of the Centuries), together with other nature, patriotic, and occasional poems rich in that lyric strain so characteristic of the poet until his dying day.

His social satires from the later years are in a somewhat milder tone than the earlier ones, partly because of the lighter touch of whimsicality and irony that the author had learned from Byron, and also because of less challenging social conditions in Iceland than in Denmark during the earlier years; these satires such as "Eden" are, however, often even more effective than before and show unmistakably that the author had not gone back on his early ideals. The *Social-Demokraten*, official organ of the Danish socialists, continued to be favorite reading material, and he actively supported the labor movement in Iceland. Further, he threw himself vigorously into the struggle for Icelandic independence, which appealed strongly to his national feeling. A poem written the year before his death, "Landvarnarmaðurinn" (The Defender of the Land), reveals that his fighting spirit was unbroken and his devotion to social reform unchanged.

The two main strains of his poetry are reflected in his major work, the narrative poem "Eiðurinn." It is made up of a series of songs on a tragic love theme and combines lyric beauty with social satire. The poetic excellence of the cycle resides especially in the purely love poems, instinct with feeling and characterized by rare mastery of form. In the satire, the Byronic influence is frequently seen in the style and the flavor of the poems, in the whimsical intermingling of gay and grave, gold and dross.

Þorsteinn Erlingsson considered himself, and was in many respects, an adherent of Georg Brandes and his Realism; in his interest in the common people and socialism he was, however, far removed from his acknowledged master. Further, he always appreciated and admired the older Icelandic poets of his day, all of whom were

Romanticists. In fact, as has been correctly emphasized, he never wavered in his Romantic admiration of the past and his devotion to the ancient Icelandic literature and culture; such was his nationalism, which, among other things, expressed itself in strong demands for Icelandic independence.

The Icelandic literary tradition had a strong hold upon him and he felt particularly deeply his kinship with the unschooled Icelandic poets and learned much from them. He was especially fond of Sigurður Breiðfjörð, whose influence can be seen in his works, and also of Páll Ólafsson. One of Þorstein Erlingsson's favorite verse forms was the quatrain, the traditional meter of the unschooled Icelandic poets, which he used with rare success. With the years he became increasingly interested in Icelandic history and studies, which always had been close to his heart, and found themes in that field. He also collected folk tales and other historical lore, which provided material for his cycle of poems "Eiðurinn" and his projected poem on Fjalla-Eyvindur, the outlaw who was later immortalized in Jóhann Sigurjónsson's drama.

Þorsteinn Erlingsson aspired to be the poet of the common man, and this he unquestionably achieved in large measure. His poems, from the time of their first appearance, became unusually popular, not least among the rank and file, as he most preferred. The new note that he struck with his radical poems and his social satires appealed to many, even if it aroused anger in other quarters. And all could delight in his brilliant skill in versification and the lyric charm of his poems. In short, through his social and political views, and perhaps even more because of his lyric art, he has had a tremendous influence. His great contemporary, the poet, Stephan G. Stephansson, acknowledged his debt to him; and his influence on the unschooled poets of his day and since cannot be measured readily. Not only in the realm of Icelandic letters, but also in the field of social and political advancement can his influence be traced. Withal, his poems may live longest because of their rich beauty.

5. Einar Benediktsson lived a life that was eventful far beyond the ordinary and, all things considered, without a parallel among Icelandic men of letters. He was born at Elliðavatn in the southwest of Iceland on October 31, 1864, son of Benedikt Sveinsson, a richly

endowed and influential political leader, and Katrín Einarsdóttir, who was equally brilliant. After graduating from the College of Iceland in 1884, Einar Benediktsson studied law at the University of Copenhagen, receiving his degree in 1892. He published and edited the newspaper *Dagskrá* in Reykjavík, 1896–1898, practiced law as a Superior Court attorney for the next six years, and served as a prefect at Rangárvallasýsla in southern Iceland from 1904 to 1907. After his retirement he traveled extensively on three continents and resided a great deal abroad, for years in England. Returning to his native land, he spent his last years there, at the farm of Herdísarvík in the south. He died on January 12, 1940. He interested himself in various business enterprises and in politics, for a time playing an important part in the Icelandic struggle for independence, where he firmly took his stand among those who made the greatest demands for political self-determination. His greatest and most lasting achievements are, however, in the field of literature, his poems constituting the high-water mark of present-day Icelandic poetry, carrying to a new and noble height the tradition of the greatest Icelandic poets preceding him.[8]

A productive writer, Einar Benediktsson published five large and important collections of poetry. His first published poem, and likewise his initial contribution to Icelandic politics, was "Bréf í ljóðum til Þingvallafundarins" (A Rhymed Letter to the Meeting at Þingvellir, 1888), annonymously printed both privately and in a Reykjavík newspaper. Although it lacks the impressiveness and the

[8] For information about his life and literary career, see further Guðmundur Finnbogason, "Einar Benediktsson," *Skírnir*, LXXIX (1905), 340–356; Þorkell Jóhannesson, "Einar Benediktsson: Drög að kafla úr íslenzkri menningarsögu," *Eimreiðin*, XXX (1924), 134–152; Kristinn E. Andrésson, *Einar Benediktsson sjötugur* (1934) and "Útsær Einars Benediktssonar," *Iðunn*, XIX (1936), 211–233; Sveinn Sigurðsson, "Einar Benediktsson sjötugur," *Eimreiðin*, XL (1934), 337–352; Símon Jóh. Ágústsson, "Einar Benediktsson 75 ára," *Lesbók Morgunblaðsins*, XIV (1939), 337–339; Sigurður Nordal, "Einar Benediktsson," *Skírnir*, CXIV (1940), 5–23; Sigurgeir Sigurðsson, "Við líkbörur Einars skálds Benediktssonar," *Eimreiðin*, XLVI (1940), 5–9; Sveinn Sigurðsson, "Og það fór þytur um krónur trjánna," *ibid.*, 10–11; Jónas Þorbergsson, "Einar Benediktsson skáld, *Tímarit Máls og Menningar*, III (1940), 7–16; Sigurður Guðmundsson, "Einar Benediktsson," in *Heiðnar hugvekjur og mannaminni* (Akureyri, 1946), pp. 101–104; Richard Beck, "Við legstað skáldkonungsins," *Almanak Ó. S. Thorgeirssonar*, LIV (1948), 54–59.

literary excellence of his later poems, this first published effort is very characteristic and clearly foreshadows his more mature and effective poems on the subject in its frank description of Icelandic social conditions resulting from centuries of oppression, its recognition of the country's rich though unused resources both on land and sea, and its uncompromising demand for political freedom.

It was not, however, until his poems began appearing in the periodical *Sunnanfari* (1891–1896) that he attracted general attention as a poet. Here were published several of his most original and memorable productions, among them his masterful and inspiring "Norðurljós" (Northern Lights). These, together with a number of other poems, made up his first published collection, *Sögur og kvæði* (Stories and Poems, 1897). Now there could be no doubt that a highly gifted poet, mature beyond his years and endowed with an uncommonly robust genius, had made his appearance on the literary stage. The collection opened with a particularly notable group of challenging patriotic poems, "Íslendingaljóð" (Songs of Icelanders), some of which still retain their popularity and doubtless will continue to do so for a long time to come, as they not only strike a familiar chord but have their roots deep in the soil of Icelandic history and culture and hold high aloft the torch of national ideals. As in his rhymed letter to the meeting at Þingvellir, but more forcefully and with greater literary skill, the poet held up before his countrymen their miserable conditions and at the same time reminded them of their natural resources and their inherent abilities, challenging them to a concerted fight for their political freedom by citing other small nations that had broken the fetters of oppression. Characteristically, he eloquently eulogized the Icelandic language in one of these poems, in lines that vibrate with love and admiration and are among his most quoted stanzas. In other patriotic poems from those years, as "Íslendingaljóð," he vigorously struck the same note calling for a national awakening to achieve regained independence and material progress. This clarion call was to resound through his poetry subsequently and is one of its strongest undercurrents.

Other collections of his poetry are: *Hafblik* (Calm Waters, 1906; second ed., 1935), *Hrannir* (Waves, 1913; second ed., 1935), *Vogar* (Billows, 1921), and *Hvammar* (Grassy Hollows, 1930).

He was also a very able translator and successfully rendered into his native tongue such famous poems as Gray's "Elegy in a Country Churchyard," Fitzgerald's "Rubáiyát of Omar Khayyâm," Poe's "The Raven," and selections from Whitman's "Leaves of Grass," as well as a number of other notable poems. His greatest achievement in the realm of translation was, however, his rendition of Ibsen's *Peer Gynt* (first ed., 1901; second ed., 1922) a remarkable piece of work that faithfully reproduces not only the form, but the spirit and the mood, of the original, its heart and soul.[9]

All of Einar Benediktsson's original poems and translations are included in the collected edition of his works, *Ljóðmæli* (Poems; 3 vols., 1945), edited, with bibliographical notes, by Pétur Sigurðsson, and containing a discriminating introduction by Guðmundur Finnbogason, dealing in detail with the poet's versification and his philosophical poems. A selection from his poems, *Úrvalsljóð*, edited by Jónas Jónsson, appeared in 1940. Another selection, under the same title, edited by Alexander Jóhannesson, was published in 1946. A significant contribution to an understanding of the poet and his works is the memorial volume by his wife, Valgerður Benediktsson, entitled *Frásagnir um Einar Benediktsson* (1942) and edited by Guðni Jónsson.

As indicated in the title, Einar Benediktsson's first book, *Sögur og kvæði* (Stories and Poems), contained some stories from his pen, generally well told, some of them masterfully. In the second edition (1935) of the book, two of the original stories were replaced by a number of the author's sketches, which had previously appeared in papers and periodicals. Especially significant is the sketch "Gullský" (The Golden Cloud), which strikingly reveals his deep mystical feeling, his sense of oneness with nature and the universe, which became increasingly important in his poetry. In later articles, in the periodical *Eimreiðin*, he wrote on philosophical and metaphysical subjects, which also are the themes of many of his most elaborate and penetrating poems.

---

[9] For a detailed discussion, see Steingrímur J. Þorsteinsson, "Pétur Gautur: Nokkrar bókfræðilegar athuganir varðandi þýðingu Einars Benediktssonar," in *Afmæliskveðja til Halldórs Hermannssonar 6. janúar 1948* (1948), pp. 115–153 (reprinted in *Landsbókasafn Íslands, Árbók 1946–47* [1948], pp. 173–211).

Einar Benediktsson has cast his net wide and the variety of his themes is commensurate with the vastness of his literary domain. His experiences and observations are frequently and memorably manifested in his poetry. Therefore he has correctly been characterized as "the Viking who on his raids and expeditions in many lands has boldly captured new and grand themes to sing."[10]

He describes graphically and with rare insight an evening in Rome, with the Tiber flowing leisurely to the sea, "slowly like the march of time"; a storm on Lake Trasimenus, under a moon "pale as the face of Hastrubal"; the Cathedral of Milan, where "the echo of silent prayers lingers in the chancel." Equally vividly and profoundly he pictures St. Helena and the fate of Napoleon. The poet walks the banks of the Thames and the Seine and from that vantage point paints unforgettable, gripping pictures of life in London and Paris. In eight lines, entitled "Við Zuydersæ" (By Zuydersee), Holland is masterfully portrayed. The gigantic machines of our day, in fact the machine age itself, are described with telling force in a poem about the factories in Newcastle-on-Tyne. A far different experience is the subject of the poem "Í Dísarhőll" (In the palace of the Goddess), in which the poet describes in a masterly and penetrating fashion the performance of a symphony orchestra in London's famed Queen's Hall. Clearly, he was endowed with keen observation and great descriptive power.

Cosmopolitan as Einar Benediktsson undeniably was, he was none the less fundamentally and vigorously national. He delighted in writing on Icelandic subjects; in fact, it has been estimated that nearly one fourth of his original poems deal with his country and nation. Here again he excels in nature descriptions. He pictured Iceland, with its striking scenic contrasts and in its changing seasonal garb, affectionately and memorably. And nowhere is his unusual artistry as a painter in words seen to better advantage than in some of these poems. Impressive in its realism is his description of the drift ice in the poem "Hafísinn" (Drift Ice), and equally graphic, but far more attractive, his portrayal of the charm and the magic of the Icelandic summer in such poems as "Fjallaloft" (Mountain

[10] Guðmundur Finnbogason, "Literature," in *Iceland 1946*, ed. Thorsteinn Thorsteinsson (1946), p. 228.

Air), "Í Slútnesi" (At Slútnes), "Lágnættissól" (Midnight Sun), and "Bláskógavegur" (The Road to Blue Forests). Deep thinker that he was, his descriptions of natural phenomena not infrequently becomc highly symbolic of human life and conditions. That is well illustrated in his group of poems "Heklusýn" (A View of Hekla), in which, in bold flashes of poetic inspiration, the country itself and the forces of nature reflect the life and the struggle of the nation for generations. His great poem "Útsær" (The Ocean), with its powerful and sweeping description of the grandeur of the sea, is equally notable for its deeper and wider significance. Elsewhere, he has interpreted Iceland, its past and future, to his countrymen in poems destined to live long. He has also drawn clear-cut and refreshingly original word pictures of a number of the leading men in the cultural and literary history of Iceland, from Egill Skallagrímsson, the great poet of the tenth century, to Björn Gunnlaugsson, the poet and the astronomer of the nineteenth century.

Reference has already been made to some of Einar Benediktsson's specifically patriotic poems, which grew out of his abiding interest in the progress of his country and his active participation in its struggle for political independence. Especially significant is his poem "Aldamót" (The Turn of the Century), a wise and spirited exhortation, in which the author spans the centuries, linking past, present, and future. His progressive spirit is here the keynote. He emphasizes the great need of capital for the material advancement of the nation and the development of the country's resources; but he also reminds his countrymen that wealth in itself is not enough, that it must serve a higher purpose if the nation is to reap lasting good fortune and happiness. In his poem "Dettifoss," notable for its descriptive quality, but even more so for the light it throws on the poet himself, he develops a similar theme, dramatically visualizing the utilization of the natural resources of Iceland, specifically its waterfalls, for the improvement of the living conditions of the people and general material progress. For the purpose of developing and utilizing water power, he organized large-scale business enterprises that for various reasons failed to achieve the projected results and made him the subject of much criticism. As far as he was concerned, these bold and extensive financial ventures enabled him to enrich his life through wide travels and prolonged residence in the great centers of culture in Europe and elsewhere; and he paid his nation inestimable dividends in the numerous great poems, rich in thought and literary excellence, that his sojourns abroad inspired. Although he emphasizes the material side, the utilization of the waterfalls for practical purposes, in "Dettifoss," he goes far beyond that and envisions a future day when man, through higher knowledge, will have mastered thought-power and thus tapped a source of unlimited spiritual strength. This approach and interpretation is thoroughly characteristic of him.

In Einar Benediktsson's patriotic poems, as well as in his poetry generally, his love of Iceland and the Icelandic cultural heritage and his unwavering and deep-rooted faith in the future and the mission of his people are written large. Time and again, in inspired and prophetic words, he reminds his nation of its historic past, its glorious heritage, and its great destiny, provided it does not fail to meet the challenge.

He was deeply immersed in the Icelandic literary tradition and particularly interested in the time-honored poetry of the unschooled Icelandic poets, whom he greatly admired. It was, therefore, not by any means accidental that he edited the poems of Sigurður Breiðfjörð with a sympathetic introduction. Einar Benediktsson's interest in the *rímur* poetry is further eloquently attested by the fact that for the express purpose of reviving that type he wrote his notable *rímur* cycle, *Ólafs ríma Grænlendings*. This work also reveals his profound interest in the Icelandic settlement of Greenland and the discovery of the North American continent, the subject of several other major poems.

Einar Benediktsson has been referred to, and not without reason, as an Icelandic Browning. His poems, even the descriptive ones, are rich in philosophic thought expressed in lofty style. Especially in his numerous more purely philosophical poems, such as "Jörð" (Earth), "Einræður Starkaðar" (Starkaður's Soliloquy), and "Stórisandur" (The Great Sand), he boldly wrestled with the deepest problems facing the mind of man: the ultimate meaning and goal of human life and the mysteries of the universe. A great deal of a mystic, monistic and pantheistic, he was profoundly conscious of the unity and continuity of life, its source of energy and powers of renewal. To him a soul appeared imprisoned in the dewdrop upon a blade of grass. His pantheism is strikingly illustrated in his poem "Dagurinn mikli" (The Last Day), in which he emphasized the presence of God everywhere and in all things, large and small. Independent of traditional interpretation of religion, he was deeply religious in the best sense of the word, and extolled the blessing of true faith and the spirit of sacrifice: "The temples of God are the believing hearts, though they be without shelter."

Einar Benediktsson is, therefore, not a personal poet in the ordinary sense of the word; his own feelings enter comparatively little into his poems. Blind passions do not surge through them like rushing streams. His poetry is much more notable for its intellectual than its emotional quality, for its vast sweep and rare penetration. And this intellectual approach, combined with the philosophical themes, tends to make his poems obscure in the opinion of a good many readers. Mental effort, careful reading, and reflection are indeed needed to retrace his thoughts, but the patient reader is generally rewarded with a generous glimpse of the poet's great visions and far-flung vistas.

His poems always bear the unmistakable stamp of his individuality and originality in style as well as in the treatment of his themes. They abound in striking and varied similes. He was a master of the use of contrasts. Frequently his elaborate and elevated verse forms were of his own invention; and although they sometimes lack lightness of touch and smoothness, they are as a rule a fitting vehicle for the subject matter; in fact, he succeeded especially well in harmonizing form and theme and in adjusting his verse line to the mood and the movement of the poem. In his excellent narrative poem "Hvarf séra Odds frá Miklabæ" (The Disappearance of the Reverend Oddur from Miklibær), one of his most interesting efforts, he brilliantly reproduced, metrically, the hoofbeats of the horse upon the frozen ground and the howling of the storm. He had great faith in the expressiveness of his native tongue, which he eulogized with fond affection; nor has this faith in the richness and the flexibility of the Icelandic language been put to shame, severely as he tested it. His vocabulary is nothing short of astounding, keeping pace with his wealth of ideas, the flight of his fertile imagination, and his penetrating understanding.

It is the great glory of Einar Benediktsson that he never shrank from attacking the themes that constituted the greatest challenge to his literary genius, straining it to the utmost; and because he thus dared to attempt great things his achievement in the realm of poetry is commensurate with his effort.

Equal to the demands upon his poetical genius was his reverence for the sanctity of his art; its realm was to him a sacred temple in which the ignoble and the insignificant have no place. His poetry is purity itself. He never cheapened his art by catering to fluctuating popular taste.

While several of Einar Benediktsson's first published poems have a strong strain of social satire, he very early parted company completely with the Realists and their social teachings and championed greater appreciation of national cultural and literary values, stressing patriotism, idealism, and progressive spirit. His articles in *Dagskrá* (1896–1897) illustrate this shift. In other words, he became a full-blooded Neo-Romanticist, spiritually akin to such contemporaries as Sweden's great national poet Verner von Heidenstam; and the mission of the two for their respective peoples was fundamentally alike—holding high the shining banner of national greatness and national destiny.

The influence of Einar Benediktsson is readily traceable in the works of his contemporary and younger Icelandic poets to the extent that he may be said to have founded "a school." Without attempting to imitate this master of the grand style, they may profitably set before them his ideal—to paraphrase S. Nordal—to enrich Icelandic literature with new themes conceived on a grand scale, adhering at the same time to the characteristically Icelandic precision of form.

"I wished that every life which serves you, my country, should be lifted to a higher vision, transforming the people's dreams into deeds," wrote Einar Benediktsson in one of his great poems ("Kveðja Skírnis"). Like Ibsen he was engaged in teaching his people to think great thoughts, and the flame of high ideals will continue to burn brightly in his poems for generations to come, challenging them to noble deeds.

6. Þorsteinn Gíslason was born January 26, 1867, at Stærri-Árskógur in Eyjafjörður in northern Iceland, but he spent most of his youth at Kirkjubær in Fljótsdalshérað in the east. He came of a good family and was, on his mother's side, a direct descendant of the Reverend Stefán Ólafsson, the leading secular poet of seventeenth-century Iceland. After graduating from the College of Iceland in 1892, he studied Scandinavian (with special emphasis on Icelandic) philology and literature for several years at the University of Copenhagen. Upon returning to Iceland he edited various Icelandic papers and periodicals and took a prominent part in the struggle for Icelandic independence, which was then at its height. Besides his prolific writing in the field of journalism, the essay, and lyric poetry, he rendered Icelandic literature and cultural life great service by publishing many of the works of the leading Icelandic writers of the day. At the time of his death, October 20, 1938, he had long been recognized and highly respected as the dean of Icelandic journalists.[11]

It is not difficult to detect his kinship with the older Icelandic poets—on the one hand with Jónas Hallgrímsson, on the other with the unschooled Icelandic poets, especially Páll Ólafsson. The relationship with Páll Ólafsson is not surprising as he grew up in his immediate neighborhood. Traces of influence from both the poets mentioned can be seen in Þorsteinn Gíslason's early poems, but he soon outgrew that stage. Like many another Icelandic student of the day, Þorsteinn Gíslason came under the influence of the Realism of Georg Brandes during his university years in Copenhagen. The influence was not, however, of long duration, but can be seen in some of his early newspaper articles in which he attacked what he considered extreme and unsound nationalism and worship of the past on the part of his countrymen. His poems, on the other hand, reveal hardly any influence from Realism, unless it is in his satirical poems such as "Grafskrift" (An Epitaph), effective in their quiet irony. And very rarely does he make the controversial issues of the day the theme of his poetry. At any rate, as his poems show beyond doubt, he

[11] Concerning his life and literary work, see also Alexander Jóhannesson, "Þorsteinn Gíslason," *Andvari*, LXX (1945), 3–25; Richard Beck, "Skáldið Þorsteinn Gíslason," *Tímarit Þjóðræknisfélags Íslendinga í Vesturheimi*, XXVIII (1946), 39–48.

quickly rid himself of the Brandesian influence and became national and idealistic in his poetry—a Neo-Romanticist who kept his feet on the firm ground of reality in good Icelandic literary fashion.

His first book, *Kvæði* (Poems, 1893), a collection of youthful efforts, did not arouse any particular attention; but with his second book, *Nokkur kvæði* (A Sheaf of Poems, 1904), although only a slight volume, he really arrived as a poet. Here are some of his finest and most original poems and his most successful translations. The reviewers were unanimous in their praise. Such was also the case when his third book, *Ljóðmæli* (Poems), appeared in 1920; a collected edition of the bulk of his poetry up to that time, it made his place as a poet more secure. He published two other books of poetry: *Dægurflugur* (Ephemera, 1925), humorous poems, that had gained deserved popularity, and *Önnur ljóðmæli* (New Poems, 1933), consisting of translations and occasional poems.

Þorsteinn Gíslason's keen appreciation of the beauty and the charm of the Icelandic landscape animates many of his best poems. He delighted in singing the praises of spring and summer. His "Fyrstu vordægur" (First Days of Spring) is a simple but thoroughly genuine description of the arrival of spring in Iceland, a lyric gem. And as a matter of fact, his purest poetry is found in similar lyrics. The grand style is not, generally speaking, his forte.

Akin to his nature poems are his descriptions of travel in rural Iceland, in which the beloved haunts of his youth in the eastern part of the country duly receive his expression of filial attachment. Outstanding among his travel poems is his "Göngusöngur" (Marching Song), a metrical masterpiece, refreshingly vigorous in spirit. His most impressive and original poems are, however, "Gjögurnes" and "Hornbjarg," in which graphic nature description and effective social satire (particularly in the latter poem) go hand in hand. Other satirical poems also achieve their purpose well. A different note is struck in his appealing poems written in the spirit of folk poetry.

Þorsteinn Gíslason was popular as a composer of occasional verses and wrote a very large number of such poems. They naturally differ in literary excellence, but are always in good taste and often exceptionally well done. Especially good is his group of poems written on the occasion of the founding of the University of Iceland, June 17,

1911; these are still generally sung at University festivities. In many of his occasional poems, the author's nationalism and idealism, his genuine love of country and faith in the future of his nation find a worthy expression; thus these poems throw much light on his view of life.

Þorsteinn Gíslason was an unusually productive and able translator. His prose translations include Bjőrstjerne Bjőrnson's *Arne* and Sir Walter Scott's *Ivanhoe*; his verse translations include major poems by Henrik Ibsen, Bjőrnson, Gustaf Frőding, and Percy B. Shelley, and a number of lesser poems. Especially noteworthy are his translations of Ibsen's important and self-revealing cycle, "Paa Vidderne" (On the Moorlands), and Shelley's celebrated poem, "The Cloud." Therefore, Þorsteinn Gíslason enriched Icelandic literature with his extensive translations no less than with his original poems. And both the choice of his translations and his own poems reveal his virile optimism, the national and progressive spirit that characterized him and his fellow laborers during the era of awakening and advancement in the history of his country.

7. SIGURJÓN FRIÐJÓNSSON is the product of the significant progressive political and cultural movement that developed in Þingeyjarsýsla in the nineties.[12] He was born at Sílalækur in Aðaldalur on September 22, 1867, but grew up at Sandur in the same neighborhood. Belonging to a sturdy farm family also known for poetic talent and literary interest he graduated from the Eiðar Agricultural School in 1887 and became a farmer, first at Einarsstaðir and since 1913 at Litlu-Laugar in his native district. He has been prominently identified with local public affairs and served as a member of the Althing from 1917 to 1922. Always a progressive and active in the cooperative movement, he has become increasingly radical in politics, a shift strikingly indicative of his responsiveness to political and cultural currents.[13]

He was equally responsive in the realm of letters. His early poems in particular reveal influence from the Scandinavian Neo-Romantic and Symbolic movements of the nineties, primarily through the

[12] See Einarsson, *Prose Writers*, pp. 82–83.

[13] See Þorsteinn Gíslason, "Sands-bræður," *Óðinn*, III (1907), 40–41; and "Sigurjón Friðjónsson skáld," *Óðinn*, XXIV (1928), 98.

medium of the Norwegian periodical *Kringsjaa,* which was widely read in Þingeyjarsýsla; and the symbolic and mystic note has ever been readily discernible in his poetry, which is only natural considering his contemplative attitude of mind. He is, in fact, a self-acknowledged representative of the Neo-Romantic Movement, which flourished in Þingeyjarsýsla toward the close of the century and first attracted general attention and found its purest and most artistic expression in the poetry of Hulda (Unnur B. Bjarklind). In a preface to one of his later collections of poetry (*Heyrði ég í hamrinum*), Sigurjón Friðjónsson has traced the origin of this move-movement not only to its foreign sources, but also to the earlier Icelandic Romantic poets and to external nature and living conditions in Þingeyjarsýsla, with its contrast of severe winters and enchanting summers. His brand of Romanticism, he informs us, is a form of "Realism," embodied particularly in the spirit of growth and love, embracing coming spring, sun, and summer. His spiritual kinship with the older Icelandic masters of the lyric, unschooled and learned alike, is also easily seen in his works, as are impressions from the folk poetry and the traditional *þulur* (rhapsodies). In his preface he also frankly recognizes his debt to Sigurður Breiðfjörð, to Steingrímur Thorsteinsson, and especially to Jónas Hallgrímsson; of foreign favorites he lists Henrik Ibsen, Maurice Maeterlinck, Leo Tolstoy, and Friedrich Nietzsche, adding that during his earlier years his acquaintance with foreign lyric poets was largely limited to translations and magazine articles. We may assume that the periodical, *Kringsjaa,* is included; it is also specifically mentioned.

Sigurjón Friðjónsson began writing poetry early and had for years contributed poems to various periodicals, but it was not until he was past sixty that he published his first book of poems, *Ljóðmæli* (Poems, 1928); a decade later appeared the first of a series of collections, *Heyrði ég í hamrinum* (Voices from the Cliff, 1939).

His close relation to the soil and his love of beauty are revealed in his numerous nature poems, which constitute the main part of his poetry. In them he frequently becomes one with the various phases and changing moods of nature, as in the delicate lyric "Síðkvöld" (Late Evening) and in the more sonorous "Áin niðar" (The Murmuring River), one of his most striking poems, in which he identifies the flowing river with his beating heart. This poem also illustrates how the love theme and nature description are frequently interwoven. On the other hand, "Sumarmorgunn" (Summer Morning) is both an attractive nature description and a truthful picture of Icelandic rural life.

"Að baki blárra fjalla" (Beyond the Blue Mountains) is, however, one of his most characteristic and beautiful poems, revealing his deep roots in his native haunts and his nostalgic feeling for them, together with his inherent optimism and his faith in the future. Generally, his poetry is, as has been well said, a hymn of praise to spring and youth.

Rightly he himself has observed that his poems are musical rather than pictorial; his strength lies in his genuine lyric touch and sensitiveness to beauty seen clearly in "Sól yfir landi ljómar" (Bright Beams the Sun on the Land), simple but haunting in quality.

Sigurjón Friðjónsson writes in many meters and is usually discriminating in their selection. Smoothness, tastefulness, and mastery of form characterize his poetry, with an undertone of sadness and longing, for the personal element is always strong. There is, however, a certain sameness about his themes and generally nothing startling or vigorous about his poems; the fires of emotion smoulder underneath, but seldom flare up on the surface. At the same time, one may say that his most artistic and appealing poems have the proverbial depth of calm waters, a mystic strain, and a suggestiveness reminiscent of the folk song.

Remarkable is the fact that he has written some of his finest poems in his seventies and eighties. Thus many of the love poems in his latest collection are exquisitely done, sheer lyrics, while others eloquently testify to his mastery of form. These later poems also clearly show that he is in league with progress and that the flame of youth still burns bright in his heart. They further reveal that, although he has been averse to the religious teachings of the established church and remained a doubter, his spirituality and inclination toward the belief in immortality have increased with the years.

His translations, many of which are from the poems of Jóhannes Jőrgensen and Erik Axel Karlfeldt, are generally very well executed and also are an indication of his spiritual affinity with the Scandinavian Neo-Romanticists and Symbolists.

Sigurjón Friðjónsson's contribution in the realm of letters is all the more notable when it is borne in mind that it has been accomplished in the hours spared from the time and energy-consuming labors of a farmer and a provider for a large family.

8. Guðmundur Friðjónsson (1869–1944), whose career has been surveyed in detail in connection with his prose writings, was the brother of Sigurjón Friðjónsson and like him was in many ways the product of the progressive and cultural awakening in Þingeyjarsýsla.[14] His unforgettable experiences during the hard years of famine in his youth unquestionably conditioned and colored his outlook upon life and are reflected in both his prose and poetry. They can be seen, for instance, in his graphic and resonant poem "Hafþők" (Ice Fields), which was included in his last verse collection. On the other hand, the new cultural and political currents from abroad that swept his native district during his early years did not leave his sensitive poetic soul untouched. His stories and poems alike amply reveal that fact. However, whereas literary impulses from abroad, and Realism in particular, stimulated and influenced him as a poet, his main source of inspiration was Old Icelandic literature and, one might add, the Icelandic tongue itself, with its rich resources. Few of his fellow Icelandic poets have indeed been as firmly and deeply rooted in the soil of the Icelandic historical and literary tradition; few have cherished and cultivated the Icelandic language in the same degree and with such fruitful results. His spiritual kinship with Egill Skallagrímsson of old and those later Icelandic poets in whom the

[14] See Einarsson, *Prose Writers*, pp. 103–109. For information about his life and literary career, see further Guðmundur Finnbogason, "Guðmundur Friðjónsson," *Vaka*, III (1929), 129–160; Stefán Einarsson, "Frá Guðmundi Friðjónssyni og sőgum hans," *Tímarit Þjóðræknisfélags Íslendinga í Vesturheimi*, XVIII (1936), 52–66, and "Guðmundur Friðjónsson við Dettifoss," *ibid.*, XXVIII (1946), 34–37; Guðmundur G. Hagalín, "Guðmundur Friðjónsson sjőtugur," *Lesbók Morgunblaðsins*, XIV (1939), 329–332; Bőðvar frá Hnífsdal, "Skáldið við Skjálfanda," *Eimreiðin*, XLVII (1941), 356–359; Þorkell Jóhannesson, "Guðmundur Friðjónsson á Sandi," *Lesbók Morgunblaðsins*, XIX (1944), 417–423, 427–428; Þóroddur Guðmundsson frá Sandi, "Úr főðurgarði," *ibid.*, XXI (1946), 109–112.

Norse spirit has been most marked and vigorous can easily be seen. It is therefore not surprising that, according to the testimony of his brother Sigurjón Friðjónsson,[15] Hjálmar Jónsson (Bólu-Hjálmar) appealed especially to Guðmundur Friðjónsson and somewhat influenced him.

Besides his extensive production in prose, he published the following collections of poetry: *Úr heimahögum* (From Native Haunts, 1902), *Haustlöng* (Fall Fancies, 1915), *Kvæði* (Poems, 1925), *Kveðlingar* (Ditties, 1929), and *Utan af víðavangi* (From Far Afield, Poems, 1942). Specimens of his poetry were included in a volume commemorating his seventieth birthday, *Guðmundur Friðjónsson sjötíu ára* (Guðmundur Friðjónsson at Seventy, 1939); and a selection, *Ljóðmæli* (Poems), was edited with an introduction by Vilhjálmur Þ. Gíslason in 1947.

Characteristically, Guðmundur Friðjónsson called his first book of poems "From Native Haunts," for, as in his stories, the themes of his poems are very largely found in his native district, which proved to his poetic genius a veritable gold mine of challenging and important material. It was a district, isolated and harsh on the one hand, but rich in impressive and varied scenery on the other, with historic traditions reaching far back into antiquity. All left their mark on the life of the people, and the unrelenting struggle for existence often resulted in pitiable and tragic fate, but in other instances bred admirable heroism. None of this was lost by Guðmundur Friðjónsson's penetrating observation and sympathetic insight; his awareness was equally alert to weather and seasonal changes, so fundamental to the farmer; and his range of interest and sympathy embraced all living things, animal no less than human. His stories and poems reveal in telling fashion how closely he was linked to the soil, for it is not difficult to identify heroes and heroines in his immediate neighborhood, although he also went farther afield, especially in his later years, and the whole country became his domain. Early in his career he also felt the need of recording his deep attachment to his native district in a notable and beautiful

[15] In the preface to his collection of poems *Heyrði ég í hamrinum* (Akureyri, 1939).

poem, "Þingeyjarsýsla," one of many in which he has sung its praises directly or indirectly.

Guðmundur Friðjónsson began writing poetry early, but few if any of his youthful efforts have been printed; the oldest poems in his first collection, published when he was thirty-three, date from 1893, when he was twenty-four years old. No mere beginner here appeared on the scene, but a mature poet, who had been tested in the crucible of hard struggle, a revolutionary in more than one sense, who fearlessly expressed his views and boldly went his own way in theme and form. The reaction was not slow in coming, for the book was severely criticized and was, in fact, made the subject of an outright scurrilous attack by the chief reviewer. To be sure, it is easy to point out excesses in the poetic diction and lack of taste in other respects, but here also was much to admire in a young poet, working under conditions highly adverse to literary pursuits; here were several poems that, because of their originality and vigor, their realism, beauty, and eloquence, have since come to be recognized as belonging among the author's most outstanding productions and have been given their rightful place in the history of Icelandic letters: such as "Bréf til vinar míns" (Letter to a Friend of Mine), addressed to a friend who was migrating to America, inspired by a fervent love of country and of the soil, eloquent and challenging; and the less sonorous, but even more touching, "Ekkjan við ána" (The Widow by the River), in which the heroism of everyday life is eulogized with sympathetic realism and genuine feeling.

And here we are at the very heart of Guðmundur Friðjónsson's poetry and outlook upon life, for he excelled in memorial poetry, thus nobly, and often very brilliantly, carrying on one of the oldest and most fundamental phases of the Icelandic literary tradition. It was Guðmundur Friðjónsson's individualism, his reverence for the sacredness and importance of the individual, together with his Carlylean respect for work and its value, that inspired these poems. Manliness, courage, faithfulness to duty, industry, endurance, and self-denial were some of the character traits and virtues that he admired most, not least in the common people. Their lot he understood best, like "The Widow by the River," who bore the heavy burdens of life with an unflinching and uncomplaining fortitude. Unforgetable in their truthfulness and sympathetic portrayal are his poems about them, such as "Þórunn Jónsdóttir," "Jónas Guðmundsson," "Jón gamli" (Old John), "Hrólfur Þögli" (Silent Hrólfur), "Björg ljósmóðir" (Midwife Björg), "Kristján Jóhannesson ferjumaður" (Kristján Jóhannesson, ferryman), "Einar í Skógum," and "Halti-Már" (Lame Már), the paper vender. With the exception of Halti-Már all were taken directly out of the life about him and have, therefore, cultural and historical, as well as literary, value. His deeply felt memorial poem about his father is in the same vein.

Although Guðmundur Friðjónsson unquestionably succeeds best in his memorial poems about the heroes of everyday life whom he knew most intimately and who were nearest to his heart, he could also appreciate fully his cherished virtues and the marks of individual greatness in men and women in public life who, in his judgment, had shown those characteristics in their devotion to duty and service to the nation. Many of his notable memorial poems are dedicated to outstanding political, church, and business leaders, educators, scientists, writers, and artists who had met the demands of their positions or other circumstances with a manful spirit. In those poems he has, without doubt, often succeeded very well in bringing out the most noteworthy and praiseworthy traits of these people. His ripe wisdom, his understanding of human nature, and his warm sympathy are nowhere better revealed than in his memorial poems, many of which possess universal appeal in an uncommon degree, testifying to his ability to transmute ordinary experiences into memorable poetry. His hero worship is clearly seen in his poems on themes from the Icelandic sagas, in which he selects those men and women who in various ways personify the character traits and virtues that he most admired. It is also apparent when he writes of leading personages from later Icelandic history.

Nature poems constitute another major group in Guðmundur Friðjónsson's poems, for nature in its changing seasons and moods was for him a rich source of inspiration. Few Icelandic poets have, as a matter of fact, equaled him in describing effectively and colorfully the rugged aspects of nature and the Icelandic scenery, the raging storms of fall and winter, which he portrays in such poems as "Haustmerki" (Signs of Autumn) and "Dettifoss." "Sendlingur" (The Sandpiper), is similar, but even more it is a touching picture of the little bird's struggle for existence and at the same time a strikingly symbolic account of the poet's own life. He was equally successful in describing spring with its gentle breezes and the northern summer in all its glory. He has, as already mentioned, portrayed his native district with characteristic vigor and colorful language in impressive poems, and he has also written a number of poems about other places of scenic, historical, or cultural interest.

Among his strictly personal poems, which are not numerous, the most deep-felt, revealing, and moving are the ones written in memory of his son, Vőlundur. Several of his poems, on the other hand, are general in theme, dealing with contemporary events and social conditions, and although these are not as a rule among his best efforts, they, like his stories and articles, attest to his wide interests.

He adheres largely to traditional and well-established meters, but there is considerable variety in his verse forms, which he handles with great skill, often more vigorously than fluently, however. Not infrequently he employs old Eddic and Skaldic meters, as well as intricate meters of later origin. Thus a whole book of his (*Haustlőng*) is written in the exacting *hringhenda* meter; it is an uneven performance, to be sure, but one which contains some excellent stanzas. The majority of his poems are, however, written in varieties of newer meters. His later works include a few sonnets as well as some interesting efforts in the infectious meter and mood of the "Rubáiyát of Omar Khayyám."

Guðmundur Friðjónsson's wealth of language and rare mastery of his native tongue are among his chief characteristics and great glories as a writer. His language was always individualistic and forceful. At first justly criticized for tending to be bombastic and excessively ornate, his poetic diction developed into a firm, flexible, personal style, which was both sonorous and colorful. He drew on two principal sources—the Old Icelandic literature and the spoken rural language. At his best, he harmonized the two strains in a happy balance and was also invariably a past master at coining new words or turning old ones to new uses. Many of his descriptive phrases are both original and beautiful and his similes are often both unusual and brilliant, although they sometimes miss the mark or, rather, overshoot it. Some of his poems would also gain in artistry and effectiveness by greater concentration. Conversely, his frequent ability to make every word count is excellently illustrated by his short poem "Niðurstaða" (Conclusion), in which he masterfully, and with engaging humility, sums up the fruits of his labors and expresses his faith in the continued longevity of the Nordic spirit.

In one of his poems he speaks of his "one-sided melodies"; and undeniably his themes are, generally speaking, rather limited in range, as a result of both the conditions under which he lived and his outlook upon life, his predilection for the heroic and the time-honored virtues. Nevertheless, his visits to parts of Iceland outside his local community inspired some excellent poems, and his later poems reveal a definite attempt on his part to extend his range.

During his formative years Guðmundur Friðjónsson came, as already indicated, under the influence of Brandesian Realism, and this is seen especially in his stories. He was, moreover, a Realist in the sense that he sought his themes largely in the everyday life about him. The influence of the Realistic Movement is no doubt seen in his critical attitude toward the church and established religion during the earlier part of his career; later in life, however, he became more religiously inclined. That his thoughts were turned in that direction by the loss of his son is seen in his group of poems, "Sőknuður" (Lamentation); but he always remained a good deal of a doubter.

Although Realism unquestionably characterized Guðmundur Friðjónsson as a writer, he was, in his poems at any rate, a great deal of a Romanticist. His love of the past, the ancient literature, and nature and his admiration of the heroic spirit are akin to the Icelandic Romantic poets and nationalists of the nineteenth century, for he became increasingly national in his attitude.

Because of his deep attachment to the soil and to rural life, and no less because of his profound admiration of the tested and time-honored virtues, coupled with the ingrained conservatism of the farmer, Guðmundur Friðjónsson was often bitterly critical of the new in contrast to the old. As a result he was not infrequently criticized for what his more radical opponents termed his reactionary views. He himself characterized these views as resistance to the seamy side of civilization, its artificiality and false values. In any event, he minced no words in expressing his hearty dislike of the superficialities of city life and his hostility to new-fangled ideas generally. All of which was in full harmony with his robust Icelandic character and Norse spirit, his avowed love of national cultural values.

Guðmundur Friðjónsson retained his mental powers and the vigor of his poetic genius unusually well, for among the poems written in his sixties and seventies there are some splendid alike in weighty content and mastery of form. Considered in its entirety his rich literary production, in poetry as well as prose, is nothing short of amazing, for, as in the case of his brother Sigurjón Friðjónsson, his writing was secondary to demanding farm labor and the support of a large family. Among Icelandic poet-farmers, of whom there have been many of note, Guðmundur Friðjónsson shares with Stephan G. Stephansson the distinction of having, in recent times, succeeded most remarkably in rising above conditions generally considered unfavorable to the cultivation of high literary art.

9. GUÐMUNDUR GUÐMUNDSSON was born at Hrólfstaðahellir in Rangárvallasýsla in southern Iceland on September 6, 1874. He came of a poor family with some literary inclination; his father, at any rate, is reported to have possessed versemaking ability. After graduating from the College of Iceland in 1897, Guðmundur Guðmundsson studied medicine for some time, but soon turned his attention to literary pursuits. From 1906 to 1909 he was engaged in journalistic work at Ísafjörður, where he served as local librarian and did some teaching as well. This proved to be a fateful and fortunate period in his career, for at Ísafjörður he met and married Ólína Þorsteinsdóttir, who was destined to exert an enobling influence upon him and inspire him to new poetic achievements. Many of his best poems date from these years and during them he also laid the ground work for major works, whole cycles of poems, which he completed later. From 1913 until his untimely death on March 18, 1919, he resided in Reykjavík, devoting himself to writing and journalism.

He was a very prolific poet and published the following collections of poetry: *Ljóðmæli* (Poems, 1900), *Guðbjörg í Dal* (Guðbjörg at Dal, 1902), *Strengleikar* (Melodies, 1903), *Gígjan* (The Fiddle, 1906),

Friður á jörðu (Peace on Earth, 1911; second ed. 1913), *Ljósaskifti* (Twilight, 1913), and *Ljóð og kvæði* (Songs and Poems, 1917). A volume of his translations, *Erlend ljóð* (Foreign Poems), was edited with a preface by Alexander Jóhannesson in 1924; and a collected edition of his poems, original and translated, *Ljóðasafn* (3 vols.), appeared in 1934, edited with an introduction by Grétar Fells.[16]

Guðmundur Guðmundsson's literary interest was awakened early, and before entering college he had achieved a local reputation for his poems. During his school years he continued to cultivate the poetic art to the extent that he became known as "the College Poet," not only to his fellow students, but nationally as well and is to this day often referred to by that fond designation.

He was a sensitive soul, deeply religious by nature and with strong mystic leanings; it was therefore, natural that the Neo-Romanticism and Symbolism of the nineties should appeal to him. His early prose efforts are definitely emotional and lyrical in spirit, and in his later poems as well those strains run strong. Nor is it difficult to trace in his poetry influences from the native Icelandic tradition and from older and contemporary leading Icelandic poets, whom he especially admired, not least from Jónas Hallgrímsson, his greatest favorite. His admiration for Kristján Jónsson, Guðmundur Guðmundsson has recorded in a sympathetic lecture (Ísafjörður, 1908), and it is easy to understand that the brooding melancholy of the former and his tragic fate should find a response in the kindred soul of his younger fellow poet.

It is a great contrast to come from the realm of Guðmundur Friðjónsson's rugged and strongly Nordic poetry, in which vigor and robust spirit are the dominating characteristics, and enter the world of Guðmundur Guðmundsson, where lyricism in its purest form reigns supreme. He was above anything else the sweet-voiced songbird among contemporary Icelandic poets. The very titles of some of his poetical collections, such as *Strengleikar* (Melodies) and

[16] Concerning his life and literary work, see also Grétar Fells, "Guðmundur Guðmundsson skáld," *Gangleri*, II (1927), 62–69; Arngrímur Fr. Bjarnason, "Endurminningar um Guðmund Guðmundsson skáld," *Lesbók Morgunblaðsins*, XIX (1944), 53–56, 61–62, 72; Einar Thorlacius, "Frá uppvaxtar-og námsárum Guðmundar Guðmundssonar skálds," *ibid.*, 87–88.

Gígjan (The Fiddle), are in themselves strikingly indicative of the inherent musical quality of his verse. Few Icelandic poets, past or present, have equaled him in mastery of delicate form and melodious language. He readily invented new verse forms to suit his mood and theme and often succeeded admirably, as in his beautiful spring poem "Vorgyðjan kemur" (The Arrival of the Goddess of Spring). His rare metrical skill is seen to excellent advantage in "Strengjagaldur" (Strong Magic); this poem is indeed appropriately named, for here is the magic lyric touch, together with flight of the imagination and deep spirituality. Many of his love poems, with a recurrent strain of underlying sadness, are among his best productions; that is not the least true of some of the group entitled "Terra Memoriae," such as "Harmslagur" (Lament) and particularly "Dropatal" (Dripping Rain), equally effective in its symbolic and musical quality, hauntingly reproducing the rhythmic movement of falling raindrops. Appealing in its simplicity is "Norðan frá hafi" (From the Northern Ocean), in a popular, traditional vein, in which the descriptive element and the love theme blend harmoniously.

Some of his nature poems, describing nature in her quieter moods—dreamy evenings and starlit nights, when stillness reigns on land and sea—are very well written, as illustrated by the group "Andante Religioso." Such poems reveal his strong feeling of communion with nature, his ingrained mysticism. On the other hand, he lacked originality and forcefulness.

Among his numerous memorial poems, the one mourning the great loss of lives at sea on April 7, 1906, is especially noteworthy for its sincere and genuinely poetical expression of the spirit of sorrow and sense of loss on the part of the nation. He achieves an even purer lyric strain in his simple and deeply felt poem "Marin Francais," dedicated to the French fishermen buried in the cemetery at Reykjavík.

Guðmundur Guðmundsson had, as an editor, championed the cause of Icelandic independence, although his chief interest lay in the realm of poetry and literature generally rather than in politics. He has written numerous patriotic poems and eulogized a number of Icelandic cultural and political leaders with varying success but always with characteristic choice of diction and mastery of metrical form.

His love of beauty and his idealism are ever in evidence in his poetry, not least during his later years, and his devotion to the temperance cause is particularly noticeable. Genuine religious feeling and heightened spirituality were also an increasingly strong element after he had embraced Theosophy, which readily appealed to his mysticism and sense of the symbolic, and had become the leader of that movement in Iceland. Earlier he had shown his pronounced moral and religious bent with his cycle, *Ljósaskifti* (Twilight), on the introduction of Christianity to Iceland in the year 1000, and still more with his challenging series of poems entitled *Friður á jörðu* (Peace on Earth), of which the introductory poem, an eloquent imploration, is particularly impressive and reveals his deep interest in world peace.

He enriched Icelandic literature with numerous and often splendidly rendered translations from the poetry of many nations, of which the translation of Tennyson's *Locksley Hall* is the most ambitious as well as one of the most successful. Guðmundur Guðmundsson's sensitiveness to beauty enabled him to reproduce in his translations the spirit as well as the theme and the meter of the originals in an unusual degree, and naturally he selected for rendition into his native tongue those poems that particularly appealed to him.

10. SIGURÐUR JÓNSSON was another significant product of the social and cultural awakening in Þingeyjarsýsla. He was born at Hólar in Eyjafjörður in northern Iceland on August 25, 1878, but grew up at Helluvað in Mývatnssveit. His father, Jón Hinriksson (1829–1921), a man of unusual gifts, was the best known unschooled poet in Þingeyjarsýsla during the latter part of the nineteenth century. A collection of his poems, *Ljóðmæli* (Poems), was published on his eightieth birthday in 1909. After graduating with highest honors from the school at Möðruvellir in 1889, Sigurður Jónsson taught for several winters, doing farm work during the summer months. From 1902 until his death February 24, 1949, he was a farmer at Arnarvatn. He occupied for years important public positions in the community and was equally prominent in the agricultural and co-operative organizations both locally and nationally.

The Mývantssveit district is noted for its varied and impressive scenic beauty, and it left its indelible stamp on Sigurður Jónsson's poetry. His attachment to his native soil is, in fact, the deepest and most fundamental note in his poems from first to last. And nowhere does that strain find a purer and nobler expression, nowhere does his poetry reach greater heights, than in his inspired hymn of praise to his native district, "Sveitin mín" (My Home District), which he wrote at twenty-one; it made him known nationally and has increasingly endeared him to his countrymen. Although the poem undeniably echoes a popular lyric by Jónas Hallgrímsson, it expresses, in such a sincere and charming fashion, love for one's locality and appreciation of its scenic beauty that people of all parts of the country have readily claimed it as their own. It has come to be known as the "National Song of Rural Iceland" and is one of the most popular songs on public occasions, especially at patriotic gatherings.

This poem alone would suffice to give the author a secure place in the history of Icelandic letters. But although it is unquestionably his greatest effort, he has published a number of other noteworthy poems, which after having appeared in papers and periodicals were collected in his two books: *Upp til fjalla* (Up in the Mountains, 1937) and *Blessuð sértu sveitin mín* (Blessed Be Thou, My Home District, 1945). Some of his nature poems are particularly impressive in their sonorousness and descriptive power, such as "Herðubreið," about the mountain that towers in its grandeur above his home district. Other poems, such as "Við sólarlag" (At Sunset), are most remarkable for the beautiful word pictures of his rural surroundings and again reveal his deep attachment to them. In these, and in his poems generally, his love of country in a wider sense is also readily seen, as is his appreciation of the Icelandic cultural heritage, the history and the literature of his nation. He said farewell to his country and to life in his beautiful and reverential "Útfararsöngur" (Funeral Song), which also breathes devout faith.

Among his poems on everyday life, the one in praise of the housewife and mother, "Húsmóðirin," describing her daily work and larger mission, is especially attractive in its truthfulness and warmth of feeling. He has also mourned his contemporaries and neighbors, like the writer Jón Stefánsson (Þorgils Gjallandi), in worthy poems; and he has written a number of other occasional poems; they are of uneven quality, as is only to be expected in poetry of that kind.

Among the latter, however, "Skautaljóð" (Skating Song) and "Glímusöngur" (Wrestling Song) are very well done and in their challenge to action reveal the author's manly spirit and healthy optimism.

Like his fellow poet-farmers in Þingeyjarsýsla, Sigurður Jónsson wrote his poetry in time spared from manifold duties and the earning of a living for a large family. In one of his poems, "Tíminn líður" (Time Passes), appealing in its simplicity and sincerity, he laments the lost opportunities and the poems that never were completed.

Sigurður Jónsson has deep roots in the Icelandic literary tradition; his spiritual kinship with the older Icelandic poets, whom he greatly admired, is easily discernible, as is their influence upon his poetry. Above anything else, however, he is as a poet a characteristic product of rural Iceland, whose praises he has sung so lavishly. Withal, he was a man of wide reading, having among other things read English literature quite extensively. From it he translated several poems, some of which are fine renditions.

11. SIGURÐUR SIGURÐSSON was born in Copenhagen on September 15, 1879, the son of Sigurður Sigurðsson, teacher at the College in Reykjavík, and a Danish mother. He grew up in the home of Dr. Björn M. Olsen, the noted scholar and rector of the College, which he attended from 1894 to 1898. He graduated from the Pharmaceutic Institute in Copenhagen in 1906. After having served as secretary to the prefect of Borgarfjarðarsýsla until 1912, be became pharmacist in Vestmannaeyjar for a number of years, where he also interested himself in public affairs. His last years he spent in Reykjavík, where he died on August 4, 1939.

His books of poems include: *Tvístirni* (The Double Stars, 1906; in collaboration with Jónas Guðlaugsson), *Ljóð* (Poems, 1912; second ed., 1924; third ed., 1933), and *Síðustu ljóðmæli* (Last Poems, 1939), edited with a sympathetic preface by Sigurður Nordal.

With his contributions to *Tvístirni*, Sigurður Sigurðsson established himself as an uncommonly promising poet, for here were poems of considerable variety and high literary excellence—nature poems like "Hraunteigur," love poems like "Hrefnuóður" (Hrefna), descriptive and narrative poems like "Útilegumaðurinn" (The Outlaw), and pure lyrics like "Við Sundið" (At the Sound) and

"Sólarlag" (Sunset). These poems are generally characterized by genuine lyric quality, strong personal feeling, originality, sure taste, and reverence for the poet's art.

Unfortunately, the great hopes which the early poems aroused were not to be realized to the fullest extent. In his second book, *Ljóð*, there are, to be sure, both beautiful and excellently wrought poems, splendid and deepfelt nature descriptions such as "Lundurinn helgi" (The Sacred Grove), "Lágnætti við Laxfoss" (Midnight at Laxfoss), and "Hjőrsey"; graphic historical portraits like "Auður"; striking memorial poems such as the one on Surgeon General Jónas Jónassen; and not least the highly personal "Í dag" (Today), masterful in its portrayal of changing moods and amazingly prophetic of the vicissitudes of the poet's later life. Nature in its quieter moods and the depths of his own soul in hours of solitude are his main sources of inspiration. As a result, the lyric element is the dominating characteristic of these poems although the underlying emotion seldom breaks the bounds of restraint and flows over. The language is clear-cut, the poetic images generally simple and tasteful. Often there is an undertone of sadness, a nostalgic longing for departed youth, with its dreams and joys, especially memorably expressed in "Skammgóð er draumtíð" (Vita somnium breve).

The collection also contained a number of successful translations, most of them from the poems of Oscar Levertin, a central figure in the Swedish Neo-Romantic movement; these translations are indicative of Sigurður Sigurðsson's feeling of kinship with the Neo-Romanticists and Symbolists of the nineties, a kinship that appears also in his own poetry.

In his preface to Sigurður Sigurðsson's last collection of poems, *Síðustu ljóðmæli*, Sigurður Nordal, the editor, suggests, no doubt correctly, that the poet's absorption in other interests and his spirit of self-criticism, for he was a great deal of a perfectionist, largely resulted in his not cultivating his poetry during his most favorable mature years. His great admiration for Einar Benediktsson may also, as Dr. Nordal intimates, have made Sigurður Sigurðsson more reluctant to write poetry and thus invite comparison with the master poet and object of his admiration. Let no one think, however, that he was a slavish imitator, for he always remained his individual self. This is clearly revealed in his last poems, which both bear the stamp of his own personality and throw bright light on his life during his last years, when wealth and good health had forsaken him; but the adverse fortune could not subdue his artistic soul and rich poetic gift. It frequently flares up in bright flashes in these last poems of his: in richly imaginative nature poems like "Hafið" (The Ocean), strongly personal poems like "Guitar," descriptive poems with a fine lyric undercurrent like "Í Hnitbjargaholti," as well as in splendid memorial and other occasional pieces. Effective in its symbolism and sincere feeling is "Krists konungs kirkja" (King Christ's Church).

These and other poems in the collection, though lacking the polish and perfection of form of his best earlier productions, show that the old flame still lived in the poet's heart, warmed him when the cold blasts blew about him in those declining years, and opened to him, at least at times, that world of dreams, that inner sanctum of the spirit, which he had described with rare mastery in his poem "Lundurinn helgi" (The Sacred Grove). And while it is to be lamented that he did not succeed in developing his unusual and vigorous poetic talent to its potential heights, with his best poems he has made a lasting contribution to Icelandic literature of the period and also, no doubt, left his mark on some of the younger poets.

12. HULDA, pen name for UNNUR BENEDIKTSDÓTTIR BJARKLIND, in whose work the literary aspect of the cultural awakening in Þingeyjarsýsla found its most lyrical and purely artistic expression, was born at Auðnir í Laxárdal in Suður-Þingeyjarsýsla on August 6, 1881, the daughter of parents of uncommon gifts and cultural attainments. Her father, Benedikt Jónsson, was the intellectual leader of the progressive and cultural movement in that part of the country, one of the founders and until his death the librarian of the remarkable district library, the fountainhead of inspiration for this political and cultural movement. His home was, therefore, a cultural center, where the gifted daughter and future poetess received full encouragement and had access to rich and varied literature, foreign no less than native. Poetic talent also appears to run strong in the family, for in the collection of poetry from the district, *Þingeysk ljóð* (1940), two of Hulda's sisters are represented by beautiful and well-written poems.

At her home Hulda had excellent private tutors in languages and other subjects, and later she studied domestic science at Akureyri and in Reykjavík and continued her language studies with noted private tutors. Her study of the Icelandic mother tongue had, as might be expected, been duly emphasized; and her knowledge of foreign languages—Danish, English, German, and later French—was far beyond the level of most Icelandic young women of that day and became for her the golden key that opened the door of the wide realm of foreign literature. According to her own testimony (in a letter to the writer), her reading included not only Icelandic poetry and prose, past and contemporary, but also the works of many of the greatest writers of all time, from Dante to Charles Dickens. She also knew the leading Scandinavian poets of the nineteenth century, such as the Norwegian masters, Ibsen and Bjőrnson, and the great Swedish poetess, Selma Lagerlőf, as well as her more immediate northern contemporaries. She was particularly attracted to Icelandic folklore, as is profoundly reflected in her poetry. Among Icelandic poets Eggert Ólafsson was a special favorite of hers, his love of rural life and culture naturally appealing to her. Her admiration for Benedikt Grőndal (the younger) was likewise unbounded; nor is it surprising, for they had indeed much in common: love of beauty, dreamy Romantic spirit, and a humble reverence for the glories of nature.

Hulda's literary work was accomplished in addition to her duties as a busy housewife and mother. She was married to Sigurður S. Bjarklind, and they resided at Húsavík, where he was manager of the co-operative store, until they moved to Reykjavík in 1935. Here she died on April 10, 1946.[17]

In view of the fact that, at least during her earlier years, she could devote only her spare time to literary pursuits and often had to fight ill health, her literary production is nothing short of amazing. Her numerous prose works, short stories, fairy tales, and sketches, and a two-volume novel, together with her several collections of

[17] For information about her life and literary career, see further Richard Beck, "Hulda skáldkona," *Tímarit Þjóðræknisfélags Íslendinga í Vesturheimi*, XXII (1940), 29–41.

poetry, reveal both the extensiveness and the considerable variety of her production, which throughout bears witness to her love of beauty, purity of soul, and rich lyric gift.

Her first published poems, which appeared in the women's magazine *Framsókn* when she was only twenty years of age and unknown outside her native district, immediately attracted favorable attention, and deservedly, for they were unusually promising in their unmistakable poetic quality, notably for the genuine lyric touch that was to become the hallmark of her later poetry. Encouraged by the favorable reaction to her first published efforts, she continued to contribute poems to Icelandic papers, especially the Reykjavík paper *Ingólfur*. Her poems aroused the interest of Einar Benediktsson, the poet, to the extent that he hailed Hulda in a beautiful poem characterized by deep insight and sympathetic understanding of her art and outlook upon life. This tribute and others like it naturally were for her a source of both gratification and inspiration. The public, on the other hand, as Einar Benediktsson says in the conclusion of his poem, was eager to learn the identity of the sweet-voiced poetess who concealed herself behind the pen name of Hulda. This was not generally known until the poet Þorsteinn Erlingsson revealed it in his brilliant article about her ("Huldupistill"), in the paper, *Þjóðviljinn* (June 15, 1905). This penetrating and masterfully written article from the pen of a highly regarded and beloved poet drew the attention of the general public to the poetess, especially to her *þulur* (rhapsodies). She was soon a favorite with poetry lovers throughout the country; chiefly because she succeeded in touching the heart of the nation by reviving, polishing, and thereby elevating to a new literary level the time-honored *þulur*, cherished poetic production of the common people.

Þorsteinn Erlingsson also devoted most of his discussion to these poems in the traditional strain, especially singling out the lovely rhapsody, "Ljáðu mér vængi" (Lend Me Wings), stressing how marvelously well the poetess had been able to recapture with unexcelled purity the spirit and the lyric charm of the old *þulur* and other folk poetry. He also praised highly her other poems in that vein, fully realizing that a new note of melodious and lyric beauty had been added to Icelandic poetry.

Hulda's first book of poems, *Kvæði* (Poems, 1909; second ed., Akureyri, 1926), was also enthusiastically received by Þorsteinn Erlingsson, who could better than most appreciate the musical magic and the sheer beauty of many of the poems included. The collection also received high praise from the poet Matthías Jochumsson, especially for the sincerity of the poems, the personal feeling, beauty and musical quality. Generally the reviews were very favorable.

In this first collection Hulda strikes the fundamental notes that were to resound throughout her poetry; she listens to the voices of nature and interprets them with deep emotion and melodious language. Here is the fragrance of flowers and birch woods, sunny spring and summer, and the murmur of bubbling brooks. The picture is generally set in the frame of the Icelandic rural scene in all its glory, which Hulda never grew tired of euloguizing, as in her beautiful poem "Dalbúinn" (The Valley Dweller). The poems in *þulur* style are, as already indicated, the most original ones in the collection. Many of the love poems are also polished in form, sincere and deep-felt.

In her next collection, *Syngi, syngi svanir mínir* (Sing, O, Sing, My Swans, 1916), Hulda retold a popular Icelandic fairy tale, which had naturally appealed to her interest in folklore. It is a cycle of poems skillful in diction and meter, not particularly impressive, but rich in poetic and beautiful pictures.

In her third collection, *Segðu mér að sunnan* (Bring Me Tidings from the South, 1920), the poetess in the main strikes the same notes as before. Here are numerous nature poems inspired by Icelandic scenery in its choicest garb, as well as poems in the enchanting, melancholy spirit of the rhapsodies and other folk poetry. Undeniably, a number are rich in lyric beauty. The range of observation is also somewhat broader than before; here are some poems, such as "Oxford," written during a sojourn abroad.

Her fourth book of poems, *Við yzta haf* (By the Outermost Sea, 1926), one of her principal collections of verse, is also, all in all, marked by the greatest variety of themes, ranging from material from ancient times to her characteristic eulogies of rural life. Although some of the poems are more vigorous than many of the earlier ones, the pure lyric quality is still the principal feature. In one of the most beautiful poems in the collection, "Helga Bárðardóttir," the poetess has indirectly portrayed herself well. Here is also found one of the most masterful poems in all her extensive production, "Krossaumur" (Cross-stitch), delicate in its thoroughly feminine touch, with its symbolic description of the daughter of the valley during the height of winter embroidering in her cloth her hopes and dreams, the glory of coming spring and summer.

Especially noteworthy for its strong personal element and emotional quality is her cycle of poems, *Þú hlustar Vőr* (Listen, Vőr, 1933), constituting what may be called spiritual autobiography, written with tender feeling and delicate lyric charm.

Her last book of poems, *Söngur starfsins* (The Song of Toil), was published posthumously in 1946. Here are many poems marked by her characteristic love of beauty, ingrained faith in goodness, and her strong national feeling. This last found memorable expression in her poem written in commemoration of the establishment of the Icelandic republic on June 17, 1944, and adjudged one of the two prize-winning poems submitted in national competition for that occasion. The title poem of the volume strikes the note effectively. The memorial poem about her beloved father is appealing in its unadorned sincerity, a devoted daughter's noble tribute to an equally devoted father, a great idealist and a friend of man.

Hulda translated into Icelandic poems by such Romantic poets as Heine, Longfellow, and Uhland, clearly revealing her literary taste and artistic sensitiveness. Her rendition of "Home, Sweet Home," which was in full harmony with her love of home and the native soil, is splendid.

In his poem to Hulda, Einar Benediktsson hailed her as "the first fruit of our new school [of poetry]." He was right in that here a new note was struck in Icelandic poetry and that here impulses from the Neo-Romantic and Symbolic movements found in many ways a true and fruitful expression.

With her revival of the *þulur* in particular, Hulda made a unique and lasting contribution to Icelandic literature and paved the way for many other poets who have since written splendid poems in that same style. And, in a wider sense, she contributed in no small measure toward making Icelandic verse-forms more lyrical, light, and flexible than before, without sacrificing traditional Icelandic features.

13. JÓHANN GUNNAR SIGURÐSSON (1882–1906), whose brief career is sketched among the prose writers as he left some stories worthy of note, is most important as a lyric poet of great promise and one of the pioneers among the Icelandic Neo-Romantic and Symbolic poets of the day.

His poems constitute the greater part of his writings included in the volume, *Kvæði og sögur* (Poems and Stories), published posthumously by his friend Benedikt Bjarnarson in 1909. These poems were written between 1897 and 1906, or from his sixteenth to his twenty-fourth year, the last ones only two months before his death. In view of that circumstance, it is surprising how mature many of these poems are, although, as is only natural, they also reveal the impressionableness of the youthful poet, who had not as yet fully found himself. Nor was it granted him to complete a number of his poetic efforts.

He was a lyric poet in the true sense of the word, and his indebtedness to Jónas Hallgrímsson, whom he greatly admired, is easily detected. He wrote a number of nature poems, often charming in their simplicity and naturalness, such as "Sólris" (Sunrise), "Rőkkurljóð" (Twilight Song), and "Kvőldbæn" (Evening Prayer), which are marked by his lightness of touch and fluency.

Much more notable, however, are several personal poems, clearly the genuine outburst of a sensitive soul saddened and torn by impending doom; his deep emotional turmoil he has expressed symbolically in such poems as "Kveðið í gljúfrum" (A Voice from the Ravine), "Óráð" (Delirium), and "Í álőgum" (Spellbound), in which he reproduces brilliantly the mood, language, and haunting rhythmic quality of the folk song. And these poems, definitely written in the spirit of the Neo-Romantic and Symbolist movements, strike a new note in Icelandic poetry and have deservedly found their place in the history of Icelandic letters of the period. They also eloquently reveal how rich a poetic talent the author possessed and what a loss the nation sustained in his death at the age of twenty-four.

14. ŐRN ARNARSON, pen name of MAGNÚS STEFÁNSSON, was born at Kverkártunga in the Langanes district in northeastern Iceland

on December 12, 1884. These were hard years in that part of the country, and his parents were compelled to break up their home because of poverty. He remained with them, however, and after his father's death in 1887, grew up with his mother at Þorvaldsstaðir in his native district. As was customary, during those early years he engaged in ordinary farm work and also had some experience as a fisherman, his interest in the sea thus being aroused in those formative years. Determined to acquire education beyond the limited foundation that he had received at home, he first attended a preparatory school in Eyjafjőrður, then the Flensborg High School in Hafnarfjőrður, graduating in 1908, and finally the Teachers College at Reykjavík, receiving his teaching diploma in 1909. On his own account, he added immeasurably to his formal education, studying languages to gain access to foreign literature—mastering, besides the Scandinavian languages, both English and German, and reading very extensively in all these. At one time he had built up a considerable library of foreign and Icelandic books. He interested himself both in geology and botany, and on his extensive walking tours gathered specimens of both minerals and plants. He was an athlete of note during his earlier years, and walking continued to be his favorite pastime as long as his health permitted. He had, in fact, covered most of the country on foot, enjoying the uncertainties and the adventures of such travels and rejoicing in the unique grandeur and rich scenic beauty, the striking contrasts of his native land, which are eloquently and memorably reflected in his poetry.

After one year of teaching in his old community (1909–1910), Őrn Arnarson made his home, with but short interruptions, in Vestmannaeyjar, doing clerical and secretarial work in winter and manual labor, such as road building, during the summer months, for outdoor work was much to his liking. When he moved to Hafnarfjőrður in 1924, he engaged in similar work, until his health broke in 1935. His working days were then practically over, although he retained his literary interest and revised or wrote some poems and assisted in preparing his collected works for publication. He died at a hospital in Hafnarfjőrður on July 25, 1942.[18]

[18] Concerning his life and literary work, see further Sigurður Skúlason, Őrn Arnarson," *Samtíðin*, II (1935), 7–9; Richard Beck, "Őrn Arnarson skáld,"

Őrn Arnarson's gift for poetry came to light very early. And no doubt his interest in versemaking was stimulated by the traditional custom of chanting for entertainment during winter evenings the popular narrative cycles of *rímur* poetry, a custom regularly observed in his home at Þorvaldsstaðir. He has himself affectionately described those winter evenings of saga reading and *rímur* chanting and the effect upon him, as well as the exciting first visit of a recognized poet, Símon Dalaskáld, of *rímur* fame. The poets were to young Őrn Arnarson glorious individuals, for they had the power and the magic of the winged word at their command.

At any rate, he made up his mind early to become a poet and during the years of his youth composed numerous verses, which, if nothing else, developed his metrical skill to a high degree. At the time of his confirmation he composed his first full-length poem. During his school years he wrote considerably, but only a few poems from that period have found their way into his collection; for he was very critical of his own efforts and, in addition, very retiring by nature and reluctant to offer his poems to the public (or even to undertake the writing or the completion of some of them) without the encouragement and urging of his friends. They were for years almost the only people familiar with his poetic ability.

His first poems, under the pen name of Őrn Arnarson (which he retained thereafter), appeared in the periodical *Eimreiðin* in 1920 and immediately attracted the attention of poetry lovers because of their newness of tone and general poetical excellence. Melodious fluency, whimsicality, and irony reminiscent of Heine, which sometimes became bitter satire, marked these early poems, together with uncommon mastery of form; these remained his main characteristics. Nor was it difficult, even in these first published poems, to detect under the harsh exterior his warm human sympathy. There was, as well, deep seriousness and submerged sadness in some of his love poems.

Tímarit Þjóðræknisfélags Íslendinga í Vesturheimi, XXI (1939), 53–63; Jóhann Gunnar Ólafsson, "Magnús Stefánsson skáld," *Helgafell*, I (1942), 159–168; Stefán Júlíusson, "Skáldið Őrn Arnarson," *Skinfaxi*, XXXVI (1945), 85–93; XXXVII (1946), 8–17; XXXVIII (1947), 15–21; and "Um skáldskap Arnar Arnarsonar," *ibid.*, XXXIX (1948), 20–31, 80–88.

All these qualities are seen to a better advantage in his collection, *Illgresi* (Weeds, 1924), of unusually even literary quality and very favorably received, and to a still greater extent in the larger selection from his total production, which was published under the same title shortly after his death in 1942, edited with a biographical sketch by Bjarni Aðalbjarnarson.

Although Őrn Arnarson cannot be considered a prolific poet, no doubt in a large measure because of his reserved temperament, adverse circumstances, prolonged illness, and rigid self-criticism, his production is by no means small. As a result the collection is especially notable for its uniformly high literary level and also reveals that the poet's world was far from circumscribed.

Here are the satirical poems from his younger years, such as "Őngulseyri," with its inimitable description of the Icelandic fishing village ruled by the Danish merchant, of the merchant himself and his wife, biting in its irony. Here also are the even more bitter social satires, like "Útlegð" (Exile) and "Skiptafundur" (Settlement of an Estate), in which, revolting against organized religion and the existing order of things, the poet lashes out at superficiality, hypocrisy, hard-heartedness, and injustice with merciless realism and gives full vent to his radical views. He was appreciative of genuine manliness, as seen, for instance, in his sonorous and sympathetic poem on "Sigurður hreppstjóri" (Sheriff Sigurður), who is to Őrn Arnarson a personification of the Nordic spirit that is still alive in the nation. In a similar fashion, "Stjáni blái," a seaman without a peer and the very embodiment of the heroism of that large part of the Icelandic nation who wrest their livelihood from the sea, becomes the subject of one of the author's greatest poems, a poem masterful in diction, pictorial quality, and metrical skill. As a matter of fact, with his satires, his poems about the sea and seamanship won him his greatest popularity. He has captured the magic power of the sea over men's minds in a charming lyric, "Sigling" (Sailing), and written a stirring seaman's song, "Hrafnistumenn," which won first prize in a general competition and became the official song of the Icelandic seamen. In these songs, as well as elsewhere in his poems, his ingrained love of the sea and his thorough knowledge of the life of the seamen as well as his sympathy for them can be seen. This sympathetic interest extended to the working class generally, whose cause he championed in his poems and embraced politically, affiliating with the Icelandic Labor Party, although he took but a small public part in politics. His positive interest in the common people and their welfare, as expressed in his radical views, no doubt was inspired by his bitter acquaintance with poverty in his youth and his constant association with working people, which moulded him and his outlook.

His sympathy reached out to animals no less than to human beings, as shown in his poem "Rjúpan" (The Ptarmigan). Its roots were deep in his sensitive nature, hidden behind the mask of gayness and banter and bearing the scars of bitter disappointments, touchingly revealed in his beautiful love poem, "Ásrún." With the years, as he saw his youthful dreams come true in increasing measure, his earlier pessimism and bitterness mellowed, and he adopted a more sympathetic view of humankind, without compromising with his long-held convictions. Penetrating in its understanding of the human heart and effective in its symbolism is his poem, "Reimleikar" (Ghosts Abroad), suggestive of Ibsen's *Ghosts* in miniature. A whole life story is masterfully told in five stanzas in his poem "Amma kvað" (Grandmother's Tale), one of his finest lyric poems.

He delighted, as already indicated, in extensive walking tours through Iceland and felt much at home in the company of the mountains, the wastelands of the interior, and the lonely headlands on the coast, far from the beaten path. And with his keen poetic insight and his sense of the beautiful, he portrays scenic Iceland, in summer and winter garb, in such notable poems as his impressive "Ljóðabréf til Vestur-Íslendings" (A Rhymed Letter to a Western Icelander), occasioned by the visit to Iceland of the Canadian-Icelandic poet, Guttormur J. Guttormsson, presenting a graphic picture of life in Iceland, and penetrating the psychology of the emigrant.

Őrn Arnarson's mastery of language and form are also strikingly seen in this poem and in an even more remarkable degree, together with his rare epigrammatic ability, in his cycle of poems, *Rímur af Oddi sterka* (1938), in the time-honored *rímur* form. Rollicking humor, eloquence, and passages of beauty and forcefulness add to the literary excellence of this work, which, with no little justification, has been called a masterpiece of its kind.

His greatest lyrical heights are found in his poem, "Þá var ég ungur" (I Was Young Then), his last poem, a heart-felt survey of his youthful years and a tribute to his devoted mother. All things considered it is probably his most beautiful and penetrating poem and is indeed a noble testament to his nation.

Traditional in his poetry, Őrn Arnarson did not, to be sure, break a new trail, but such poems as his last one and his other best efforts will, nevertheless, ensure him a long life in Icelandic letters because of their literary artistry. He is the kind of a poet who is likely to gain in stature with the passing of time.

15. Jakob Thorarensen was born at Foss in Vestur-Húnavatnssýsla in northern Iceland on May 18, 1886. Scholarly interest and poetic talent characterized both branches of the family; on his father's side he was not far removed from Bjarni Thorarensen, the great poet of the earlier half of the nineteenth century, and on his mother's side he was closely related to the gifted poet Stefán Sigurðsson frá Hvítadal, his contemporary. While Jakob Thorarensen grew up mostly in Hrútafjőrður, he also spent a considerable part of his youth in Reykjafjőrður in the Strandir district. This rugged country, with its steep and barren mountains, which enclose the fjord on three sides and rise in imposing grandeur toward the open sea, has left its impact on his poetry, personality, and outlook upon life. So also have the seasonal changes with their great contrasts and the northern weather. And one must not forget the people he associated with in his youth, which was marked by the hard struggle for existence no less than by the harsh surroundings. Other factors also played a part in moulding him during those formative years; his sojourn first with his maternal grandfather, Gísli Sigurðsson, and later with his paternal grandfather, Jakob Thorarensen, were, according to his own testimony, both memorable and fruitful for him. Gísli Sigurðsson was steeped in Icelandic lore and poetically inclined. Jakob Thorarensen was a man of action and strong personality. The latter, therefore, probably aroused in the future poet an admiration for wholeheartedness and manliness, whereas the former, with his accounts of adventurous shark-fishing expeditions

fraught with danger, probably furnished him with the idea for his later impressive poem on the subject.

In his youth Jakob Thorarensen did ordinary farm work and, as was customary, occasionally took part in fishing expeditions. In 1905 he moved to Reykjavík, where he has resided ever since. For a number of years he has been a carpenter by trade, especially engaging in housebuilding; but lately he has devoted himself almost entirely to his poetry and other literary pursuits. He is a self-educated man, but he has read widely and has acquired a very large and significant private library, not least in the Icelandic field. He has twice made journeys abroad, as reflected in some of his poems, and read foreign literature extensively, but Icelandic literature has primarily moulded him and been his chief source of inspiration.[19]

Jakob Thorarensen's early poems, published in the periodical *Óðinn*, drew attention to him because of their marked individuality. Here was a young poet daring to go his own way in thought and form and, therefore, likely to make his mark in the realm of letters.

The promise was made good, in no small measure, in his first collection of poems, *Snæljós* (Snowblink, 1914). Through these poems there blew a fresh and invigorating breeze; there is in them the tang and the surge of the sea, the sweep of the mountains and the moorlands; and what is still more significant, the life of the people, its hard struggle against the elements, is here portrayed with faithful realism and in striking pictures. Not that all these poems are equal in literary merit or significance, but here as early as 1914 were several of the poet's finest and most characteristic productions, bringing out more clearly those qualities that had characterzied his first published poems—his originality in treatment of themes and diction, his vigor, realism, and frankness, and his humor, which often takes the form of scathing irony. And these have continued to be his principal characteristics as a poet, although with the years he has gained in maturity and penetration, and his views have also undergone some changes, as evidenced by the titles of his books: *Sprettir* (Spurts, 1919), *Kyljur* (Breezes, 1922), *Stillur* (Calm

[19] For information about his life and literary career, see also Guðmundur G. Hagalín, "Jakob Thorarensen," *Óðinn*, XX (1924), 13–17; Vilhjálmur Þ. Gíslason, "Jakob Thorarensen skáld," *Eimreiðin*, LII (1946), 87–98.

Weather, 1927), and *Heiðvindar* (Winds from a Clear Sky, 1933). These volumes are extensive and naturally somewhat uneven in excellence, but here are numerous poems of a high order, notable especially for their intellectual quality and vigor in thought and expression.

Jakob Thorarensen has written graphic nature descriptions, and in these it is often the rugged, awe-inspiring aspect of the Icelandic scene that appeals most strongly to him, as in "Stigahlíð" and "Svőrtuloft." This is evident also in his excellent poem "Sogn," the result of a visit to that historic and scenic part of Norway; here, as elsewhere, external nature stimulates him to contemplation about human life. The northern winter, in its darkness and awe, has likewise inspired such poems as "Skammdegi" (Winter Days), while its grandeur is the theme of "Stirndur himinn" (Starlit Sky), sonorous and pictorial, with a deep contemplative strain. The softer aspect of nature and the seasons does not escape him, as can be seen in several spring and summer poems alive with genuine rejoicing.

He has also written impressive historical poems, in which he has clothed with the flesh and blood of reality such heroic saga figures as Guðrún Ósvífursdóttir, Hildigunnur, Snorri Goði, and Sturla Sighvatsson. These and others like them from later centuries are men and women after the poet's own heart, of no ordinary make, strong-minded and whole-souled. In such poems, no less than in his memorial poems on those contemporaries whom he has considered worthy of his eulogy, he often succeeds very well in picturing his subjects frankly and honestly in simple, bold strokes. Among his poems on Icelandic saga women the one about Ásdís á Bjargi, Grettir's devoted mother, is particularly attractive; it is a hymn of praise to motherly love and sacrifice, not unlikely reminiscent of the poet's deep attachment to his own mother.

Jakob Thorarensen excels particularly in his narrative poems, which tell the life story of various types of people and interpret their characters in illuminating flashes that throw into relief their most fundamental traits and fateful moments. His deft irony not uncommonly adds to the effectiveness of the picture. In such poems, no less than in his historical and memorial poems, he often portrays proud people of forceful personalities and strong feelings, as in

"Hrossa-Dóra," memorable alike for its descriptive quality, dramatic force, and rhythmical effect.

He describes sympathetically, in a few characteristic strokes, the heroes of everyday life, such as the chimney sweep. Elsewhere he portrays just as truthfully, if ironically or critically, people of an entirely different breed, the idlers and others whom he heartily detests. For manliness and other heroic qualities appeal most strongly to him, and his admiration for these characteristics inspired his great poem "Í hákarlalegum" (A Shark-fishing Expedition), with its truthful and impressive picture of those dauntless men who, in their open boats, brave the storms and the raging seas on those uninviting expeditions in the midst of winter.

Calm realism characterizes Jakob Thorarensen's poetry. His keen insight into the seamy side of life finds frequent expression in irony and social satire, often bitter and relentless and apparently lacking in warmth; but a closer look reveals the undercurrent of sensitiveness and sympathy with the victim of the social system, as in the poem "Hann stal" (The Theft). And this sympathy extends to animals who, like the human creatures, fight their hard battle for existence and in addition not infrequently suffer from man's inhumanity. Deep moral consciousness, therefore, goes hand in hand with social satire in many of Jakob Thorarensen's poems and may, in fact, be said to be at the very root of that satire, interwoven with his sense of justice.

He has pondered the problems of life, and his attitude finds expression in numerous contemplative poems, outspoken and critical, but always honest and ultimately positive rather than negative. His realism and skepticism have not permanently bred in him that dark pessimism that finds expression in such poems as "Skaflar" (Snow-drifts). Though at times badly shaken, his faith in manliness and human sympathy, in life and in his country, remains; and although the future sometimes appears to him "enveloped in mist" and uncertain, he retains his faith, as seen in "Ný tíð" (New Time) and elsewhere, even though his enthusiasm is somewhat tempered by his cautious realism. An outright individualist, deeply conscious of the personal responsibility involved, he urges meeting the demand in an unflinching and manly spirit through faithful labor. This challenge to action is the message in many of his poems, as "Dagur"

(Day), striking in its symbolism. Strong as his sense of duty is, his faith in beauty in all its forms is even more limitless and finds expression in his poem "Feguró" (Beauty). Although he recognizes the inability of human thought to fathom the mysteries of the universe, his reverence for its Author, as well as for life in all its manifestations, is both implied and expressed in his poems.

He is not a personal poet, for hardly ever does he bare his own soul in his poems; they are, therefore, much more notable for their intellectual than their emotional quality, the descriptive element rather than the sweep of the imagination. He is not, therefore, a lyric poet. Frequently he is a skillful master of varied, melodious, and even intricate verse forms, old and new. These verse forms and his vigorous, rich language are characteristic, although at times greater smoothness and surer literary taste would have been desirable. Imbued with the spirit of time-honored virtues and cultural values, Jakob Thorarensen is of the Icelandic literary tradition, spiritually akin to the nineteenth-century Icelandic poets, not least to Grímur Thomsen (although they are unlike in many respects) and in some ways to his cousin Bjarni Thorarensen.

Because of their vigor, concentration, humor, and penetrating insight, Jakob Thorarensen's best poems constitute a characteristic and significant contribution to Icelandic literature and have, notably in the case of such poems as "Í hákarlalegum," (A Sharkfishing Expedition), cultural-historical importance no less than high literary merit.

16. Jónas Guðlaugsson (1887–1916) belonged to a family in which poetic talent has proved unusually common; both his father, the Reverend Guðlaugur Guðmundsson (d. 1931), and his younger brother Kristján Guðlaugsson (b. 1906) have published collections of poems of some merit. Very early Jónas Guðlaugsson began writing verse; and while in college, which he entered at the age of fifteen, he attracted attention with his poems and his bold dreams of future literary greatness.[20]

His first book, *Vorblóm* (Spring Flowers, 1905), appeared when he was only eighteen, most of the poems included having been written

---

[20] For his biography and prose works, see Einarsson, *Prose Writers*, pp. 134–136.

during 1904. Naturally, these youthful efforts are in many respects immature as well as imitative of older Icelandic writers, but they reveal a lyric vein that gives promise of greater achievements.

With his share in the collection, *Tvístirni* (Twin Stars, 1906), published with Sigurður Sigurðsson, Jónas Guðlaugsson gave further evidence of his lyric talent, especially in some of his nature and love poems; in others his patriotism and love of freedom found vigorous and eloquent expression. But his production still suffered from immaturity and lack of originality.

These faults are less noticeable in his next book of poems, the last published in Iceland, *Dagsbrún* (Dawn, 1909). He has a firmer grip on his themes than before, although he is as yet neither particularly profound nor original. But the genuine lyric touch, personal experience clothed in an artistic garb, is often here. Smoothness and descriptive excellence characterize several of his nature poems. Some of his satirical verses, which clearly show that he read Heine to good advantage, are likewise of special interest. In general this collection reveals him as a "dreamer of great dreams," in "Mig langar" (I Long), one who is indeed highly ambitious personally, but who also cherishes high hopes for the future of his country and nation. For him the north is a fountain of spiritual strength, and this thought is beautifully expressed in the poem "Einbúinn" (The Hermit), perhaps the best one in the whole collection. Another noteworthy poem from those early years is "Æskuást" (Youthful Love), possessing both sincerity of feeling and imaginative quality.

With his three collections in Norwegian and Danish, published in Kristiania and Copenhagen, *Sange fra Nordhavet* (Songs from the North Sea, 1911), *Viddernes Poesi* (Poetry of the Moorlands, 1912), and *Sange fra de Blaa Bjærge* (Songs from the Blue Mountains, 1914), especially with the two later ones, Jónas Guðlaugsson definitely established himself as a lyric poet of note. The freshness and the vigor of his poems appealed to genuine lovers of poetry and the literary critics alike; the latter were also generous in their praise of his mastery of form.

In *Sange fra Nordhavet* are poems that appeared originally in Icelandic in his collection *Dagsbrún*, such as "Einbúinn" (The Hermit), and the delicately wrought lyric "Svanir" (Swans), imbued with the deep longing of the poet's heart. The major part of the collection consists, however, of new poems, a number of which were inspired by the author's beloved native land and his concern for its future. Among these "Thingvellir" is particularly impressive, a strikingly poetic expression of the lament of the Icelandic people for their lost freedom.

In *Viddernes Poesi* are melodious poems on similar themes, forcefully revealing the poet's love of country and his burning desire for a reborn, free Icelandic nation. Akin in subject matter are his "Vinland" and his songs in praise of Eric the Red and Leif the Lucky. Still more numerous are the nature poems, descriptive of the shifting seasons and showing that the poet was equally capable of giving artistic expression to the stillness of a winter day, the surging sea of northern lights, the boisterous arrival of spring, and the glory of a summer sunset. Born lyricist that he was, such poems, of course, reflect his mood at the time. So also do his love poems, in which nature descriptions are dexterously interwoven into his deep-felt songs in recollection of her whom he has loved and lost.

The poems in *Sange fra de Blaa Bjærge* are related in theme to those of *Viddernes Poesi*, but the poet's hand is frequently surer than before; mood, theme, and verse form blend more harmoniously. As in his earlier poems, Iceland, the land of his hopes and dreams, is very often, directly or indirectly, the source of his inspiration; and nowhere does he reach higher in lyric beauty, His love poems, of which there are several, have a new note; they are now joyous and optimistic, for the poet has found one who returns his love. This spirit of optimism is evident elsewhere, as in his jubilant "Maj" (May Song). He faced the future with a new faith and hope, although shadows and sunshine still alternate in his songs, for he had had a full share of disappointments and lack of appreciation.

A Neo-Romanticist in his literary tendency, as seen for instance in one of his more notable youthful efforts, "Hóladans," Jónas Guðlaugsson was primarily a lyric poet. This lyric quality is also a marked element in his prose works. Though self-exiled from his country, he was Icelandic to the core, loving his native land with the fervency characteristic of his tempestuous nature. It was in complete harmony with the main interest of his all-too-short life and the recurrent theme of his poems that the novel on which he was working at the time of his death should have the title *Fædrenes Land* (The Ancestral Land).

17. Jakob Jóhannesson Smári was born at Sauðafell in Miðdalir in western Iceland on October 9, 1889, the son of the Reverend Jóhannes L. L. Jóhannesson, a philologist of note. His grandfathers on both sides were known for their versemaking ability, and on his mother's side he was related to the poetess Vatnsenda-Rósa. After graduating from the College of Iceland in 1908, he studied Scandinavian philology at the University of Copenhagen, receiving his M.A. degree in 1914. Since then he has resided in Reykjavík; for many years he has taught Icelandic language and literature in the College. He has written a large number of articles and essays on literary and cultural subjects, book reviews, and textbooks on Icelandic grammar and has translated several prose works into Icelandic.

The title of his first book of poems (1920) was *Kaldavermsl*, meaning "a spring with even temperature the year round," symbolic of the tranquil quality of the poems. With this volume Smári established himself as a lyric poet of rare mastery, equally adept at clothing in melodious form nature and love themes or contemplations on the deepest problems of human existence. He grew up in a district noted for its scenic beauty, which no doubt stimulated the deep love of nature that is one of his fundamental characteristics. And there, in his lovely and beloved childhood haunts, he received the inspiration for some of the finest poems in his first collection, the cycle of poems entitled "Sonnettusveigur til Íslands" (A Wreath of Sonnets to Iceland). These and several other sonnets in the collection already stamped him as an Icelandic master of the form, which has remained his favorite and which he has used with increasing virtuosity until it has become in his hands a highly reponsive and many-stringed instrument.

The love poems included in the first book are also charming in their delicate lyric quality and pure beauty. Above anything else, however, the poems in this collection are characterized by that deep spirituality, the search after the ultimate truth, which is fundamental to Smári's nature. At that time it found a particularly poetic and striking expression in the poem "Hillingar" (Mirage), describing the enchanting islands of Waak-al-Waak, rising from the sea on the misty, distant horizon and drawing the poet's spirit to them with irresistible magic.

The same general qualities, in even a greater degree, characterized his next book, *Handan storms og strauma* (Beyond Storms and Currents, 1936), and the title strikes at the very heart of the poems, for the poet's world is far removed from the turmoil of everyday life. Here we listen to the soft melodies from the harp of a poet endowed with profound sensitiveness of soul, who hears "silent voices" bring soothing messages to his tired mind and sees eternity smile, as in a pleasant dream, beyond the turbulent stream of the finite world.

At the same time, Smári further shows, as he had in his earlier poems, an unusually keen eye and sure taste for colors in all their shades. Also apparent is his ability to select words and phrases that as a rule clearly portray the thought and fit naturally into the framework of the verse form. His poems, especially many of his sonnets, are rich in nature descriptions, which eloquently reveal him as a master painter in words.

In spite of his rare faculty for describing nature in all her grandeur and moods, changing according to the time of the day and the seasons, Smári remains pre-eminently the poet of the inner reality rather than the external. Mysticism, old and new, together with later psychological tendencies, have largely moulded his view of life, as his poems strongly reflect. The mystic and the dreamy quality are constantly the deep and haunting undercurrents. The spiritual side receives the emphasis, even when the theme is an objective one, as in the excellent sonnets "Kvőld" (Evening) and "Sólskinsdagur" (A Sunny Day), the latter ending with the lines: "Out at the horizon the lands of sunshine await, enveloped in the golden dream of summer's mist," reminiscent of those distant and enchanting islands of Waak-al-Waak.

The collection contains many of the author's poems, such as "Drottning Berglandsins" (The Queen of the Mountain Land), in which musical and descriptive quality blend artistically, and his sonnet "Þingvellir," in which the poet's finest qualities, mastery of form, pictorial wealth, and deep insight, unite to make a lyric gem.

Smári's latest book of poems, *Undir sól að sjá* (Looking toward the Sunset, 1939), which appeared on his fiftieth birthday, further emphasized the uniform and unusually high lyric quality of his poetry. It also revealed that within its limits there is considerable variety, as he finds his themes not only in the realm of nature but also in various other phases of everyday life and in his inner self, for his poetry is highly personal. And the poems generally have in common that touching undertone of sadness and longing that is so fundamental a characteristic and finds artistic expression in such sonnets as "Gömul minning" (An Old Memory). There are many others in a similar vein, like the one entitled "Gras" (Grass), illustrative of the fact that the poet finds themes worthy of his lyric genius in the humble grass growing along his path. Unquestionably, however, one of the finest lyrics in the book is "Násíka" as the name suggests, on a theme from the *Odyssey*.

Besides his original poetry, Smári has proved himself a productive and able translator of both prose and verse; included among his translations is Rudyard Kipling's famous "If."

The kinship of Jakob Smári with the Neo-Romanticists and the Symbolists is not difficult to see, although, as he himself has revealed in a letter to the writer, [21] he acknowledges indebtedness to influences from many sources, ancient and modern, Icelandic and foreign, the principal ones being Socialism and psychical research. He is not as vigorous a poet as some of his countrymen and is certainly a great contrast to such a virile and rugged figure as, for instance, his contemporary Jakob Thorarensen. Smári is a lyricist of unusually delicate gift, which is seen in his polished vocabulary and metrical form and especially in his mastery of the sonnet. A mystic, endowed with uncommon insight and all-embracing sympathy, he is deeply conscious of the unity of life, the presence of the Divinity in every little flower, and equally convinced of the ultimate victory of the powers of goodness in the universe. All this is but another way of saying that behind and beyond the simplicity of his poems there is often greater depth than may appear at first sight. At any rate, he has written some of the finest lyrics in present-day Icelandic poetry.

18. Besides the major literary figures already discussed, and others, such as Sigurður Jónsson, who have been included with them because

[21] June 24, 1931.

of some special achievement in the field, many more poets of merit flourished during the latter part of the nineteenth century and the first quarter of the twentieth. Although unlike in many respects and not by any means all equal in importance, they represent in varying degree the main literary trends of the period; some lean toward Realism, whereas others, and the great majority, are primarily Romantic and Neo-Romantic. All of them, however, are national in spirit, and adherence to the native literary tradition is not infrequently their principal characteristic. This interest finds expression in selection of both themes and meters and in some cases in a deliberate effort to revive cherished traditional literary forms.

From the ranks of the learned and professional group of the period, whose poetry was the by-product of their scholarly and cultural interest, the four considered briefly below deserve special mention.

Bjarni Jónsson frá Vogi (1863–1926), who had received his professional degree in classical philology and German at the University of Copenhagen in 1894, was for the next decade an instructor in German in the College of Iceland and later lecturer in classical languages in the University of Iceland. Journalism was another of his interests. For years he took an active and prominent part in Icelandic politics, serving from 1908 until his death as a member of the Althing, where he proved himself a champion of both Icelandic independence and cultural matters.

A representative selection from his original poems, which had previously appeared in various publications and collections, is included in *Úrval* (Selections, 1916). His fervent love of country is expressed in a number of patriotic poems, which constitute the bulk of the original poems and are the most characteristic, together with the memorial poems on Icelandic cultural and political leaders. Mastery of form and especially choice language—for the poet was a purist in that respect—characterize these poems generally, rather than marked poetic inspiration. Here are, moreover, some significant and successful translations from the works of Norwegian and German poets. It was in the field of translation that Bjarni Jónsson made his principal contribution to Icelandic literature, with his excellent renditions of Arne Garborg's poem cycles *Haugtussa* and

I Helheim and the translation of Goethe's *Faust* (Part I), generally faithfully and ably executed.

GESTUR, pen name of GUÐMUNDUR BJŐRNSSON (1864–1937), graduated in medicine and surgery from the University of Copenhagen in 1894, served as lecturer in the Medical School and district physician of Reykjavík until 1906, and from then on for a quarter of a century as Surgeon General of Iceland. He was a man of unusual versatility and wide interests; for years, he was a prominent and influential member of the Althing and a prolific writer in his own field and on political and cultural subjects.

His literary interest also found an outlet in a number of poems which he contributed to various publications under the pen name of "Gestur." A selection from these, *Undir ljúfum lögum*, edited with a preface by Alexander Jóhannesson, appeared in 1918. They are particularly notable as an experiment in the use of varied metrical forms and rhythm, containing both some innovations original with the author himself and revivals of Icelandic folk and medieval poems. The author wrote the majority to specific tunes and emphasized the harmonizing of the text and the melody, often succeeding very well. Likewise many of his numerous translations are both accurately and fluently rendered, sometimes admirably, as in the case of Bjőrnstjerne Bjőrnson's renowned poem "Olaf Tryggvason."

Gestur possessed great metrical skill and at times reached the heights of genuine lyric poetry, as in "Sorgardans" (A Dance of Mourning), in which a universal theme, masterful form, and an undercurrent of deep emotion go together. He also succeeded excellently in capturing the rhythmical effect and the mood of the medieval ballads in such poems as "Hólamannahőgg" (The Blows of the Men of Hólar), one of his most impressive efforts.

SIGFÚS BLŐNDAL (b. 1874) received his professional degree in classical philology and English at the University of Copenhagen in 1898 and served in various capacities as a librarian in the Royal Library in Copenhagen, 1901–1941. He has played a prominent part in the activities of leading Icelandic and Danish literary and cultural societies, edited a number of works, written on Icelandic literature for the *Encyclopaedia Britannica,* and contributed numerous articles, reviews, and poems to various periodicals. His greatest scholarly achievement, however, is his Icelandic-Danish Dictionary, *Islandsk-dansk Ordbog* (1920–1924), a monumental work.

A collection of his poems, *Drotningin í Algeirsborg og önnur kvæði* (The Queen of Algeirsborg and Other Poems), was published in 1917. Several of these poems, in particular the title poem, reveal considerable narrative vigor and descriptive ability. "Draumur Hannibals" (Hannibal's Dream) is also a forceful and impressive poem. "Seinasta sigling Jóns Indíafara" (The Last Voyage of Jón Indiafarer) is, however, probably the finest poem in the collection, since the author has succeeded especially well in interpreting Jón's state of mind as he lies on his deathbed; by incorporating some of Jón's language he has given to the poem an authentic flavor. The fact that Blöndal had edited Jón's autobiography clearly served him well when he came to write this poem. Among his translations the renditions from Greek poetry, of Tennyson's poem "The Cobbler," and of selections from Dante's *Divine Comedy* are particularly noteworthy.

LÁRUS THORARENSEN (1877–1912) was a grandson of the poet Bjarni Thorarensen. He graduated from the College in Iceland in 1901 and from the Theological School in Reykjavík in 1905. After teaching at Ísafjörður for a five-year period, he served as pastor in the Icelandic settlement in the Gardar district in Pembina County, North Dakota, until his health broke in 1912. He was anxious to return to Iceland, but died on shipboard on June 11, 1912, and was buried at sea. Many of his poems were originally published in various papers and periodicals. A collection of these, together with other poems of his, did not, however, appear until 1948, edited with an introduction by Arngrímur Fr. Bjarnason.

Unlike his distinguished grandfather, whose poetry is generally characterized by rugged originality in thought and style, Lárus Thorarensen is above all else a singer, a lyricist who paints beautiful pictures in his poems, thoroughly Romantic and national in spirit, a direct heir of the earlier nineteenth-century Icelandic poets. He is untiring in singing the praises of his native land and delights in nature descriptions, in which his fine sensitiveness and love of beauty are evident. Some of these poems, written to popular music, have been widely sung. He translated, smoothly and faithfully, several poems by Scandinavian poets, including H. C. Andersen's well-known "Det Dődende Barn" and Anders Hovden's eloquent tribute to Matthías Jochumsson.

From the large group of more or less unschooled poets, who during the period carried on in their realm of activity the characteristic literary tradition of the Icelandic nation, the following five may be singled out for brief consideration.

PÁLL JÓNSSON ÁRDAL (1857–1930), largely a self-educated man, who wrote some short plays worthy of mention and therefore has been briefly considered among the prose writers, was a lyric poet of greater merit, with two good-sized collections of poetry to his credit: *Ljóðmæli* (Poems; Akureyri, 1905) and *Ljóðmæli gömul og ný* (Poems, Old and New; Akureyri, 1923), the latter a selection from his total production. He is definitely in the tradition of the nineteenth-century Icelandic poets, in many ways recalling Steingrímur Thorsteinsson, his favorite poet. Primarily a Romanticist, he wrote numerous nature poems, some of which are written to popular tunes and have enjoyed considerable public favor, not least his spirited travel poems. Like his gifted master he has a strong satirical vein and often hits the mark effectively in his satires. But he is generally at his best in his shorter poems and quatrains, many of which are splendidly done. His poems are always marked by good taste, smoothness, and fluency.

JÓN ÞORSTEINSSON (1859–1948), a self-educated farmer in the Mývatn district in northern Iceland, was another one of those representatives of national culture who ably carried on the literary tradition in Þingeyjarsýsla. A collection of his poems, *Ljóðabók* (Book of Poems), edited by Ólafur Marteinsson, was published in 1933, with a brief biographical introduction. They are generally characterized by smooth-flowing rhythmic quality, keen observation, closeness to the soil, and frequently bright spots of light humor. His tribute to Iceland, "Í dúfulíki" (In the Shape of a Dove), is original in its approach to the theme and breathes genuine patriotism. "Hvítur sauður, svartur sauður" (White Wether, Black Wether) is charming in its vivid and truthful description of Icelandic animal life. Like his fellow traditional poets, Jón Þorsteinsson often succeeds particularly well in the use of the quatrain, which lends itself so excellently to improvisation and general observation.

INDRIÐI ÞORKELSSON (1869–1943) was another self-educated farmer in Þingeyjarsýsla and an outstanding example of its much admired cultural and literary traditions. He not only, by his own efforts, became a widely read man and genealogist of note, but, aside from the heavy daily work necessary to support a large family and his active participation in local public affairs, found time to write much poetry of great merit.

Many of his verses had long been widely known when his sons had the happy idea of publishing, on the occasion of his seventieth birthday, a collection of his poems, *Baugabrot* (Fragments, 1939), with an introduction by his son, Indriði Indriðason. Although not exhaustive, the book contains an extensive representation from the fruits of more than forty years' cultivation of poetry, composed largely when he was busy with his farm work, as he preferred to devote whatever leisure time he had to genealogy and other historical lore.

Wisely, the themes of his poems are generally drawn from everyday life; the limitation in range is made up for in authentic flavor, bearing throughout the marks of the poet's observant eye. Further, they are characterized by great metrical skill, mastery of language, and, at best, not inconsiderable emotional and imaginative quality. These characteristics, together with his deep sense of his relation to the soil, are seen in his poems about his home community, such as "Heimasveitin" (My Home Community). His exhortations, like his well-known "Syngið, bræður" (Sing, Brothers), reveal his buoyant progressive spirit and idealism, whereas his many memorial poems attest his warm human interest. His poem about the poet Bólu-Hjálmar probably constitutes his greatest effort; marked by penetrating and sympathetic insight into the tragic life and fate of that roughhewn genius, it is at the same time a scathing indictment of his age. Steeped as Indriði Þorkelsson was in the Icelandic literary tradition, he is particularly successful in his quatrains.

JÓN S. BERGMANN (1874–1927), a farmer's son from northern Iceland, was likewise largely a self-educated man, for years a fisherman and sailor, but also engaged in public-school teaching and office work. His interest in the sea and seafaring is seen in the very title of his second collection of poems, *Farmannsljóð* (Sailor Songs, 1925), dedicated to Icelandic seamen and containing several poems on sailing. The title of his first collection, *Ferskeytlur* (Quatrains, 1922), is even more characteristic, for in the realm of the time-honored and popular quatrain, with its stern demand for concentration, he excels particularly. It serves him equally well for expressing his unfailing optimism and manly spirit for whatever life might bring; for satirical purposes; and for nature descriptions, in which he had few peers among his fellow epigrammatists. Thus, in one of his quatrains, he masterfully describes the drift ice, from time to time the unwelcome guest to the shores of Iceland; he is, however, equally successful in describing nature in her milder aspects.

Andrés Björnsson (1883–1916) came of solid farm stock in northern Iceland and always remained deeply rooted in the rural soil. He graduated from the College of Iceland in 1905, and studied Icelandic philology at the University of Copenhagen for some time. On his return to Iceland he engaged in journalism and secretarial work until his untimely death. In respect to training and profession he, therefore, may be said to belong to the formally educated poets of the period. However, without denying poetic value to his longer poems, often highly personal and less frequently descriptive in nature, as in the case of his fine poem "Drangey," he achieved his greatest distinction with his masterful use of the quatrain. This favorite medium of the unschooled poets became in his hands the ideal vehicle for serious or satirical expression; nor has anyone summed up more succinctly, within its four verse lines, the fundamental mission of that characteristically Icelandic meter in the poetry and the cultural life of the nation. His splendid memorial poem of Páll Melsted, the historian, is in the same traditional vein.

Andrés Björnsson's deep appreciation and understanding of Icelandic poetry and the native literary tradition in general is further seen in his popular lecture, "Rím í mæltu máli" (Rhyme in Spoken Language) and his article "Alþýðuvísur" (Folk Verses), which are included in the collection of his writings, *Ljóð og laust mál* (Poems and Prose, 1940), edited by his younger brother, Andrés Björnsson, with a biographical introduction by Árni Pálsson.

Andrés Björnsson was also an actor of no mean ability and the author of a popular humorous drama; his early death, therefore, cut short a career that held promise in other fields besides the realm of letters.

Although these five poets, carrying on the literary tradition of the unschooled class, happen to come from the northern part of Iceland, let no one think that that region alone produces poetry, for other poets, not to mention mere versifiers, are found throughout the country. As an illustration, mention may be made of KOLBEINN HÖGNASON (1889–1949), a farmer in Kollafjörður in southern Iceland, who published no less than five collections of poems. These reveal not only uncommon metrical skill but other poetic abilities as well. Here are numerous quatrains and more ambitious efforts—nature descriptions and historical, memorial, and other occasional poems. Especially noteworthy is his poem commemorating the establishment of the Icelandic Republic in 1944.

Nor would any historical survey of the poetry of the period be complete without some account of the contribution made by Icelandic women besides the poetess Hulda—women who, though burdened with domestic work, found time for writing much poetry of genuine merit, and who in the main belonged to the self-educated or unschooled class.

ÓLÖF SIGURÐARDÓTTIR (1857–1933), the greater part of her life a housewife in Eyjafjörður in northern Iceland, was a midwife by profession; otherwise she was entirely self-educated. In spite of adverse circumstances, her love of beauty and interest in literature would not be denied, and bore fruit in considerable literary production. Her slight first collection of poems, *Nokkur smákvæði* (A Handful of Verses, 1888), although immature in some respects and bearing marks of the influence of her favorite poet Steingrímur Thorsteinsson, attracted attention because of the sincerity of feeling and the mastery of form that generally characterized it. These qualities, together with a more mature outlook upon life, a surer touch, and a greater variety of themes, are to be seen in her second collection, under the same title, which appeared at Akureyri in 1913 and was favorably reviewed. Extensive selections from these collections and her poems from later years, as well as her prose writings, are included in *Ritsafn* (Collected Works, 1945), edited with an introduction by the Reverend Jón Auðuns.

In that collected edition, therefore, a fuller and truer picture can be had of her literary production. Her many deep-felt personal poems, not least her love poems, reveal a sensitive soul, bearing the scars of bitter experience, but, especially in her later years, able to rise in hope and optimism above emotional storms and disappointments. The smooth fluency that always marks her poems is seen effectively in her splendid nature poems, like "Sumarkvőld 1908" (A Summer Evening 1908), which also reveals her descriptive ability. Some of her very finest and most original efforts are found, however, among her quatrains, of which "Tárið" (The Tear), has long been recognized as a little masterpiece. Included in her collected works are some well-written sketches and short stories, together with a frank and revealing description of her childhood home, which is of considerable cultural-historical importance.

Ólína Andrésdóttir (1858–1935) and Herdís Andrésdóttir (1858–1939), twin sisters and farm wives, were born and grew up in Breiðifjőrður in western Iceland, a district renowned for its scenic beauty and historical traditions, as well as for being a center of culture. They also belonged to a family noted for its cultural and literary interest and ability; a near relative was Matthías Jochumsson, the great poet.[22]

Both self-educated, these unusually gifted sisters had, with their lifelong interest in literary and cultural values and with their retentive minds, stored up a virtually inexhaustible fund of information, particularly national lore in prose and verse. The traditional Icelandic strain is, therefore, fundamental in their published poems, *Ljóðmæli* (Poems, 1924; second enlarged ed., 1930), which bear at the same time the unmistakable stamp of their strong individualities, for they were both women of no ordinary mould, possessing true nobility of soul, clearly reflected in their poems.

Among Ólína Andrésdóttir's poems the ones in the *þulur* form

[22] See Sigurður Nordal, "Herdís Andrésdóttir," in *Áfangar* (*Svipir*) (1944), II, 174–178.

stand out because of their delicate lyric quality and rich contents. Also noteworthy are her beautiful nature poem, "Til næturinnar" (To the Night), and her love poem, "Svarað bréfi" (A Letter Answered), which is of rare poetic quality. Among her sister's poems, several of the autobiographical ones, like "Leiddist mér að lúta smáu" (I Was Weary of Little Things), and the delightful "Upptíningur" (Scrapings), may be singled out for similar qualities.

Generally adhering to traditional meters, both sisters used the popular quatrain with rare skill, sure taste, and usual mastery of form. Their poems were as a rule composed in the course of the day's work and often for special occasions, but they unfailingly show that they are the result of an inner need for expression. Here are the wisdom garnered by ripe and dearly bought experience, a noble outlook upon life, and abiding religious faith, reminiscent of their beloved kinsman and poet, Matthías Jochumsson.

Both the sisters were likewise noted for their great storytelling ability, and from their vast store of folklore and other cultural-historical information many tales and other accounts have fortunately been recorded for posterity.

Theodóra Thoroddsen (b. 1863), wife of the noted editor and political leader Skúli Thoroddsen and a first cousin of the sisters Ólína and Herdís Andrésdóttir, has, besides her sketches and stories, which give her a place among the prose writers, published a notable collection, *Þulur* (1916; second ed., 1938). In this charming cycle of poems she uses the traditional, flexible form with consummate lyric touch, even when the meter is highly intricate, as it often is. And without breaking the unity of the mood, here are interwoven into an enchanting mosaic some of the most attractive features of Icelandic folklore, creatures of the popular fancy portrayed against the colorful background of the Icelandic landscape in its varied seasonal garb. Elsewhere, on the wings of her fertile imagination, the poetess takes her readers into the world of dreams. Romantic as her world is, and ostensibly remote from the reality of life, the innermost longings of the human heart and the fate of the stepchildren of fortune are here symbolically, sympathetically, and artistically interpreted.

And to illustrate further how common the gift of poetry has been in the family of Ólína and Herdís Andrésdóttir, one may also mention another cousin, although a more distant one. Halla Eyjólfsdóttir (1866–1937), a farm wife, published two collections of poems, several of which have become widely known as texts to popular musical compositions by Sigvaldi Kaldalóns, the noted composer. Especially notable is the beautiful "Svanurinn minn syngur" (My Swan Sings).

VI

Contemporary Currents

ALTHOUGH a number of the earlier poets continued their literary activity into the period from 1918 to 1940, and in some cases published their principal works during those years, they have been considered with the writers of the previous generation, because they represent the main literary tendencies of that time and belong to it spiritually and culturally.

Many of the new poets who appear on the scene in the course of this period also continue in some respects the Neo-Romanticism of the poets preceding them, but the lyric strain is still more pronounced and the fires of passion burn more fiercely in their poems. For these poets, the products of the rootlessness and the disillusionment of the First World War and postwar years and their search for new values, are primarily concerned with expressing their inner life, laying bare their own souls in which the storms of emotion run the gamut from exuberant joy to the darkest pessimism and world-weariness. For many of them, in fact, suffering, actual or imagined, is the hallmark of genius. Beauty, dreams, love, enjoyment of the hour to the fullest—these are their chief watchwords.

Often their productions are definitely in the spirit of "art for art's sake," the emphasis being on poetic themes and literary artistry. They stress naturalness in poetic diction and form, for with their attitude in which feeling dominates, they need a flexible medium, unrestricted elbowroom, for the free play of their emotional outpourings and flights of the imagination. And the most gifted among these, at any rate, succeed brilliantly in developing metrical rhythm and form to new heights, thereby greatly enriching the literature of their country.

Generally speaking, the national note is strong in the poetry of the period. It manifests itself in an interest in various phases of the native culture; these poets, however, do not so much hold up past glories as a challenge to present achievement (as the Romantics did), but rather they analyze the national character, especially in the folk poetry and the folklore, in which the soul of the nation had most fully and characteristically revealed itself.

These fundamental qualities are prominent in the poetry of the two great pioneers of the period, Stefán Sigurðsson frá Hvítadal and Davíð Stefánsson, who both became highly articulate spokesmen of their generation and deeply influenced a whole school of poets.

During the latter half of the period, under the impact of progressive and radical political tendencies from abroad, increasing class and social consciousness at home, and the influence of the economic depression of the day, the older poets, while remaining faithful to their artistic creed, strike a more serious note than before. Others in the group, like Jóhannes Jónasson úr Kőtlum, together with new poets of the younger generation, such as Steinn Steinarr, revolt against existing conditions, vigorously embrace leftist political views, and champion them outright in their poetry.[1]

1. STEFÁN SIGURÐSSON frá Hvítadal was born at Hólmavík in northwestern Iceland on October 11, 1887, but lived during the greater part of his youth at the farm home of a cousin in the same vicinity and later at Hvítadal, with which he is chiefly associated. He and Jakob Thorarensen, the poet, are closely related, although unlike in many ways as poets.[2]

Stefán Sigurðsson was apprenticed to a printer at Ísafjőrður in 1905 and continued learning that trade in Reykjavík, but he was compelled to give it up because of ill health, which dogged him until the end of his days. The years 1912 to 1916 he spent in Norway, traveling extensively and working at, among other things, ship-

[1] For a detailed discussion of the social and cultural-historical background of the period, see Einarsson, *Prose Writers*, pp. 156–161, 206–209.

[2] For information about his life and literary career, see also Halldór Kiljan Laxness, "Stefán frá Hvítadal," *Iðunn*, XVIII (1934), 1–16.

building in Bergen. Finally he was forced to enter a sanatorium where he bravely fought off a long siege of grave illness. Upon his return to Iceland, he settled down in his native district, married, and became a farmer and the sole supporter of a large family. He died on March 7, 1933.

The appearance of his first book of poems, *Söngvar förumannsins* (The Wanderer's Songs, 1918; second ed., 1919), was no ordinary literary event and further confirmed the admiration that he had previously won in poetic circles. It brought a new strain into Icelandic poetry, refreshingly personal and rich in sheer lyric magic of mood and form. And these poems found an enthusiastic and general response, especially in the hearts of visionary and poetically inclined youth, whose dreams and longings they embodied fundamentally and strikingly.

From first to last these poems are the personal expression of the poet himself, revealing his emotional life in all its fluctuations. That note is struck in the opening poem, "Vorsól" (Spring Sun), one of the finest in the collection. After a winter of illness and gloom, the poet, lifts his heart in new hope and an inspired hymn of praise and gratitude to the spring sun with its rejuvenating and healing powers. In another poem on the same theme, however, the arrival of spring moves him to tears and lamentation, reminding him only of departed youth and past joys. Thus are these poems closely interwoven with his inner life, directly reflecting the waves rising and falling in his sensitive soul.

Sorrow and sadness are dominant in many of his poems, and nowhere more memorably or more masterfully expressed than in "Hjartarím" (Heart Rhyme), deep in feeling, penetrating, and brilliant in metrical form; this poem is very characteristic of the poet himself, and, perhaps better than any other poem of his, it interprets the state of mind of the younger generation, which hailed him as its gifted and chosen spokesman.

And his sorrow and sadness are all the more touching because they are thoroughly genuine, as is not always the case with the young poets. But his melancholy, brooding state of mind was rooted directly in his own fate; it was the outburst of his soul, tormented by years of physical illness, often of the gravest nature, with resultant disappointments and disillusionment. There is in these poems the awareness of impending death, but to the poet's great glory he did not succumb passively and abjectly to his sense of doom; he never became the victim of utter or protracted world-weariness. For gloomy and melancholy as many of these poems are, they also have a deep and steady undercurrent of love of life and joy in living and a nostalgic longing for happiness, accentuated by the fact that the poet has largely been denied them. This is especially seen in his love poems, where he relives his youth and past joys, as in "Seytjándi maí" (May Seventeenth) and "Hún kyssti mig" (She Kissed Me), both among the most beautiful poems in the collection, vibrant with youthful ecstasy; and the purest pearl of them all is "Erla."

Furthermore, with the worldliness and flaming passion, there is in some a marked strain of spirituality and deep religious feeling, particularly impressive in "Aðfangadagskvőld jóla 1912" (Christmas Eve 1912), the humble outcry of a wounded heart, expressed in masterful form, sonorously echoing the ringing of church bells. Profound religious expression and great literary art here go hand in hand. The author's devoted love of poetry and art is expressed beautifully and in an inspired fashion in "Drottningin í Sólheimum" (The Queen of the Sun Realm).

Not only did this first book of Stefán Sigurðsson arouse general interest and admiration because of its unusually rich emotional quality, the impassioned personal expression of sorrow and joy; its importance lay even more in its literary artistry, original use of natural and beautiful language, with new rhythm and new verse forms. His sojourn in Norway had been fruitful in many ways; it had enlarged his horizon and opened his eyes to new themes, and his acquaintance with the rich Norwegian lyric poetry of his day and earlier had stimulated him. The influence of the Norwegian masters, such as Ibsen and Per Sivle, is seen in his poetry; in particular was Wildenwey a favorite of his. He adopted their verse forms and adjusted and developed them to his own taste, until they had become for him a characteristic and highly personalized medium of expression. His literary pioneering consisted expecially in introducing these exquisite and much imitated meters into Icelandic poetry; for it is not difficult to trace his influence in that respect on a number of younger and lesser poets, who could not, to be sure, equal the master, but who had his example as a reminder and a challenge.

With his first book, which was received with equal enthusiasm by the literary critics and the reading public, Stefán Sigurðsson took his place among the leading contemporary poets of the nation and was recognized officially by the award of a governmental stipend.

This did not, however, enable him to devote himself exclusively to literary work. For reasons of health and other considerations, he became a farmer in his native district, where the struggle to support a large family made great demands upon his precarious health, and he only managed to eke out a meager living. But neither poverty nor illness could break him. He did not let adverse circumstances conquer his proud spirit and human dignity, and the love of beauty and joy in living continued to flame in his soul.

That his poetry was for him a refuge and lifted him above his environment is seen in his next book, *Óður einyrkjans* (The Song of the Lone Worker, 1921); at the same time, in themes and mood, the book is conditioned and colored by his circumstances and his life as a farmer. In the opening poem, "Bjartar nætur" (Bright Nights), which is one of the finest and in many ways the most revealing in the book, memories from the early years of wandering alternate and intermingle with strains of sorrow and joy and blend with an even more pronounced idyllic description of Icelandic rural life. The indescribable magic of the nightless northern spring breathes through this poem. It is rich in the fragrance of the soil; but above anything else it is aflame with the poet's deeply ingrained love of sun and summer, which gave his soul wings in illness and adversity and inspired his best poems. In a sense, therefore, the wanderer and the dreamer of dreams and the earthbound farmer and tiller of the soil clash in this poem, and that inner conflict is much in evidence elsewhere in the book. Many of the other poems are in the vein of the earlier ones, but the memories have lost their glow and color and no longer find an outlet in new and refreshing meters. The love poems, for instance, have neither the pure lyric quality nor the delicacy of those in the first volume, but are more coarse-grained.

All in all these poems are more earthy and objective than the poet's first fruit, and the range of themes is greater in that he now often goes outside his immediate personal experience. He turns to folklore and fairy tales for inspiration and finds there material that gives his imagination a free rein; such poems are characterized by his unfailing mastery of form and often by an ability to capture in a high degree the spirit of the folk literature.

His religious feeling, heightened by sickness and the lurking shadow of death, finds an expression in two notable poems, of which the closing poem in the book, "Líf" (Life), one of the very best, is especially revealing in its deeply felt and sincere declaration of faith and its keen understanding of the value of suffering for spiritual growth.

Perhaps the most remarkable thing about the collection as a whole is the revelation of the poet's heroic attempt to rise above his adverse conditions. And he does so in no small measure, although many of the poems lack the fire of inspiration, the lyricism, and the literary artistry of the earlier ones.

In view of Stefán Sigurðsson's deep-rooted religious faith, circumscribed conditions, and growing interest in old cultural values, it is not surprising that he should find a spiritual refuge in the Roman Catholic faith, which he embraced formally in 1923. The fruit of that change of heart is found in his next work, *Heilög kirkja* (Holy Church, 1924).

This eulogy of the Catholic Church, in sixty stanzas, is written in the sonorous *hrynhenda* form, reminiscent of sacred poems by medieval Icelandic writers such as Brother Eysteinn Ásgrímsson and Bishop Jón Arason. This hymn of praise to the Church, the poet's confession of faith, is masterful in its metrical excellence and at times reaches great poetic heights, where the emotional quality is on a level with the technical mastery in diction, poetic similes, and meter.

The poet's next book, *Helsingjar* (Geese, 1927), is a continuation of the new phase of his development, for the first half consists of religious poems that show that he had found in the newly adopted faith both a consolation for his soul and a firm religious foundation. Effective in form, these poems generally suffer from the strict adherence to traditional teachings, although occasionally they rise to truly inspirational poetry, as in the cycle of poems "Guðsmóðir"

(Mother of God) and especially in the closing poem "Salve Regina." A marked characteristic of many of these poems is a purity of soul achieved through suffering.

In the latter part of the book there are many poems in traditional verse forms on time-honored themes, revealing Stefán Sigurðsson's increased interest in the past and perhaps also his growing sense of kinship with the soil. His great metrical skill is, as ever, in evidence, but generally the inspiration is not commensurate, except in a few poems such as "Það vorar" (Spring Is Arriving) and "Fram til heiða" (Up in the Moorlands), instinct with love of nature and poetic charm. Two poems of the book, however, tower above the others, like majestic mountains, "Þér konur" (You Women), an inspired and eloquent tribute to womankind, and "Þér skáld" (You Poets), an equally eloquent and impressive expression of the author's devotion to the poets and the poetic art.

Among his poems written after the publication of *Helsingjar*, the cycle *Anno Domini 1930* (published in book form in 1933, with a biographical sketch by Sigurður Skúlason), which was written in commemoration of the thousandth anniversary of the Icelandic Althing, is the most notable. Here the poet describes the settlement of Iceland and surveys the history of the nation with sympathetic insight and in an appealing poetic form. A collected edition of his works, *Ljóðmæli* (Poems), appeared in 1945, edited with an excellent introduction by Tómas Guðmundsson, the poet.

Sharing the fate of many of his Icelandic fellow poets, Stefán Sigurðsson could not, because of external circumstances, develop his genius to its fullest; he had, however, enjoyed the rare privilege both of becoming the spokesman of his generation and of finding a corresponding response in its heart with his youthful poems. The finest of these, as well as his best poems from his later years, have an established place in contemporary Icelandic literature because of their high poetic quality and literary artistry.

2. Davíð Stefánsson was born at Fagriskógur in Eyjafjörður in northern Iceland on January 21, 1895. His father was a leading farmer and a member of the Althing. His mother belonged to a well-known literary family; she was a sister of Ólafur Davíðsson, noted folklorist and author. Davíð Stefánsson graduated from the

high school at Akureyri at the age of sixteen, but had to interrupt his studies because of ill health, often of the gravest kind; and as a result he did not enter the College of Iceland until 1916, graduating in the spring of 1919. He made frequent and extensive journeys abroad. Since 1925 he has been district librarian at Akureyri and is both a great book lover and an enthusiastic collector, as is reflected in some of his poems.[3]

His first poems, which appeared in the periodicals *Iðunn* and *Eimreiðin* (1916), were a great revelation to poetry lovers, not least the younger generation, so unusual was their new strain in its simplicity and naturalness and rare poetic quality. The interest became still more general with the publication of his first book of poems, *Svartar fjaðrir* (Black Feathers, 1919); it not only cast its spell upon impressionable and emotional youth, but found an equally warm response in the hearts of the older generation. Most assuredly, these poems struck a new and resonant note in Icelandic poetry; at the same time they had such a wide appeal, to young and old alike, because they came in reality from the very heart of the nation itself; in spirit, mood, and language they had their roots deep in the soil of Icelandic folk poetry, and their subject matter was not infrequently from the same realm of folklore. Nevertheless, they were the new, personal creation of the poet himself, although he stood on a solid national foundation both in his selections of themes and in their treatment. Therefore, with these poems he became a great pioneer in present-day Icelandic poetry, and his influence can be seen in the works of many of the younger poets.

His strong and fruitful interest in folklore is not difficult to explain, for such interest had been uncommonly general in his family; his uncle, Ólafur Davíðsson, and the poet's mother, a great-souled and gifted woman, steeped in national lore, no doubt greatly stim-

[3] For information about his life and literary work, see also Friðrik Á Brekkan, "Ungir rithöfundar: Davíð Stefánsson frá Fagraskógi," *Iðunn*, XVI (1932), 29–42; Guðmundur Daníelsson, "Davíð Stefánsson frá Fagraskógi," *Nýjar Kvöldvökur*, XXXIV (1941), 97–106; Halldór Kiljan Laxness, "Davíð Stefánsson fimmtugur," *Lesbók Morgunblaðsins*, XX (1945), 25–27; Richard Beck, "Davíð Stefánsson skáld," *Tímarit Þjóðræknisfélags Íslendinga í Vesturheimi*, XXVII (1945), 51–68; Sigurður Guðmundsson, "Davíð Stefánsson fimmtugur," in *Heiðnar hugvekjur og mannaminni* (Akureyri, 1946), pp. 105–132.

ulated his interest in that field. "His kinsmen collected and wrote down, the poet infused a new breath of life, new spiritual contents, new warmth into, the strange lore and the old embers, the dead superstition and popular beliefs of our ancestors," writes Sigurður Guðmundsson.[4] He rightly adds that the great general popularity that the poet has enjoyed largely stems from the same source.

Equally correctly it has been emphasized that Davíð Stefánsson has carried forward the work of his predecessors in freeing Icelandic poetry from the shackles of intricate and stereotyped verse forms and overly ornate language, an inheritance from the Skaldic and *rímur* poetry, and in replacing such verse forms and poetic diction with lighter and more flexible meters and simple and natural language. His contribution has been very great and influential, although, fortunately, he has not gone to the extreme of throwing overboard the characteristic and time-honored alliteration in Icelandic poetry; and when he so desires he can handle the more involved traditional verse forms with ease and skill. Further, in his rich and varied production, he has amply demonstrated how pliant an instrument the Icelandic tongue is, both in vigor and rhythmic effect, responsive alike to his most delicate lyric touch and gentlest moods and to his most forceful and passionate emotional outbursts.

His poem, "Mamma ætlar að sofna" (Mother Wants to Sleep), the opening poem in *Svartar fjaðrir*, is in theme, mood, and meter characteristic of the most unique element in Davíð Stefánsson's poetry, the new, fascinating, and influential strain, which he introduced into contemporary Icelandic letters. Here are the lightness of touch, simplicity in presentation, and musical rhythm that characterize his poems, together with the dreamlike beauty and deep undercurrent of heartache and sadness that enrich and elevate them.

Another of his first published poems, "Svefnljóð" (Lullaby), also masterfully illustrates the same qualities, and in his first book there were many others in a like vein. The poems in the spirit of folklore and on folk themes are numerous and characteristic, ranging from the concentrated "Brúðarskórnir" (The Bridal Slippers), where a tragic love story is dramatically told in three stanzas, through the

[4] Sigurður Guðmundsson, *Heiðnar hugvekjur og mannaminni* (Akureyri, 1946), p. 126.

strikingly original "Á Dökkumiðum" (On the Dark Fishing Grounds), ominous in tone, to the impassioned and exotic portrayal of "Abba-labba-lá," "dark of cheek and brow," a dangerous but alluring witch in the forest. Elsewhere he peoples his poems with ghosts and other strange creatures from the world of folklore and frequently captures in an uncanny fashion its spirit of horror no less than its haunting sense of doom.

His love poems, which endeared him especially to the younger generation, reflect the poet's changing moods, sometimes fiery and sensuous in their praise of women and worldly pleasures, at other times tender and lyrical, as in "Mánadísin" (The Moon Godess), in whose presence "the silence of the night speaks the secret language of the heart."

An even more contemplative chord is touched in the poem "Moldin angar" (The Fragrant Earth), where the descriptive and subdued emotional elements are softly entwined. Here, as elsewhere, is the deep undercurrent of sadness, which often expresses itself in a strong desire to be released from an evil spell, as it were, perhaps harking back to the long days of illness, loneliness, and despair, when the poet lay at death's door. This theme is most strikingly expressed in "Krummi" (The Raven), one of the finest and most original poems in the collection. The poet warns his readers not to despise the raven's raucous song, "for hearts that love the sun may beat within breasts tented with black feathers." The tragedy of being under an evil spell that cannot be broken, of never seeing one's dearest dreams realized, is here symbolically and touchingly pictured. The black raven who has no greater desire than to rise in song like the swan must endure his tragic fate until his heart breaks. The poem, only three stanzas in length, is constructed with great skill and the folk-lore mood adds to its effectiveness and appeal. Akin in theme is "Myndhöggvarinn" (The Sculptor), the misunderstood master who in his rage "cut in the hard rock his divine dream and most heart-rending lamentation." This is the first of the author's impressive and sympathetic poems about pioneers in various fields; such men are after his heart and their struggles provide a fruitful theme.

Like Stefán Sigurðsson, his contemporary and fellow pioneer, Davíð Stefánsson celebrated joy in adventurous living, with love accorded the place of honor, in his early poems; the two poets also shared the deep and recurrent undertone of sorrow and sadness. On the other hand, Davíð Stefánsson's themes are much more varied, for in his first book he touches many chords on the lyre; even the humorous note is not entirely neglected. Above anything else, however, these poems mirror his turbulent emotional life in all its fluctuating moods. Although his poetry in many respects is inspired by and draws on Icelandic folklore, he is pre-eminently of the present. Even in a wider sense than Stefán Sigurðsson, he is representative of his generation, and while resembling him in lightness of touch and naturalness, Davíð Stefánsson's forms in mood, meter, and verse are more varied and the national note much stronger and more fundamental. His genius had been stimulated from abroad by his acquaintance with older contemporary Neo-Romantic Scandinavian poets. In his early poems can be seen the example of the great Swedish lyric poet Gustaf Fröding by whom he was challenged and inspired in thought and form without becoming a slavish imitator of his master. Nor is he unacquainted with Norway's Wildenwey.

The publication of *Svartar fjaðrir* not only marked the beginning of an epoch in present-day Icelandic poetry, but also established its young author as a national poet of first importance. With his later works he has solidified his prominent literary position and added to his reputation. He has been an exceptionally prolific poet; by 1940 he had published no less than six large collections of poems, the first four of which were published in a second collected edition in two volumes, *Kvæðasafn*, as early as 1930. This also eloquently bespeaks his great general popularity, greater than that of any other Icelandic poet now living. Naturally, such a large production is somewhat uneven in literary excellence and merit. Undeniably, however, in all his six collections are to be found many original, beautiful, and impressive poems destined to live long in Icelandic literature.

In his second book *Kvæði* (Poems, 1922), there is a greater variety in themes than in his first collection, which was not by any means circumscribed in that respect. Here are extensive and forceful narrative poems along with such appealing and lilting nature descriptions as "Sigling inn Eyjafjörð" (Sailing into Eyjafjörður), in which the sight of his scenic and beloved native haunts moves the poet to pour out his devotion in a hymn of praise. Deeply felt and delicate love poems alternate with satires and poems in folklore strain.

In recognition of his remarkable first book Davíð Stefánsson was awarded a poet's stipend, which made it possible for him to travel to Italy and spend some time there. Numerous poems, inspired by this visit, set their special stamp on this new book, which consists of lyric nature descriptions, graphic pictures from the daily life of the people, and striking character sketches. Some, in particular the love poems like the impassioned "Tína Rondoní," are aflame with southern fire, whereas others are humble supplications instinct with religious feeling. In the unique poem "Með lestinni" (On the Train), the poet succeeds in reproducing masterfully, with vivid realism, the speed, the milling of the crowd, the noise, and the rapidly shifting scenes on a train journey. The poem also has a deeper symbolic significance, "for, like life, the train runs its measured, set course."

The spirit of the wanderer, so fundamental in Davíð Stefánsson's poetry, is a dominant note in many of these poems. In one, "Svefnkirkja" (The Church of Sleep), he sums it up in the words: "All my life is a pilgrimage and a search." Yet, in the midst of the busy cities and the scenic glories of historic Italy, his heart fills with loneliness and longing for his native Iceland where his mission as a poet lies, for the simple joys of rural life, because at heart he largely remains the son of the mountain valley that he often paints in glowing Romantic colors in his poems.

The restless, adventurous spirit, however, soon flares up again in his soul, and his next and third collection of poems, *Kveðjur* (Greetings, 1924), opens with the swift-flowing "Eg sigli í haust" (I Sail in the Fall), which has the emotional fire of old, although now the poet not infrequently appears in a calmer mood. Here also are stirring and colorful poems from his sojourn in Italy, realistic descriptions of the misery that greeted his eyes, in dramatic contrast with the scenic grandeur and the imposing historic monuments. The historical poems, such as "Jóhannes skírari" (John the Baptist), are inspired and impressive; eloquence and imagination characterize all of them, but each has its own mood and corresponding verse form. The contents of the collection range from the beautiful hymn, "Á föstudaginn langa" (On Good Friday), to poems in folklore spirit and effective satirical and humorous pieces. Clearly, here is a great variety in theme and meter, and the poet's art expresses itself not least in his ability to harmonize the metrical garb with the theme and the mood.

The collection *Ný kvæði* (New Poems, 1929) further reveals his poetic and spiritual development; a surer grip on the most demanding form, richer idealism, and deeper and wider sympathy unquestionably make the book one of his very best works. Here are several historical poems conceived on a grand scale, like "Hallfreður vandræðaskáld" (Hallfred the Troublous Poet), in which the poet is primarily concerned not with reproducing the historical atmosphere, but rather with interpreting the inner life of his heroes. He often succeeds very well, although his subjective approach tends to result in their largely becoming creatures of his imagination and his spokesmen. Other historical poems are on love themes, with a corresponding gentler touch. Gentle also are the personal poems in the collection, not least the enchanting lyric "Nú sefur jörðin" (The Earth Sleeps), in which sensitive interpretation of the beauty of nature and sincere religious feeling blend intimately. In a different key, but highly memorable, are his graphic poems from his visit to Russia.

The sense of social injustice, expressed in such earlier poems as "Jóhannes skírari," is more pronounced than before; and so is the widening human sympathy, which finds a beautiful and masterful expression in the poem "Konan, sem kyndir ofninn minn" (The Woman Who Keeps My Hearth Fire Burning), which may be said to have become a classic already.

In the next book *Í byggðum* (Among Human Habitations; Akureyri, 1933), the prize-winning cycle of poems commemorating the millennial of the Icelandic Althing, occupies the place of honor; lyrical and eloquent in its noble patriotism, it is an impressive poem, in which a broad view of the history of the Icelandic nation, together with deep insight into its life and fate, are expressed in inspired and memorable passages. Above all, however, it is a reminder and a challenge to action. That challenge is still more forcefully expressed in the outspoken social satires that constitute a major part of the book and show that the poet has been deeply moved by contemporary developments and events. These satires may be looked upon as a continuation of his earlier poems in that vein. But the revolutionary spirit is stronger, the prophetic inspiration greater, and the reformatory zeal more merciless, in poems like "Vőkumaður, hvað líður nóttinni?" (Watchman, What of the Night?), a graphic portrayal of prevailing world conditions, with a warm undercurrent of sympathy for the oppressed and the suffering, "the martyrs who with bent backs stand foremost in the battle line for truth." Here are many other stirring social satires, such as "Kornhlaðan" (The Granary), which decries the unfair distribution of wealth with striking effectiveness. Nor do the shortcomings of the established church, as the poet sees them, escape the whiplash of his satire. On the other hand, his genuine and deep religious feeling is beautifully expressed in "Við leitum" (Our Search), in which he declares: "Lost is the soul, though it possesses gold, if its longing for the divine is dead."

Davíð Stefánsson's social satires do not, however, reveal an adherence to any special political teaching or group; they are written from a higher vantage point, on a broader basis, and thus their general appeal and lasting significance are increased.

Besides the notable social satires, the collection contains lyric nature poems and the splendid humorous poem "Sálin hans Jóns míns" (My Jón's Soul), on a folk theme, in which humor and seriousness alternate happily, illustrating once more the author's mastery of mood and meter.

Frequently in this book as elsewhere in his poems, Davíð Stefánsson's Romanticism is much in evidence. Here is his love of distant and dreamlike beauty, which finds an outlet in poems like "Bláfjőll" (Blue Mountains), with its eulogy of valleys and mountains, of rural charm and peace. Conversely, he castigates his countrymen sharply for the increasing tendency to turn their backs upon the rural life with its fruitful challenge to the manly spirit; and in "Dalabóndi" (Valley Farmer) he paints a touching and sympathetic picture of the farmer who, upon the insistence of his children, was compelled to leave the farm where he had his deep roots and lifework and move to the village on the sea coast.

Although a number of fine and noteworthy poems are included in the poet's latest book to be considered here, *Að norðan* (From the North, 1936), the main characteristics remain the same: the light touch in meter and language, the wealth of ideas, and the emotional warmth. Social satires are still in evidence, but the nostalgic longing for the soil is even more pronounced in joyous poems eulogizing life close to Mother Earth. The human sympathy remains strong and deep, as seen in the poem "Vitavőrður" (The Lighthouse Keeper), whose prayer is that he may save and guide the wayfarer. Beautiful and deep-felt is the poet's tribute to his devoted mother, to whom he owes an inestimable filial and cultural debt.

"Í ormagarðinum" (In the Snake Pit) is one of the finest poems in the collection; it is the ancient story of Gunnar Gjúkason interpreted in a symbolic and highly poetic manner and with sad and touching feeling that tugs at the heart. Original in thought and soft as a gentle breeze in rhythm and flowing diction, with theme and form artistically blending, is the closing poem in the book, "Lótusblóm" (The Lotus Flowers), about a family group in India that has turned its back on all worldly turmoil and devotes itself to contemplating the glory of God and the wonders of nature. The closing lines are characteristic of the mood and thought of the poem: "Life is but nothingness, unless the heart possess its sacred Lotus flowers."

Summing up, it is safe to assert that inspiration, penetration, and rare mastery of form characterize many of Davíð Stefánsson's poems, and that frequently they are likewise original both in theme and form. Sufficient variety is also found within his extensive production, but the undercurrent of many of his poems, in one form or another, is a deep and all-embracing sympathy, rising out of his keen sense of justice. This sympathy finds a climactic expression in his matchless poem "Konan, sem kyndir ofninn minn," in which he extols the woman's human dignity and self-sacrificing spirit and thereby true human worth, which he eulogizes time and again in his poems. It is then only natural that he is unmerciful in his denunciation of hypocrisy, deceit, and calumny, for they are the very denial of manliness and human worth.

An elevated philosophy of life and great poetic art thus frequently join hands in Davíð Stefánsson's poetry. In addition to his youthful poems, which were such a startling innovation in Icelandic poetry, he has contributed to the literature of his country a large number of other characteristic and significant poems, which reveal not only rich emotional quality, always fundamental with him, but mastery of form, creative imagination, and sympathetic insight as well. The continued general appeal of his poems resides in those combined qualities.

3. The example of Stefán Sigurðsson frá Hvítadal and Davíð Stefánsson released a flood of poetry in a similar vein; a whole host of young poets followed in the wake of these two poets, imitating them in selection of themes, mood, and form, but lacking their freshness, maturity, emotional quality, and literary artistry.

Some of these young poets, however, later found themselves and their literary mission. Thus, KRISTMANN GUÐMUNDSSON (b. 1902), who was one of the first to appear on the scene with his collection of poems, *Rökkursöngvar* (Twilight Songs, 1922), which showed a promising lyric gift, soon turned to writing fiction and has achieved distinction and fame in that field; he has, therefore, been considered among the major prose writers.[5]

Even more characteristic of the group, in themes and mood alike, was SIGURÐUR GRÍMSSON (b. 1896), who also in 1922 published his collection of poems, *Við langelda* (By the Evening Fire). Here the Byronic world-weariness typical of these young poets, but without genuineness of feeling and vigor, is expressed in one lamentation after another. Nevertheless, and admitting lapses of taste for which the book was severely criticized at the time, the true lyric strain is here also in evidence, both in the natural and fluent form and in individual poems. For instance, the one entitled "Karlinn" (The Old Man) is effective in its symbolism; and in "Á heimleið" (Returning Home) the tragic theme is sincerely felt and well developed in four short stanzas. However, the poet has not, as far as is known, cultivated his talent to any extent since that time; this remains his only book of poems.

During the same period (1922–1925) a number of other lyric poets, who later were to achieve literary recognition in varying degree, published their first collections of poems. These poets will be dealt with in some detail chronologically, together with the other most noteworthy ones who joined the ranks later and who in some ways, as will be pointed out, represent new literary tendencies.

4. JÓHANN JÓNSSON was born at Staðarstaður in the Snæfellsnes

[5] See Einarsson, *Prose Writers*, pp. 190–198.

district in western Iceland on September 12, 1896. After graduating from the College of Iceland in 1920, he went to Germany the following year, where he studied literature and aesthetics at the universities of Leipzig and Berlin during the next four years. He never returned to Iceland, residing mostly in Germany until his untimely death in Leipzig, September 1, 1932, after protracted illness.

During his college years he was noted for his dramatic readings of literature as well as for his poetry; but aside from a translation into German of one of Gunnar Gunnarsson's novels (*Jón Arason*) and some literary fragments, his production consists of a few poems, most of them from his school years.

However, this handful of completed poems, originally published in papers and magazines, several of them in the periodical, *Vaka* (1928), have the hallmark of genuine lyric poetry, personal and deeply felt; in mood, however, they are characteristic of the prevalent trend among the younger poets of the day, as in "Landslag" (Landscape), in which vivid description and deep emotional quality go hand in hand, and "Vőgguvísur um krumma" (Cradlesong about the Raven), in which the poet makes an original and effective use of a folk song theme. This ingrained mood of sorrow and sadness, rooted in the tragic experience of the poet himself, who did not see his dreams come true, finds its deepest and most memorable expression in "Sőknuður" (Lament). This poem is concentrated and close-knit, because of the unbroken unity of the pattern in atmosphere and rhythm; it is, however, unrhymed and was one of the few notable examples of free verse in Icelandic literature at the time. This poem alone is a sufficient reminder of what an uncommonly promising poet Jóhann Jónsson really was.

5. Jón Magnússon was born at Fosskot in Borgarfjőrður in southern Iceland on August 17, 1896, the son of parents of small means. At an early age he lost his father and grew up with his mother in historic and beautiful Þingvallasveit, which left an indelible stamp on his poetry and outlook upon life. He was a cooper by trade, and, having worked as such in Reykjavík and elsewhere for many years, he became one of the founders and the manager of a furniture store in Reykjavík, filling that post until shortly before his death on February 21, 1944. He was a self-educated man but a great book

lover; and he was widely read, especially in the rich literature of his nation, although his literary interest also extended farther afield.

Jón Magnússon was young in years when he began writing verse, while herding sheep or attending to other necessary farm work. Throughout his life he could devote only the time spared from his daily duties to literary pursuits; his production in that field is therefore all the more admirable, as he published five good-sized collections of poetry.

His first book, *Bláskógar* (Blue Forests, 1925), was a promising beginner's work, generally in good taste and of a marked lyric quality. Its highest level is reached in the title poem, inspired by the scenic beauty and the historic associations of his youthful haunts in the Þingvalla district and revealing his close attachment to the soil, always fundamentally characteristic of him and his poetry.

His next book, *Hjarðir* (Flocks, 1929), showed that he had gained in vigor, range of themes, and artistic touch, for here are many splendid poems. His rich sympathy with the less privileged and neglected—and he knew whereof he spoke—is touchingly revealed in the poem "Bjőssi litli á Bjargi" (Little Bjőssi at Bjarg), which presents a simple but vivid picture, whereas "Hőggin í smiðjunni" (Anvil Blows) is characterized by its strong personal quality and rhythmic effectiveness. His portrayal of the Icelandic court poet of old in "Hreiðar heimski" (Simple Hreiðar) is impressive in its sonorous language and similes taken directly from the Icelandic scene. Impressive also is his poem on another Icelandic poet, "Sigurður skáld á Őndverðarnesi" (Poet Sigurður at Őndverðarnes), striking in both its rhythmic and its pictorial quality. Here also are excellent nature poems, such as "Sumarnótt" (Summer Night) and "Haust" (Autumn). A deeper contemplative note is struck in "Moldir" (Earth), in which the poet ponders his sad youth and the early loss of his father but closes in a characteristically optimistic vein.

Jón Magnússon's third book, *Flúðir* (Skerries, 1935) shows him undertaking new and larger themes. In the opening cycle of poems, "Vígvellir" (Battlefields), on the ever timely theme of war and peace, the poet often succeeds in painting terse and memorable word pictures of the horrors and the terrible fruits of war; these poems further reveal his awareness of the problems of the day and his human interest. Much more concentrated, however, and richer in poetic quality is "Þorkell í Hraundal," a poem about the husband of Helga the Beautiful, the heroine of *Gunnlaugs saga ormstungu*; it is written with sympathetic insight and deep though restrained feeling. All in all, the most significant part of the book is the group of poems entitled "Úr ævisögu Björns sýslumanns" (From the Life Story of Prefect Björn), generally rich in poetic beauty and narrative excellence.

In its entirety this splendid narrative poem appeared as the author's next book, *Björn á Reyðarfelli* (Björn at Reyðarfell, 1938). His earlier poems had unmistakably revealed Jón Magnússon's deep roots in the soil whence he had sprung and the lasting impression made upon him by the rural environment of his youth, together with his life-long belief in the validity of rural cultural values. It is, therefore, no accident that he sets the stage of this cycle of poems in rural Iceland, in fact, in the very district where he was born, and bases it on an actual happening, although he adjusts his material to suit his artistic needs. He selects the high points in the story of his hero, dwelling on the fateful events, linking the individual poems together effectively with prose passages that fill in the gaps in the narrative.

It is the story of Björn, the scion of a prominent family, who marries the woman of his heart against his father's wishes; he becomes a cotter on a deserted farm in the moorlands, where he wages his battle with overwhelming obstacles in a spirit of unfailing heroism. He is a man of no ordinary mould and Icelandic to the core, proud in his dealings with other men, but humble before his God. With deep sympathetic understanding the poet interprets Björn's inner life, not least in the closing poem, "Á grafarbakka" (On the Brink of the Grave), in which Björn settles his account with himself and his fellow men. The author's sound and noble view of life is also clearly revealed; the worth of the individual and whole-souledness are what count most with him.

The cycle is uniformly well written, in choice language, with theme and verse forms blending tastefully, both in the more vigorous parts and in the lyrical nature descriptions, many of which are particularly beautiful. In both theme and treatment this cycle is a notable work, the most important Icelandic epic of the day and a lasting monument to many of the finest qualities in the Icelandic national character. The story of the poor cotter, who refuses to submit passively to adverse conditions but bravely faces the greatest odds, becomes in the poet's interpretation symbolic of the fate and the struggle of the Icelandic nation, which, to paraphrase his own words, has withstood the raging storms of the ages and emerged victorious because it remained true to its best self.

Jón Magnússon's last book of poems, *Jörðin græn* (The Green Earth) was published posthumously in 1945; at the same time a collected edition of his poems appeared. The title is characteristic of his love of Mother Earth, and the opening poem "Land og þjóð" (Land and Nation) reveals his keen understanding of the close relationship between man and his native soil. His fervent patriotism and love of freedom are forcefully expressed in "Frelsi" (Freedom), ringing challenge to national unity. How deeply the events of the war years moved him, not least the fate of the northern countries, is seen in "Norðmenn" (Norwegians), yet he never lost his faith in the future. Here also are splendid memorial poems such as the impressive eulogy on the poet Einar Benediktsson.

Manliness and courage were ever among Jón Magnússon's most admired virtues, as reflected in his prize-winning poem "Sjómannaljóð," a tribute to the Icelandic seamen. They are still more clearly revealed in the group of poems on Páll at Svínadalur, a heroic figure, akin to Björn at Reyðarfell; this series contains graphic descriptions and passages of great beauty.

Jón Magnússon was a religious man in the truest sense of the word, as is evident in his poems generally and especially in the three hymns in this collection, two of which have deservedly been included in the new edition of the Icelandic hymnal.

Although he was not left untouched by the contemporary trends in Icelandic poetry, he follows primarily the tradition of the Icelandic poets of the previous century, including the unschooled group whom he greatly admired and cherished, in full harmony with his national spirit. Within his largely traditional form, he succeeded in writing notable and personal poems, attesting his good taste, mastery of form, and genuine if subdued feeling, for his was not the flaming passion of Stefán Sigurðsson and Davíð Stefánsson. With his epic poem *Björn á Reyðarfelli,* Jón Magnússon also made a significant contribution to present-day Icelandic literature; and several of the poems in his cycle about that other heroic figure, Páll at Svínadalur, which he did not, unfortunately, live to complete, are among his most appealing productions and definitely show that he did not reach the peak of his poetic powers. Between the poet and the man there never was any cleavage; his wholeheartedness and idealism enchance his poetic warmth and attractiveness.

6. Sigurður Einarsson was born at Arngeirsstaðir in Fljótshlíð in southern Iceland on October 29, 1898. After his graduation from the College of Iceland in 1922, he studied theology at the University of Iceland, graduating in 1926. He has made several study trips abroad and has behind him a long and varied public career, including several years as lecturer in theology at the University and as a member of the Icelandic Althing (1934–1937). At present he is serving as pastor at Holt in the Eyjafjalla district in southern Iceland. A lecturer and essayist, he is also the author of several books and has translated a number of prose works into Icelandic.

His only collection of poems, *Hamar og sigð* (Hammer and Sickle, 1930) struck a note new in the prevailing trend in Icelandic poetry. It was programmatic and prophetic in the sense that it anticipated the poets who during the following decade, under the impact of economic and political developments, turned leftish in their views. He does not write on the personal themes characteristic of the poets of the day; and in the initial poem, "Stefnuskrá" (A Program), he forswears and even holds up to ridicule such favorite themes as flowers, blue sky, the childhood valley, disappointed love, and lamentations. He indeed completely turned his back on them and writes of everyday life about him—the modern age as reflected in macadam city streets, steam trawlers, cement and steel, and whirring machinery—and above all about the new day that he sees dawning for the working class. Characteristically, he designated his poem written for the millennial of the Icelandic Althing in 1930 as the "Millennial Song of the Icelandic Working Class." They are his chosen people and about them he writes his poems—the struggling cotter, the girl selling newspapers on the street, the street urchin who has no other playground, the man out of work, the crews manning the fishing schooners. Such are the subject matter and the temper of these poems, with their realistic pictures from the daily struggle for existence of the common people. At the same time the poet equally vigorously reminds the working class of the fundamental part they play in the social structure and challenges them to rise and meet the dawning day that is theirs. Written in an outright socialistic spirit, which had gripped the poet and inspired him to write these poems in an amazingly short time (between April 15th and November 5th in 1930), they are aflame with the enthusiasm of a new social gospel; nor did they fall on deaf ears, for other poets were soon to take up the challenge.

But although these poems were new in theme and spirit and came like a refreshing gust of wind, they are traditional in form and do not lay any claim to literary artistry; the author himself states in a postlude that for him the message is the important thing. Neither is his interest in the working class and its struggle for justice and a rightful place in the sun limited to his native Iceland; the poem that from the point of view of literary art is considered the best in the book is "Sordavala," a glowing tribute to the memory of Finnish soldiers who fell on the battlefield in the cause of the working man.

7. Jóhannes Jónasson úr Kőtlum was born at Goddastaðir in the Dalir district in western Iceland on November 4, 1899, the son of poor parents; his father was a cotter at an isolated place in the mountains, where the future poet grew to manhood. After intermittent early schooling, he attended the Teachers' College at Reykjavík, graduating in 1921; during the next decade he was an itinerant teacher in his native district; then he became a public school teacher in Reykjavík for several years. He has of late devoted himself primarily to literary pursuits. In his younger days, according to his own testimony, the local branch of the Young People's League, a national organization dedicated to patriotic and progressive purposes, meant a great deal to him culturally and idealistically, and its influence can be traced in his poetry.[6]

His first collection of poems, *Bí bí og blaka* (Sleep, Baby, Sleep, 1926), was in many ways rather immature. On the one hand it was

[6] Concerning his life and literary career, see Sigurður Einarsson, "Ungir rithőfundar: Jóhannes úr Kőtlum," *Iðunn*, XVI (1932), 353–358.

somewhat in the prevailing Romantic and national trend; on the other it showed a close spiritual kinship with the older Icelandic poets. Thus the young poet wrote a cycle of fifty verses, "Háttalykill" (A Key of Meters), each in a different old verse form; in this fashion he carried on an ancient and persistent Icelandic literary tradition, generally speaking very successfully, and revealed his fluent metrical skill. On the whole these early efforts are also marked by a pleasant lyric touch. Of the individual poems the ones on themes from the *Laxdæla saga* deserve to be singled out, especially "Melkorka," which presents a clear and sympathetic picture of the heroine, the Irish-born king's daughter. The poet makes effective use of refrains from old folk songs, and some of the poems on folk themes are among the most successful in the collection. Youthful enthusiasm, idealism, and love of the soil run through these poems.

Very much in the same spirit is his next book, *Álftirnar kvaka* (The Swans Sing, 1929), the lyric note ringing true and strong through the nature and personal poems, which make up the larger part of the collection. "Jónsmessunótt" (Midsummer Night) is, however, more forceful and has a greater sweep than the earlier poems, and "Pílagrímur" likewise is in a more vigorous vein in its vivid portrayal of the pilgrim's journey and its effective symbolism. Romantic as these poems generally are in theme and mood, in their nationalism and idealism, the poem "Ef ég segði þér alt" (If I Told You All) reveals the poet's awakening social consciousness, his growing concern for the oppressed and the suffering; he cannot sleep "because the sorrow from the east and south and west bursts in upon his soul." Here is, so to speak, the first gust of wind preceding that storm of social satire and challenge to the working class that was to surge in full force through his later poems.

In the meantime he first attracted national attention with an entirely different kind of a poem, his inspired and patriotic cycle commemorating the Millennial of the Icelandic Althing, for which he was awarded second prize and which put him on level with the leading poets of the day, as Einar Benediktsson and Davíð Stefánsson jointly received first prize.

His next book, *Ég læt sem ég sofi* (I Pretend Sleeping, 1932), is, however, far removed in theme and tone. By the impact of economic and political developments, and perhaps also by the example of Sigurður Einarsson, he was now thoroughly awakened from his Romantic dreams to the cold reality of the world about him, and he aligned himself with the leftist cause. He hurls out bitter social satires, such as "Arðránsmenn" (Profiteers) and "Atvinnulaus" (Out of Work), which like many others forcefully bespeak his adherence to the new social gospel. The group of poems entitled "Karl faðir minn" (My Old Man), although of unequal merit, is superior from a literary point of view. It is, as the title suggests, inspired by the poet's own bitter experiences during his early years and is therefore strongly personal; the portrayal of his father is both refreshingly realistic and sympathetic without being sentimental. In this collection the poet wrestles with larger themes than before, and his earnestness is everywhere in evidence, but some of the lyric quality has been lost; the poems are more roughhewn, no doubt because the poet is now primarily concerned with his mission.

With his next book, *Samt mun ég vaka* (Yet, I Will Stay Awake, 1935), his conversion to Communism is complete. That same year he was one of the founders of the leftist organ *Rauðir pennar* and wrote the opening poem, "Frelsi" (Freedom), which is included in this collection. Though somewhat uneven, it is one of the most impressive of the social poems in which, with burning conviction and enthusiasm, he mercilessly assails prevailing conditions and abuses, espouses the cause of the working class, and challenges it to greater action. Although some of these poems are forceful and contain splendid poetic passages, the message not infrequently overshadows the literary quality.

On the other hand, here are a number of poems that show that the poet has regained his former lyric strain—such poems as "Lind fyrir vestan" (A Fountain in the West) and "Maíkvöld" (A May Evening), and not least the strongly personal ones, like "Útlendingur" (A Stranger) and "Glókollur" (Towhead), in which the poet succeeds in merging his social views with genuine poetic quality. Several poems, such as "Brúna höndin" (The Brown Hand), with its description of the horror of Nazism, and "Félagi Dimitroff" (Comrade Dimitroff) are foreign in theme. But the national note, always characteristic of the poet, is generally strong in his social poems, as for instance in "Frelsi" (Freedom), with its bright illuminating flashes of Iceland and its history pointing forward to his next book.

This was *Hrímhvíta móðir* (1937), a series of poems surveying the history of Iceland, centering around those men and women and events that contributed most to the political and cultural advancement of the nation and especially of the common people, the least privileged. The book is a large and worthy undertaking and, all in all, a notable achievement, for these poems are often impressive both in thought and in the elaborate poetic garb in which the poet has chosen to clothe them. His burning hatred for oppression flames forth here, as does his equally wholehearted admiration for all those who, whatever their station in life, courageously rise against the oppressor and exemplify the ideas of freedom and justice. Naturally, Jón Sigurðsson, Iceland's noble-minded and stouthearted champion of freedom and cultural ideals, receives a glowing and extended tribute, but richer in sheer lyric beauty is the splendid poem on Jónas Hallgrímsson, the pioneer poet and herald of a new day for the nation. This poem illustrates once more how splendidly the poet can succeed when he deals with lyric themes.

As might be expected, in view of the author's deep social consciousness and his devotion to the cause of the working class, the struggle of this class against foreign governmental oppression and internal injustice and its battle against the elements are graphically and touchingly portrayed in several poems. Nowhere does he, however, reach greater poetic heights than in the closing poem, "Þegnar þagnarinnar" (Citizens of the Land of Silence), a deep-felt and penetrating tribute to the unknown soldiers in the struggle of the Icelandic nation for its existence, regained freedom, and cultural advancement. Deep-rooted patriotism and vigorous progressive spirit are the under current of these historical poems from first to last.

He strikes the same eloquent and lyrical note in "Mitt fólk" (My People), the opening poem of his next book, *Hart er í heimi* (Woe Is in the World, 1939), and in others in a like vein. However, as the title of the book indicates, the poet has been deeply disturbed by world and national conditions and especially by the victories of anti-democratic movements abroad and the threat of an impending war; his heart goes out to the struggling working class in other lands.

His emotions are revealed in many of these poems, stirring social satires ablaze with his reformatory zeal. Sincere as these poems are and noteworthy as they may be in other respects, the poet succeeds still better from a literary point of view when he turns his attention to themes from his own land, especially when he sings about rural life and the soil to which he is linked with unbreakable bonds; there are his cultural and spiritual roots. His "Ástarkvæði til moldarinnar" (A Love Poem to the Earth) is, as its title suggests, an impassioned hymn of praise to Mother Earth; that deep-rooted feeling of kinship with the soil finds a still more direct and beautiful expression in his poem "Heimþrá" (Homesickness), in which the nostalgic longing becomes a pure lyric outpouring of the heart.

The longest and, all things considered, the greatest poem in the book is "Stjörnufákur" (Star Steed), in which the poet tells the life story of an Icelandic horse from its birth and youth in the freedom of the Icelandic moorlands, through its capture and its days of bondage, to its death in an English coal mine. All this is told with deep and touching feeling, alternating between lyricism and eloquence, and imbued throughout with the author's characteristic love of liberty; the exiled Icelandic horse never forgets his native haunts, but yearns for them and his lost freedom. The general symbolic significance is obvious.

In his next book, *Eilífðar smáblóm* (Eternity's Flower, 1940), the last one published within the time limits of this volume, he has largely gone back to his first love, lyric and nature poems; social satire plays a minor part, and most often only an indirect one. The war-torn world of men and the fate of justice and truth in such a world have compelled the poet to withdraw from the arena and turn to Mother Nature and her peace and beauty for relief and inspiration. Here he writes in an engaging but difficult form, the simple, short lyric, in which every word must be an integral part of the mood and the pattern; and although not by any means equally successful throughout the book, he sometimes achieves lyric art of a high order, especially in such delicate and genuinely felt nature poems as "Fyrsta jurt vorsins" (The First Springflower), masterful in pictorial and emotional quality.

In the foregoing rapid survey of Jóhannes Jónasson's extensive production, we have followed him on a long road of development as a poet, from the beginning stage of the romantically minded youth with his love of nature and rural life, through the mature phase when, under the impress of contemporary events, he became a fiery social and revolutionary poet, to the still later stage when wearied by world conditions, although unchanged in political views, he turned back to nature and life close to the soil for consolation and inspiration. At heart he had always remained a son of the soil, attached to both his youthful haunts and his native land. These feelings have also remained deep and resounding strains in his poetry. And in some of his finest efforts he has succeeded in blending them, together with his profound social consciousness and idealism, into splendid poetry, characterized by his rich lyricism and mastery of form. Such poems and his pure lyrics, of which there are a considerable number, constitute his noteworthy contribution to Icelandic literature of the day.

8. Jón Helgason was born at Rauðsgil in Borgarfjörður in the south of Iceland on June 30, 1899. On his graduation from the College of Iceland in 1916, he studied Icelandic philology at the University of Copenhagen, receiving his M.A. degree in 1923 and his Ph.D. degree in 1925. After teaching at the University of Oslo, 1926–1927, he became curator of the Arna-Magnean Collection in Copenhagen, two years later succeeding Dr. Finnur Jónsson as Professor in Icelandic Language and Literature at the University of Copenhagen; since that time he has served with distinction in that dual capacity. An indefatigable research worker, he has, besides his university teaching, published a number of books in his field and rendered Icelandic scholarship an especially great service with his splendid editions of Icelandic manuscripts and medieval Icelandic poems, and numerous shorter scholarly contributions to learned and literary publications.

Jón Helgason has been known for years, not least in academic circles, for his humorous and satirical poems, many of which have, by word of mouth spread far and wide in his native Iceland; skillful and effective as these are, they, nevertheless, would hardly have sufficed to ensure him a lasting place in the literary history of his country. The full measure of his poetic gift was revealed (and came as a pleasant surprise to Icelandic poetry lovers generally) with the publication of his collection of poems, *Úr landsuðri* (From the Southeast, 1939).

The first part of the book is pretty much what one might have expected from the poet in the light of his previous performance, as here are some of his humorous and satirical pieces, though many well-known ones are deliberately omitted by the author. Fortunately, he has included several, particularly those in which the satire is of a general nature, and holds up to biting ridicule certain faults and excesses in the Icelandic national life and character. This is simply another manifestation of his great pride in his nation and its cultural achievements, his deep love of his native land; he wants his countrymen to live up to their unique and rich cultural and literary traditions, which have elevated their small country to a place of honor among the nations of the world. The positive side of that sound love of country, entirely free from cheap chauvinism, is the surging undercurrent, the heart and soul, of the most notable serious poems in the collection. These made it such an unexpected and gratifying literary event.

The stage of Jón Helgason's daily labors is set in the historic surroundings of the Arna-Magnean Collection, where the precious treasures of his nation, the ancient Icelandic manuscripts, are housed. The editing and interpreting of them is his chosen task, his principal mission in life, and the deeper he has entered into that labor of love, the more clearly he has come to see revealed in those old literary treasures the life and the history of his nation. Like his older colleague, Dr. Jón Þorkelsson (Fornólfur), he has found his themes and inspiration in the world of his scholarship, although the two are unlike in other respects. The literary by-product of his penetrating scholarship is nowhere more masterfully embodied in poetic form than in his poem "Í Árnasafni" (In Árni's Collection), all things considered, his greatest poem. With deep insight he here describes how the yellowed, old codices, the labors of thousands, take on life, how the mists of the centuries clear away, and his struggling nation, in its cultural endeavors, often fighting for its very existence, emerges from the faded pages of the treasured manuscripts. The poet has the feeling that the old chronicler is standing by his side, and despite the vastly different conditions under which their labors are done, he keenly feels their spiritual kinship. Thus this remarkable poem becomes a deep-felt personal expression, the author seeing his destiny and his labors mirrored in the fate of the scribes of old and their work. This deep sense of the fleetingness of life, which is characteristic of the poet, gives strong universal appeal to the poem and adds much to the historical insight, the description of the national life, and the effective metrical form.

With his keen understanding of the historical and cultural implications of his labors, it is not surprising that Jón Helgason is also deeply conscious of his responsibility as a preserver and interpreter of the ancient manuscript treasures, as expressed in his poem "Til hőfundar Hungurvőku" (To the Author of Hungurvaka). In "Máríuvísur" (Verses to Mary) he identifies himself with the old writers to the extent of imitating their language and style and achieves an authenticity that is convincing and appealing. Here is a striking example of his great mastery of the Icelandic language and Icelandic verse forms.

Clearly his roots lie deep in the Icelandic cultural soil, and, like many an Icelandic poet before him in his self-exile abroad, he has found for his love and nostalgic longing for his country an outlet in his poetry, most memorably in his beautiful sonnet "Í vorþeynum" (In the Spring Thaw), in which his feeling of being a stranger in a strange land is strikingly expressed in the closing lines: "Foreign rain drips from the eaves of the house, strange winds moan at its door." With equal tenderness and poetic excellence his attachment to the native soil is expressed in the poem "Á Rauðsgili" (At Rauðsgil), inspired by a visit to the haunts of his youth.

With Jón Helgason's background, training, and devoted absorption in his scholarly work, it is only natural that his preoccupation with the traditional literary values should have left its mark on his poetry; but at the same time it bears the strong stamp of his personality and rich poetic gift, in originality, concentrated thought, vigorous language, and not least genuine though restrained emotion, sparked by his longing for the land across the sea, which is inseparably interwoven with his daily work, his deepest satisfactions and dreams.

9. Tómas Guðmundsson was born at Efri-Brú in Grímsnes in

southern Iceland on January 6, 1901. On his graduation from the College of Iceland in 1921, he studied law at the University of Iceland, receiving his degree in 1926; he then practiced for some time and since 1929 has done office work in the Statistical Bureau of Iceland.

He was in his day one of sixteen college "poets," whom he celebrated in a notable poem. His first collection of poems, *Við sundin blá* (By the Blue Sounds, 1925), was very much in the spirit of the prevailing tendency among the young poets of the time, on such themes as nature in its Romantic moods, love, and dreams that never came true. At the same time, these youthful efforts of his were smooth-flowing, in good taste, and written with considerable metrical skill. They did not, however, attract any wide attention. Yet, in retrospect, one can see in them certain characteristics pointing forward to his later production, especially a love of life and beauty that was to become such a dominant strain in his poetry.

Eight years passed by, and no doubt many thought that he was going to share the fate of most of his fifteen schoolmates, who had transferred their adolescent devotion to the muse into more prosaic channels. Not so Tómas Guðmundsson, for in his next book, under the attractive and characteristic title, *Fagra veröld* (The Beautiful World, 1933), he burst upon the literary scene with such mature personal style and form, such newness in theme and lyric artistry, that these poems took the reading public by storm; the collection appeared in a second edition before the year was out, and a third was called for the next year. After the book had been out of print for several years, a fourth, illustrated edition appeared in 1946. Several of the poems have been translated into the Scandinavian languages, English, and German, and the majority of them were published in a French translation by Dr. Pierre Naert in Paris in 1939.

The poet's "Beautiful World" is above anything else the world of his precious memories from his college days in the young Icelandic capital, lying fallow in his mind for years and now blossoming forth in all their beauty, through the Romantic haze of distant enchantment. Against that background and in that light the present is portrayed, for the poet's soul responds in an outburst of song to everything about him recalling the past. And when he contemplates those bygone days, his heart fills with a melancholy longing that imbues his poems with a gripping undertone of sadness. The mood is brilliantly expressed in the opening poem, "Gamalt ljóð" (An Old Song), which he closes with this supplication to Night: "Take my grief and transform it into a song to sooth the sorrowful longing for all that was and never returns." The spirit of youth still lives in his heart, and like Omar Khayyám he continues to enjoy the passing hour to the fullest, because he realizes the fleetingness of life and of worldly pleasures.

The poems center around Reykjavík, and more specifically around its main thoroughfare, Austurstræti, the heart of the city, which the poet has made the particular subject of one of his most excellent poems. Here the description is really little more than the frame for the cherished picture from days past, which the street, so dear to the poet, evokes in his mind.

Elsewhere in his poems he has painted graphic and charming word pictures of Reykjavík in its summer and fall garb and of the harbor with its many-sided and ceaseless activity. In such poems he has caught the pulse beat of the growing capital, which had taken him, the country boy, to its heart, and which he, in turn, was the first to interpret in vivid poetry of lasting quality, thereby putting it permanently on the literary map of the nation. These poems have an attractive Romantic tinge, but are no less characteristic for their whimsical quality, because the poet delights in looking at the city life, and at life in general, with a good-natured glint in his eye. This is excellently illustrated in his poem "Húsin í bænum" (The Houses in Town), in which he ponders quizzically upon all the houses under construction and why. Sometimes this whimsicality has a more sober note, as in "Hótel jőrð" (Hotel Earth), in which the poet, with striking symbolism, compares the sojourn of man on earth with a stay at a hotel, where ultimately all have to face the great Bill Collector, Death.

Nowhere does the poet, achieve greater poetic beauty than in the purely lyric poems, such as "Japanskt ljóð" (A Japanese Song), a delicate Romantic phantasy, and in "Haustnótt" (Autumn Night), equally Romantic in its lyricism, but having a deeper emotional undercurrent.

Throughout the book the poet is primarily the perfectionist, possessing in an uncommon degree the choicest language, the ability to construct a poem effectively, and not least the rare gift of clothing his thoughts and feelings in a corresponding artistic form.

In appreciation of his book, *Fagra veröld*, both because of its high literary quality and even more because of its original and fascinating portrayal of Reykjavík, the city government awarded Tómas Guðmundsson a travel stipend, which enabled him to visit Italy and the Mediterranean.

In his next book, *Stjörnur vorsins* (The Stars of Spring, 1940), there are a number of poems, and some of the most beautiful ones in the collection, which are inspired by that memorable and stimulating visit. Here also are several poems harking back to *Fagra veröld* in theme and spirit, such as "Skólabræður" (School Mates) and "Post jucundam," constituting a further flowering of the deep-rooted memories of youthful days and joys and showing that the virtuosity in form is undiminished. In these poems and throughout the book the sparkling humor is both a fundamental and an attractive quality; and it is even richer and more fully developed than before. This is best illustrated in such inimitable poems as "Þegar ég praktiseraði" (When I Practiced) and "Víxilkvæði" (A Promissory Note). In the first the poet describes with lyric irony his experiences as a practicing attorney, his wait for the customers who never arrived, and how at last, to while away the dragging hours, he resorted to writing poetry on his official stationery until it was all used up, and then, of course, there was nothing to do but to close the law office for good. The latter poem is unique, for it is the delightfully humorous story, in autobiographical form, of the checkered career of a promissory note, which is to be renewed for the fourtieth time. Vividly the poet personalizes his prosaic subject and with his characteristic whimsicality makes it symbolic of human life.

His rare ability to interweave rich lyricism and sparkling humor is brilliantly used in "Garðljóð" (Garden Song), from the Italian journey, and "Jónsmessunótt" (Midsummer Night), in folklore spirit, describing the elves celebrating on Midsummer Night and written in a light, dancing rhythm admirably suited to the theme.

It is in the purely lyric poems that the chief literary value of the book lies. In "Við Miðjarðarhafið" (By the Mediterranean), he describes colorfully the scenic beauty of those regions and still more penetratingly the poetic inspiration and insight that came to him in those historic and romantic surroundings. In "Í klausturgarðinum" (In the Monastery Garden), also the fruit of the Italian journey, the poet's deep desire to recapture the dreams and ideals of his youth and make them a new and vital reality in his life is portrayed with delicate sensitiveness. Masterful in diction and similes, the poem exemplifies in the highest degree his ability to find an adequate and artistic expression for his intermost thoughts and feelings. The greatest lyric height is, however, reached in "Þjóðvísa" (A Folk Song), in which he tells a touching love story with such delicate simplicity and penetrating insight that no attempt at retelling it does any justice to it whatsoever; it must be read and relived in the original language.

The lyric and ethereal magic of Tómas Guðmundsson's literary artistry, therefore, finds a magnificent expression in this and other poems in the collection, and with those and his finest poems in *Fagra veröld,* he has reached a level of perfection in form and the expression of poetic beauty new in Icelandic literature—indeed a major achievement.

In the opening and closing poems of the book, "Aladdín" and "Eftirmáli" (A Postscript), both among the most beautiful lyrics included, he expresses once more his brooding over departed youth and its world of dreams, together with his searching for beauty and happiness, which he continues to find in the enjoyment of the hour. Underneath, nevertheless, there is always the feeling of the unstableness and fleeting nature of worldly joys, of the imminence of Death.

Negative as this fatalistic view of life may seem to some, there is in the poems of Tómas Guðmundsson an uncommonly great aesthetic satisfaction, for he not only has the ability to find romantic beauty in life about him, even in the most unlikely places, but he also has the still rarer gift of sharing that discovery with others in artistic and poetic form.

While his principal contribution to Icelandic literature consists in his original poems, mention may also be made of the selections from the Arabian Nights, *Arabískar nætur* (1934), which he translated with Páll Skúlason.

10. Magnús Ásgeirsson was born at Reykir in Lundarreykjadal in Borgarfjörður in southern Iceland on November 9, 1901. Graduating from the College of Iceland in 1922, he studied Icelandic philology at the University of Iceland for some time afterwards engaging in clerical work, journalism, and literary pursuits.

He began his literary career as one of the young poets who appeared in the wake of Stefán Sigurðsson and Davíð Stefánsson, with the publication of a slender volume of poems, *Síðkveld* (Late Evenings, 1923), original and translated, which promised little beyond fluency in language and verse forms. This remains his only book of original verse; a few poems published later indicate unmistakably that he could have made his mark in the field of original poetry had he chosen to do so. Instead, and fortunately for Icelandic literature, he has devoted himself to translating poetry from many lands and languages into his native tongue.

His first collection of translations, *Þýdd ljóð*, appeared in 1928, only five years after the publication of his juvenile poems; but he had clearly found himself and come a long way in mature literary artistry, although he had not yet acquired the mastery characteristic of his later work. Quite naturally the necessity for wrestling with the rendition of foreign poetry into corresponding Icelandic form has developed his own literary talent.

Deservedly, his first collection of translations was favorably reviewed and equally well received by the reading public, and it laid a secure foundation for his later work in the field, which has gained him increased popularity and esteem. Four more volumes of his translations had appeared before 1940 (in 1931, 1932, 1935, and 1936), and they contain hundreds of poems by over a hundred poets, especially from the northern countries, but from Germany, England, many other European nations, and the United States as well. Naturally, in such a vast body of translations, all the renditions are not of equal merit, but the amazing thing is that as a rule, they are executed uncommonly well and often masterfully. Only a translator possessing rare command of language and metrical skill of a high order, together with flexibility, insight, and imagination, could have achieved such results, for these translations range from restrained classics, through the tenderest lyrics, to modern burlesque. All of these types Magnús Ásgeirsson handles with ease, as well as with painstaking care and the deep sense of responsibility characteristic of the conscientious translator. Thus he hardly ever changes the metrical form of his translations, indeed a fundamental factor, considering how intimately related theme and meter are in all truly lyric poetry and how much of the mood of the poem is inherent in the metrical pattern. Often he likewise succeeds admirably in giving his translations an Icelandic flavor by localizing them, without sacrificing the mood and the spirit of the original, and in that respect he carries to new heights the tradition established by some of his greatest Icelandic predecessors.

Magnús Ásgeirsson's interest in social problems and world affairs, together with his political leanings and general outlook upon life, is reflected in his choice of translations, many of which are satirical in spirit and theme, although otherwise vastly different and not by any means of equal poetical value or general significance.

His translations of "The Ballad of Reading Gaol" by Oscar Wilde, "The Twelve" by Alexander Bloch, selections from *The Spoon River Anthology* by Edgar Lee Masters, and "The Rubáiyát of Omar Khayyám" may be singled out as they are, in the main, excellently done.

Magnús Ásgeirsson has not only greatly enriched Icelandic literature with his numerous and generally splendidly rendered verse translations; he has also been a source of inspiration to the younger poets, who have found both challenging examples and intellectual stimulation in the poems of foreign masters whose work he has rendered into Icelandic. This indebtedness some of the younger poets have publicly acknowledged. It is not difficult to trace in their poems influences from the translations of Edgar Lee Masters, Carl Sandburg, and others.

Magnús Ásgeirsson also has to his credit a number of significant prose translations.[7]

---

[7] Concerning him and his translations, see the introduction to his *Ljóð frá ýmsum löndum*, ed. Snorri Hjartarson (1946).

11. Guðmundur Böðvarsson was born on September 1, 1904, at Kirkjuból in Borgarfjörður in southern Iceland, and has lived all his life there and in the immediate neighborhood; a farmer's son, he took over the parental land in 1932 and has farmed it ever since. Except for limited rural school attendance in his youth, he is a self-educated man, for whom like so many of his Icelandic fellow poets, wide and intensive reading has taken the place of extended schooling.

His poems, which appeared in the periodical *Eimreiðin* in 1930 and the years following, at once attracted the attention of poetry lovers because of the strong personal and lyric quality. His first book, *Kyssti mig sól* (The Sun Kissed Me, 1936), was, therefore, awaited with interest in poetry circles and more than lived up to the promise of the earlier poems. In reality, the publication of the book was no ordinary literary event, for these poems were the product of a virtually unschooled, hard-working farmer, living in an isolated rural district that he had never left for any length of time. Considering that circumstance, the generally high literary quality, vision, and wide-awake social awareness were all the more remarkable.

Guðmundur Böðvarsson lives in one of the most beautiful regions of inland Iceland, and his deep roots in the soil and his love of nature are everywhere evident in these poems. They are rich in poetic descriptive passages, in striking word-pictures and similes taken directly out of the poet's rural environment as it changes its appearance with the seasons. The prevailing mood of these poems, which are generally highly contemplative in spirit, is one of alternating sorrow and joy, fear and hope. This is seen in the title poem with its reminiscences of a past summer, which, in spite of all, sings in the poet's heart. As he says in his poem "Í október" (In October), he does not forget the yellowed bushes in the lava field, but for the long journey he would like to choose as company "the soft murmur of the springs which never freeze."

The personal and contemplative note, strong as it is, and the sensitively felt nature descriptions are not by any means the only chords struck. In such poems as "Sveitaskáld" (A Rural Poet) the author reveals his ability in characterization, in this case no doubt largely autobiographical and hence all the more significant for the light it sheds on his own life and development, the conflict between the poet and the farmer within him, between his artistic nature and the unrelenting struggle to make a living; to his great credit, he appears to have solved that problem very happily, as he is both an excellent poet and a successful farmer.

He is also an unusual poet in that his alert social consciousness and progressive spirit extend far beyond his rural district; like his fellow poet and farmer, Stephan G. Stephansson, he is deeply moved by prevailing world conditions and contemporary events, as seen in his social satire, "Spánskt kvæði frá 17. őld" (A Spanish Poem from the Seventeenth Century), whose title is merely a thin camouflage for a direct reference to current conditions. The same human interest is a strong undercurrent and finds far more artistic expression in the original and splendidly constructed opening poem, "Til þín, Mekka" (To You, Mecca), where, in the guise of a Mohammedan faithful, the poet pours out to Allah his lament over social injustice in the world. Akin in spirit is the closing poem, "Ok velkti þá lengi í hafi" (And They Were Cast about the Sea), dramatically describing the hopes and disappointments of the sailors when the expected land is never sighted. Assuredly the poet's Romanticism, a rich strain in these poems, is sorely tried and tempered by the disturbing conditions in the larger world about him. But even if doubts sometimes assail him, the sunlight of hope breaks through the gloom, beautifully revealed in the poem "Vísur um birkilauf" (Verses about a Birch Leaf), describing a withered and windblown birch leaf that becomes to the poet a precious reminder of summer and his cherished dreams. Here is also illustrated his genuine poetic ability to see the large in the small.

In his next book, *Hin hvítu skip* (The White Ships, 1939), Guðmundur Bőðvarsson's further poetic development is seen in his selection of larger themes as well as a deepened and widened human interest; the love of nature, the lyric touch, and the choice language are here as before. At times, however, he appears more concerned with expressing his thoughts and feelings than with polishing his form, with the result that some of the poems are rather loose-knit, even when they are original in theme, like "Gamall skór" (An Old Shoe), and contain splendid passages. Here are, however, many of his finest poems up to that time.

Characteristically, they are often closely linked to the Icelandic scene and the changing seasons, the poet seeing his hopes and dreams reflected in the moods of external nature, as in the fine lyric "Hið daglanga sumar" (The Summer of Long Days), where the magic of the summer evokes the tenderest recollections in his heart. Elsewhere in his nature poems, the recurring strain of doubt and sadness mingles with the rejoicing or finds an expression in lamentations over departed springtime and summer. That note is the undertone in the strikingly symbolic poem "Rauði steinninn" (The Red Stone); the poet saw a stone shining like a ruby in the dust of the road as he and his company rode by, but he neglected to pick it up and was never able to find it again. Here the poet succeeds particularly well in harmonizing thought and form.

Also original and well constructed are the deeply felt personal poems "Vísurnar við hverfisteininn árið 1936" (Verses Composed at the Grindstone in the Year 1936) and "Smiðjuljóð" (The Song of the Smithy), which illustrate how effectively the poet can make use of themes from his daily life to symbolize both his own experience and the fateful events of the larger world that crowd in upon his sensitive soul. His interest in world events and his deep human sympathy, which are so strongly reflected in these two remarkable poems, find a still more direct expression in "Varðmenn" (Guards), in which, indirectly at least, he aligns himself with those fighting for a new social order of peace, justice, and brotherhood. This deepening sense of social and moral responsibility is also seen in "Vor borg" (Our City), in which he describes the temple he wishes to build with his life and poetic art and the social structure he desires to see rise on a firm foundation

"Vor borg" is an excellently constructed poem, but nowhere does Guðmundur Böðvarsson's rich poetic gift find a purer expression than in some of his short lyrics, such as the one entitled "Ljós" (Light), about the little light that gleams alone at the bedside of an old man and bravely keeps out the darkness and it horrors. The symbolic significance needs no elaboration.

With these first two collections Guðmundur Böðvarsson took his place in the forefront of the younger poets of the day, for in many splendid poems he succeeded in expressing his deep-rooted love of beauty and his unconquerable idealism. Original and well-wrought personal poems and nature descriptions transform the material of his everyday life into the precious metal of genuine poetry. In other words, he has not only reconciled himself to his conditions, but through the understanding of the beauty of his environs and the positive and productive nature of his work as a farmer he has found a compensation for those youthful dreams that he was not allowed to see realized. The title poem of his second collection concludes with these words of mature wisdom: "Praised be the dream, which is endless and never realized."

12. Guðmundur Ingi Kristjánsson was born on January 15, 1907, at Kirkjuból in Bjarnardalur in Őnundarfjőrður, western Iceland, where his father has farmed all his life, and where since early manhood, the poet himself has been a farmer. He comes from a family in which versemaking ability is unusually common.

Beyond the rural school level, his education included a year at one of the Icelandic district schools modeled upon the renowned Danish Folk High Schools and another at the Co-operative School in Reykjavík. Culturally, he is in addition the product of the Icelandic Young People's League, which was for many rural young people of his generation a source of inspiration and idealism. At an early age he became active in the local branch of the League and has for years played a prominent part in the work of the chapters in his part of the country. These associations proved very stimulating for his budding poetic talent.

According to his own testimony, he began writing verses at the age of seven and has cultivated the poetic art ever since. Before the appearance of his first book, *Sólstafir* (Sunbeams, 1938), he had already attracted attention with his poems in papers and periodicals, for they generally struck a different note from the prevailing trend. The themes were mostly taken directly from rural life and work. And it was this new note that set his book apart and made it find a ready response in the heart of many of his countrymen, the farm population and rural youth in particular.

The keynote of the collection is effectively struck in the title poem, alive with joy in rural life and farm work in the sunny summer. The theme is further elaborated in the beautiful poem, "Vornótt" (Spring

Night), about the sower, who, in his implicit faith in the earth, entrusts his seed to its care. Then follow poems about the hay harvest, the waving field of barley, and other phases of farm life; the sight of his flock of sheep inspires the poet to an enraptured outburst; the milk, the kale, and the salad, all that sustain the farmer, take on a romantic hue in his eyes; even the mechanized farm equipment, which lightens the farmer's toil and increases his harvest, becomes the burden of the poet's rural hymn of praise. His close kinship to the soil is clearly seen here as elsewhere in his poetry.

As he himself says in "Vornótt," it is the neglected land that has challenged him, for he feels he has a God-given mission to cultivate the soil, to build for future generations who will reap the fruit of his labor. And he wants to sing his love for the land and rural life, as well as his faith in the soil and his native country, into other hearts.

Although the poems on farm life and work are most characteristic, Guðmundur Ingi Kristjánsson also writes love poems, akin to the former in being less ethereal and more down to earth than is commonly the case, occasional poems, and finally poems on historical themes.

It is, however, with his rural poems, warmed by his enthusiasm and idealism, that he has made his special contribution. There is about them the breath and the fragrance of the earth. They are genuinely felt, though somewhat uneven, for the poet does not always succeed in clothing his emotions and thoughts in equally poetic garb. He has admitted the inspiration received from his favorite poet, the Danish Jeppe Aakjær, beloved singer of rural Jutland.

13. Steinn Steinarr, pen name of Aðalsteinn Kristmundsson, was born in 1908 at Laugaland in Norður-Ísafjarðarsýsla in western Iceland but grew up in the Dalir district, the country of Stefán Sigurðsson frá Hvítadal and Jóhannes Jónasson úr Kötlum. As a youth Steinn Steinarr went to Reykjavík, but lack of means prevented him from continuing his education. As the economic depression was at its height, it was difficult for him to find work, and besides he was hampered by a physical disability. Hence, poverty and hunger were his lot, moulded him and his outlook upon life, and are reflected in his poems.

He is one of that proletarian youth that he salutes and challenges to action in the opening poem of his first book, *Rauður loginn brann*

(Red Burned the Flame, 1934). He dedicates the book to "my comrades and acquaintances in Reykjavík, who have for years fought like heroes at my side for the necessities of life—and not as yet been victorious." These words are highly revealing with respect to the genesis, the subject matter, and the mood of these poems.

Their themes are taken directly out of everyday life and generally they are revolutionary in spirit, bitter social satires in thoroughly leftist, Communistic vein. In form they are as a rule simple and sincere, often genuinely lyrical, as "Hin hljóðu tár" (The Silent Tears), in which fervent social satire finds effective poetic expression. Of the poems in free verse, and there are many, "Mold" (The Earth) and "Stiginn" (The Stairs), although unlike, are especially noteworthy in thought and poetic quality, whereas "Minning" (Remembrance), a splendid lyric, and "Veruleiki" (Reality) are particularly significant for the light they throw on the poet's life and spiritual development; the doubt, characteristic of his later poems, is already beginning to gnaw at his heart. Although Steinn Steinarr had not as yet found himself and was under the influence of some of his older contemporary Icelandic poets, these first poems revealed unquestionable literary ability and lyric gift.

In his next book, *Ljóð* (Poems, 1937), the poet had very largely outgrown the immaturity of the beginner's stage and had virtually rid himself of the influence of his Icelandic contemporaries. On the other hand, he had clearly been stimulated by the example of foreign poets, contemporary and past, especially in form. Generally short, simple and unadorned in language, these poems are very often in free verse; they are constructed with great care, for the poet takes his art seriously, but they are not all equally successful. Some of them, however, are original in thought and concentrated in form, like "Sement" (Cement) and "Marmari" (Marble), whereas others, such as "Vor" (Spring), are rich in poetic beauty. Several of the most lyrical and best poems in the book are in a more traditional form, such as "Columbus," a fine poetic interpretation of mankind's instinctive search for the unknown.

In subject matter and mood these poems differ greatly from the earlier ones. Revolutionary spirit and social satire are no longer the central elements, but are now implied rather than expressed. The gnawing doubt, which already had shown its hideous head in the poet's first book has now gripped his soul, and the recurrent theme of these poems is a dark hopelessness; life has no purpose and offers only misery and death. No doubt the hard fate that the poet had endured has bred in him that gloomy view of life, expressed with characteristic sincerity of personal feeling and in poetic form in the poem "Ekkert" (Nothing).

The note of pessimism runs strong through the poems in Steinn Steinarr's next collection, *Spor í sandi* (Footprints in the Sand, 1940), many of which are abstract in thought and experimental in form and do not always achieve their artistic purpose. Here are, however, a number of poems marked by deep emotional feeling and sheer lyric quality, such as "Hvíld" (Rest), "Síesta," "Ljóð" (A Song), and "Heimferð" (Homeward Journey); the last two express penetratingly the gloomy pessimism of the lonely wayfarer (as the poet presents himself in many of these poems) for whom life is nothing more than *vanitas vanitatis*.

Relieving the somewhat monotonous recurrence of the pessimistic theme are several humorous poems, generally good-natured and refreshing, in which the poet sometimes achieves the desired effect by blending whimsically medieval and modern expressions, as in "Brúðkaupskvæði" (A Nuptial Poem). Elsewhere he succeeds excellently in combining the humorous and the melancholy element.

Steinn Steinarr has himself acknowledged his indebtedness to such Icelandic poets as Jóhann Sigurjónsson and Jóhann Jónsson; influences from both contemporary Scandinavian poets and American poets like Edgar Lee Masters and Carl Sandburg are also traceable in his poetry. His poems have, however, not least in his third book, increasingly acquired his own personal stamp in thought and style. And although the range of their themes is rather limited, their growing individuality, the frequently high lyric quality, and mastery of form have gained him a special place among contemporary Icelandic poets, with promise of greater things to come.

14. Guðfinna Jónsdóttir frá Hőmrum was born at Arnarvatn in Mývatnssveit in northern Iceland, on February 27, 1899. She spent her first and most formative years there and at Grímsstaðir in the same vicinity and the rest of her youth at Hamrar in the Reykjadal

district, with which she is associated. Both Grímsstaðir and Hamrar are noted for their scenic beauty and naturally moulded the sensitive soul of the future poetess. The surroundings at Hamrar, with their impressive and varied mountain scenery, were especially dear to her and are reflected in her poems. At an early age she showed an uncommon appreciation of poetry, and a still greater musical inclination and ability, which was stimulated by a sympathetic interest on the part of her parents, especially her music-loving father. In spite of adverse circumstances, she was able to realize her childhood dream of studying music and pursued her studies both in Reykjavík and Akureyri. She came to be recognized as one of the finest organists outside the capital. Failing health and other difficulties prevented her from continuing her musical studies, and during her last years she was a music teacher at Húsavík, choir director, and church organist, as long as her health and strength permitted. She died at a sanatorium in Eyjafjőrður on March 28, 1946, after a long illness.

Guðfinna Jónsdóttir was a mere child when she began writing verses, but in her retiring way she kept those efforts to herself. However, when her failing health prevented her from devoting her attention to her beloved music, she found in poetry an outlet for her pent-up emotion and began cultivating the poetic art with characteristic seriousness. Her training in music had naturally developed her sense of rhythm and form, and musical quality is fundamental in her poems, for they are lyric poetry in the full sense of the word, personal and deep-felt.

She first attracted general attention with a few poems published in the collection *Þingeysk ljóð* (1940), which stood out because of their high poetic quality and workmanship.

Her delicate lyric gift was further unfolded in her first book, *Ljóð* (Poems, 1941). Although she wrote on common themes, nature and everyday life, she possessed the sensitiveness and insight to endow these with fresh beauty and to present them in a new light, with literary artistry in form and diction. Uniformly these poems are short, and they generally achieve their purpose well, having the necessary concentration and unbroken mood. There is in them a deep undercurrent of sympathy and reverence for life.

The poem "Rokkhljóð" (The Humming of the Spinning Wheel) is a fine example of these qualities and illustrates especially well the ability of the poetess to give a new and deeper significance to an everyday occurrence. Into the description of the spinning itself, she delicately weaves a picture of the thoughts and dreams of the women at the spinning wheel, of how their lives become interwoven so to speak with the thread that they are spinning. As a result the poem takes on a symbolic meaning. The joy in work is here also a refreshing note.

Her poems are rich in striking similes and pictorial quality, particularly the nature descriptions, such as "Ljóssins knőrr" (The Ship of Light), a hymn of praise to the midnight sun, standing guard over the drowsy sea and the earth clothed in the green garb of spring.

Even the titles of some of these lyrics reveal the musical interest of the author, and the influence from that source is naturally still more fundamental in the poems themselves; in one of them for instance, she uses symbolically the various types of string instruments. But this kind of symbolism is perhaps most striking in the poem "Heiðakyrrð" (Moorland Calm), in which, to the inner ear of the poetess, the voices of nature blend into the symphony of eternity.

Throughout these poems there is a strain of sadness and longing, deepened by the awareness of imminent death, but that feeling is entirely free from sentimental self-pity.

Guðfinna Jónsdóttir's next and last book, *Ný kvæði* (New Poems, 1945), has all the fine lyric characteristics of her earlier poems, but is still richer in emotional quality and depth; consequently, a number of her very best poems are found here. Some of these are memorable pictures taken directly from Icelandic rural life, like "Íslenzkir skór" (Icelandic Shoes); the shoes, in her penetrating handling of the humble theme, became a striking symbol of the struggle and the fate of the nation. Her keen understanding of the close relationship between the soul and the soil is revealed in such poems as "Maður og mold" (Man and Soil).

Her horizon and human sympathy were, however, far from limited to her native land; the storms of her turbulent time, the years of the Second World War, had moved her deeply. Her heart goes out to the oppressed nations, as seen in her deep-felt poem on the fate of Poland, "Harpa Chopins" (Chopin's Harp), in her first book, and in her magnificent tribute to the Norwegian nation, which is among her later poems. This wide human sympathy is still more penetratingly revealed in "Þagnarmúr" (The Wall of Silence), about that rocklike wall of misunderstanding that has been built up between the nations and will not be destroyed until the music of brotherly love, imprisoned in the hearts of men, is released from its bondage. "Viðlag" (Refrain) is related in mood and spirit, but is even more strongly colored by the musical approach so characteristic of the poetess, reaching its climax in the poetic expression that the soul of man is "a refrain in God's poem."

Tenderly she expresses the deepest longing of her heart in "Fjallið blátt" (The Blue Mountain), and characteristic of her faith, idealism, and love of beauty is the touching closing poem, "Með sól" (With the Sun), in which she comforts herself with the thought that she is making her journey in the inseparable company of the sun.

Her poems are, as has been indicated, generally characterized by sure literary taste, choice and often vigorous language, and elevation in theme and spirit; and they are not infrequently accompanied by that undertone that gives to lyric poetry its indefinable charm.

Besides Guðfinna Jónsdóttir frá Hőmrum, many other women of the middle-aged and younger group have published poetry of merit. Margrét Jónsdóttir (b. 1893), a public school teacher by profession, has to her credit two collections of poems, often with a fine lyric strain, though not particularly original or vigorous. Specimens of the poems of thirty Icelandic women, illustrating their contribution to the present-day literature of their country, are included in the collection *Það mælti mín móðir* (So Spake My Mother, 1936), edited with a preface by Sigurður Skúlason.

15. Of the numerous other poets who have published books of verse during the period three more will be considered briefly.

Guðmundur Frímannsson Frímann (b. 1903) is a farmer's son from Húnavatnssýsla in northern Iceland and is largely self-educated. A cabinet maker, he has for years plied his trade at Akureyri, but he has continued to cultivate his literary interest and has published three collections of poetry.

His first book *Náttsólir* (Night Suns), appeared in 1922. He was one of the group of young poets inspired by the example of Stefán Sigurðsson frá Hvítadal and Davíð Stefánsson. His youthful efforts are largely love poems in the prevailing trend of the time, immature in many respects and lacking in originality, but generally smooth in verse form and containing some promising glimpses.

His second book published under the rather far-fetched title *Úlfablóð* (Wolf Blood, 1933) and the pen name Álfur frá Klettastíu, came eleven years later. It is more mature, contains some good nature poems, and shows an increasing mastery of form, especially in the selection of original and personal meters. Lyrical in tone, the characteristic mood of these poems is one of a subdued feeling of sadness.

This chord is also struck often in his third and best book, *Störin syngur* (The Sedge Sings, 1937), which echoes his nostalgic longing for his native river valley, the subject of several of these poems. Akin in spirit are his nature poems, lyrical in quality as before and frequently written in original and appropriate verse forms. So also are his other poems, both the attractive descriptions of rural life and those about various unfortunates whose fate appealed to the poet's human interest. Some of the individual characterizations are, however, the most refreshing and striking in the book, especially the delightful description "Drukkinn bóndi úr Skyttudal" (The Tipsy Farmer from Skyttudalur), with its realistic and individualistic picture of the tipsy farmer and itinerant reciter of poetry.

These latest poems of Guðmundur Frímann show that he is steadily gaining a more personal form of expression in themes and meters.

KJARTAN J. GÍSLASON frá Mosfelli (b. 1902) is a clergyman's son, from the Grímsnes district in the south of Iceland. His first book, *Næturlogar* (Night Flashes, 1928), contained some well-written and promising poems, but the young poet had not as yet developed a personal style in themes and treatment.

This he has done to a much greater extent in his second book, *Skrjáfar í laufi* (Rustling Leaves, 1936). There are two primary strains in his poems, which are always lyrical and light in touch. On the one hand, he delights in painting good-natured, whimsical word pictures of life in Reykjavík and of human life in general, which often hit the mark very well. On the other hand, his poems are inspired by his deep-rooted attachment to his native haunts and to the soil, and he has affectionately described rural life in such poems as "Hirðing" (The Hay Gathered In), an excellent picture of haying in his youth. That he can handle an historical theme is seen in the longest poem in the book, "Áning" (Resting on the Road), in which the descriptive and the narrative elements are effectively interwoven.

With his first collection, *Eg ýti úr vör* (I Embark, 1933), BJARNI M. GÍSLASON (b. 1908) showed some promise, not least in the patriotic and nature poems. A short time later he went to Denmark, where he has since been engaged in lecturing and writing in Danish on Icelandic subjects. His second book of poems, *Ekko fra Tankens Fastland* (Echo from the Spirit's Mainland; Ry, 1939), was favorably reviewed by Danish papers. Many of these poems are in a pleasant, lyric strain, with the poet's native Iceland as a recurrent theme.

16. ICELANDIC POETRY, 1940–1950. This survey is, as the title states, limited to the period 1800–1940. Since 1940, many of the established poets, old and young alike, have published new books, which, especially in the case of the most notable younger ones, have revealed their poetic gifts and literary stature more fully. Gifted new poets have also appeared, whom it would have been tempting to include. But any discussion of poetry published during the last decade would go far beyond the prescribed limits of the present volume. Suffice it to say that the latest literary developments in the realm of Icelandic poetry indicate that this form of literary expression, cherished by the Icelanders, continues to flourish.

VII

American-Icelandic Poets

THE historical background of the emigration from Iceland to North America during the last quarter of the nineteenth century has been sketched sufficiently in the parallel volume on the prose writers, and emphasis has, naturally, been laid on the significant fact that the Icelandic immigrants brought with them not only uncommon literary interest but also the alert consciousness of a time-honored and rich literary tradition.

To their everlasting honor, they have also, in spite of adverse circumstances, vigorously maintained the literary tradition of the homeland, not only in prose, but to a much greater extent in poetry, which has for centuries been the traditional Icelandic form of literary expression.

The literary production of these American-Icelandic poets is all the more remarkable in view of the fact that the majority of them are entirely or largely self-educated and that they have cultivated their literary interest in the time they could spare from earning their living at various occupations or from discharging exacting public duties.[1]

As most of them belong to the older generation, they represent the literary trends prevailing during their formative years in Iceland, where many of them grew to manhood. Romanticism runs strong in their works, although the Realistic strain is also a dominant note in

[1] The designation "American" is used here in the continental sense, even though the great majority of the poets concerned have been or are Canadian-Icelanders.

the poetry of some, and still others are thoroughly in the tradition of the unschooled poets. In varying degrees, these poets have selected themes from their new environment and have been stimulated, not to say influenced, by cultural and literary currents in the adopted country. In that fashion the old and the new meet and mingle in their poetry and, since it is written in the Icelandic language, make it all the more noteworthy as a contribution to Icelandic literature. That is, of course, particularly true of such poets as Stephan G. Stephansson and Guttormur J. Guttormsson, who have pictured their Canadian surroundings and interpreted their experiences of the pioneer life most extensively and penetratingly.

1. Sigurbjőrn Jóhannsson was born at Breiðumýri in Suður-Þingeyjarsýsla in northern Iceland on December 24, 1839. He emigrated to Canada in 1889 and settled on a farm in Argyle, Manitoba. He died in 1903. He was the father of the poetess Jakobína Johnson (see below).[2]

Self-educated, Sigurbjőrn Jóhannsson was already a man of fifty when he left his native Iceland and was as a result thoroughly in the tradition of the Icelandic unschooled poets in themes, spirit, and fluent metrical skill. Much of his poetry was written in Iceland, where he had won a reputation for his ready versemaking ability; the rest of his poems are from his later years in Canada. An extensive selection was published in *Ljóðmæli* (Poems; Winnipeg, 1902), consisting largely of various occasional poems; it is characteristically Icelandic in containing many rhymed letters and *hestavísur*, verses in praise of horses, together with a large number of quatrains, in which the poet is often at his best. On the other hand, some of these poems and epigrams deal with pioneer life in Canada. Among the personal poems, the opening one, "Til landa minna" (To My Countrymen), addressed to his prospective readers, is the most significant, not least because of the honest portrayal of the poet's life and the adverse conditions under which he labored and wrote his poems.

Other poets of the older generation, who were also overwhelmingly

---

[2] For information about him and his poetry, see Guðmundur Friðjónsson, "Tveir Þingeyingar," *Tímarit Þjóðræknisfélags Íslendinga í Vesturheimi*, VIII (1926), 21–25; Sigurður S. Christophersson, "Skáldið Sigurbjőrn Jóhannsson, endurminningar," *Almanak Ó. S. Thorgeirssonar*, LIIII (1948), 36–40.

in the native Icelandic tradition, deserve to be mentioned. EYJÓLFUR EYJÓLFSSON WÍUM (1855–1931) is especially remembered for his impressive and deeply felt tribute to Iceland, "Minni Íslands," antiquated in mood and thoroughly Icelandic in language and verse-form. BALDVIN HALLDÓRSSON (1861–1934) was a master of the traditional quatrain, which has, of course, been the effective medium of many other American-Icelandic poets. The *rímur* poetry has had its representative in NIKULÁS OTTENSON (b. 1867), who in his *Minni Nýja Íslands* (A Toast to New Iceland; Winnipeg, 1934) records in characteristic Icelandic fashion the names of Icelandic lake captains in New Iceland in Manitoba; the book is, however, far more noteworthy for its historical value, and as a literary curiosity, than for its poetic quality. Among the women of the pioneer generation, ÚNDÍNA, pen name of HELGA S. BALDVINSDÓTTIR (1858–1941), attracted attention with her highly personal poems in American-Icelandic publications.

2. STEPHAN G. STEPHANSSON was born on October 3, 1853, at Kirkjuhóll, a small farm in Skagafjőrður in northern Iceland; his birthplace has since been abandoned, as have the two other small farms in the neighborhood where he spent his youth. His last three years in Iceland he worked as a farm hand at Mjóidalur, farthest upland in the Bárðardalur district in the northeast. His parents, though poor, possessed both intellectual alertness and cultural appreciation. Literary interest and marked poetic talent had also characterized his forebears, and on his father's side he was related to the poet Benedikt Grőndal (the Elder).

In 1873, at the age of nineteen, Stephansson emigrated with his parents and other kinsfolk to America. Three times he became a pioneer; first, after working for a year as a day laborer near Milwaukee, he went to Shawano County, Wisconsin; again, after 1880, to Pembina County, North Dakota; lastly, in 1889 he settled permanently in Alberta, Canada, near the village of Markerville.[3] His

[3] Concerning his life, see also his autobiographical sketch "Stephan G. Stephansson: Drőg til ævisőgu," *Andvari*, LXXII (1947), 3–25; and Baldur Sveinsson. "Stephan G. Stephansson sjőtugur," *Iðunn*, VIII (1923), 4–21. Concerning his literary career and poetry, see Guðmundur Friðjónsson, "Stephan G. Stephansson," *Skírnir*, LXXXI (1907), 193–209, 289–314, and "Lífsskoðun Stephans G. Stephanssonar," *Skírnir*, LXXXVI (1912), 44–63; Ágúst H. Bjarnason, "Skáldið

participation in the development of that frontier community, as well as his attitude toward his adopted country, are well described as follows:

With this district he identified himself for the rest of his life. He came to it a man of thirty-six, in the prime of his strength, with a family of little ones about his knees. Here, too, he died on August 19, 1927, a white-haired veteran of seventy-four, with a rich life-record behind him. He was one of the first organizers of the Markerville school-district; he took an active part in every community enterprise; and he contributed generously out of his poverty in aid of every good cause. He considered himself categorically a Canadian, but in his heart he linked up that allegiance with an unfailing affection for the far-off island of his birth.[4]

As his poems abundantly reveal, Stephansson became deeply attached to his new neighborhood and has immortalized its scenic beauty, in all its seasonal variety, in some of his most beautiful and inspired poems.

He began writing poetry at a very early age; the oldest poems in his collected edition are from the years 1868–1869; his first published poem, a farewell to Iceland, appeared in the paper *Norðanfari* at Akureyri, August 9, 1873. After 1890 his poems appeared regularly in the Icelandic weeklies and periodicals in Winnipeg. His first collection of poems, *Úti á víðavangi* (Out in the Open Air), was published in Winnipeg in 1894; it is a slight book, but contains, in the original form, such splendid poems as "Greniskógurinn" (The Spruce Forest). In 1900 his important cycle of poems, *Á ferð og*

Stephan G. Stephansson," *Iðunn*, II (1916–17), 356–378; "Heimför Stephans G. Stephanssonar skálds 1917," *Almanak Ó. S. Thorgeirssonar*, XXIV (1918), 21–59; Jóhannes P. Pálsson, "Stephan G. Stephansson: Nokkur orð um skáldið og manninn," and Jóhann M. Bjarnason, "Endurminning um Stephan G. Stephansson," *Tímarit Þjóðræknisfélags Íslendinga í Vesturheimi*, IX (1927), 37–45, 46–51; Sigurður Nordal, "En isländsk bondeskald: Stephan G. Stephansson," *Bygd och folk*, (Stockholm, 1929), Vol. II (an Icelandic translation, "*Alþýðuskáldið*," by Benjamín Kristjánsson appeared in *Tímarit Þjóðræknisfélags Íslendinga í Vesturheimi*, XIII [1931], 52–58); Jónas Þorbergsson, "Stephan G. Stephansson," *Iðunn*, XVIII (1934), 161–177; F. Stanton Cawley, "The Greatest Poet of the Western World: Stephan G. Stephansson," *Scandinavian Studies and Notes*, *XV* (1938), 99–109; Jón Magnússon, "Andvökur hinar nýju," *Eimreiðin*, XLVI (1940), 212–224.

[4] Watson Kirkconnell, "Canada's Leading Poet, Stephan G. Stephansson: 1853–1927," *University of Toronto Quarterly*, V (1936), 264–265.

flugi (En Route), was printed in Reykjavík. The three first volumes of his collected edition, *Andvökur*, were published in Reykjavík, 1909–1910; volumes IV to V in Winnipeg, 1923; and volume VI in Reykjavík in 1938, with a preface by his literary executor, the Reverend Rögnvaldur Pétursson of Winnipeg. Three more special publications of his poetry remain to be listed: *Kolbeinslag* (The Lay of Kolbeinn; Winnipeg, 1914), a historical poem on a sixteenth-century folklore theme; *Heimleiðis* (Homeward Bound; Reykjavik, 1917), a group of poems inspired by his triumphal visit to Iceland in 1917 as guest of the nation; and *Vígslóði* (The War Trail; Reykjavík, 1920), a cycle of poems on the First World War, strongly pacifistic. An extensive selection from his poems, *Andvökur* (*Úrval*; Reykjavík, 1939), was edited with a detailed introductory evaluation of the man and the poet by Sigurður Nordal; and a smaller selected edition, *Úrvalsljóð* (Reykjavik, 1948), was edited by the poetess Hulda. His works in prose, including the large and significant collection of his letters and articles, *Bréf og ritgerðir* (Reykjavík, 1938–1948), have been dealt with in the history of the prose writers of the period.

A hard-working farmer, who had his full share of the struggles and griefs of the pioneer life, and the supporter of a large family, Stephansson, nevertheless, succeeded in becoming one of the most prolific as well as one of the greatest poets Iceland ever produced; although vastly different, he may be ranked with such giants as Matthías Jochumsson and Einar Benediktsson, his most illustrious contemporaries. Considering the conditions under which Stephansson did his writing, his literary achievements are astounding; they presuppose unusual genius, irrepressible creative urge, and an untiring devotion to the poetic art. The title of his six-volume work, *Andvökur*, tells the story. *Andvökur* means "wakeful, or sleepless nights." These poems, filling some 1,800 pages, are the result of labor while others slept; hours of rest were sacrificed to the expression of that rare creative power that long days of hard toil only strengthened and awakened more fully.

Stephansson's productivity, great as it was, is not, however, the most amazing thing about him; the range and variety of his themes are no less impressive—his sweep, wide horizon, and great store of knowledge. All this becomes most remarkable in the light of the fact that the poet never had any formal education, his schooling in Iceland having been most elementary. He was primarily self-taught, and through selective reading continued his self-instruction in language and literature all his life. The sagas, which he had read as a youth in Iceland and retained firmly in his memory, were a particularly fruitful source of information and inspiration to him. "As he matured intellectually, incidents from the Eddas, sagas and legends, appeared to him in a new light, more penetratingly understood, and became themes for his poems."[5] He also quotes the Scriptures, draws upon Oriental lore, and frequently reveals his acquaintance with the works of other poets, foreign and Icelandic. Professor Kirkconnell's sympathetic visualization of the great poet-pioneer engaged in his creative literary pursuits is worth reproducing:

> The Stephansson farm-house was probably unique in Alberta in having a separate room devoted solely to its master's studies and poetic labor. By evening lamp-light in that snug sanctum, after the day's farm tasks were done and he had washed and changed his clothes, he would sit at his table far into the night, blissfully unaware of the passage of time as he wrought with the materials of his poetic art. His beloved books were at his elbow, and all the ages were brought to one imaginative focus of experience as he lived through another instalment of creative exaltation. In the earlier log-cabin years, however, this studious privacy was not available; and some of his best poems were even composed in the railway construction camps where he sometimes toiled in order to enable the family to survive stark poverty.[6]

In the foregoing account of Icelandic poetry, consideration has been given to a number of Icelandic farmers who, in the face of the most adverse circumstances, succeeded through tireless perseverance not only in attaining a high level of self-education but also in making a significant contribution to the literature of their country. All things considered, Dr. Sigurður Nordal is no doubt right in his contention that Stephan G. Stephansson is the most remarkable example of Icelandic poet-farmers, not only because of his vast and unique literary production, but even more because he had to overcome

[5] Sigurður Nordal, introduction to his edition of *Andvökur* (1939), p. xxxviii.
[6] *Op. cit.*, p. 271.

greater difficulties than any of his brother poets within the farmer class.[7] And he succeeded admirably in resolving the clash between the insistent demands of his daily duties, which he never shirked, and the creative poetic urge within him; in other words, he rendered unto Caesar what was Caesar's and unto God what was God's. Of course, the conflict was not achieved without a prolonged and hard inner struggle, revealed in his poem "Afmælisgjőfin" (The Birthday Gift), in which he lays bare his soul in an imaginary exchange of words with the Goddess of Poetry, who reproaches him for having neglected her because of his devotion to his daily tasks. The greatness of the poet is seen not only in how well—with great sacrifice—he succeeded in solving the conflict between his creative urge and his daily work, but no less in how he elevates those tasks by his genius, making them a source for his spiritual strength and the wings of his soul, in that he translates those everyday experiences into poetry of high imaginative and intellectual quality.

As already indicated, Stephansson spent all his mature years away from his native land, but he was linked to it and its cultural traditions with unbreakable bonds. Iceland always remained for him both "Mother and land of memories," and he has recorded his deep affection in some of his most excellent poems. His profound attachment to the native soil was deepened by his long sojourn in another land, and this made him still more conscious of the close kinship between the motherland and its children everywhere. That feeling is forcefully and memorably expressed in a noble tribute to Iceland ("Úr Íslendingadags ræðu"), his most widely known poem, the opening lines of which may be translated: "Though you travel all over the world, your thoughts and your dreams bear the stamp of your homeland"; and in graphic and original word pictures he goes on to illuminate the spiritual kinship of the sons and daughters of Iceland to the characteristic and most impressive scenic features of their native land. Nowhere, however, is the warmth of affection greater than in his poem "Ástavísur til Íslands" (Love Verses to Iceland). Bathed in the glory of the midnight sun, the country rises before his poetic vision, and in the true spirit of a devoted son offering a heart-

[7] *Op. cit.*, p. xvii.

felt homage to a beloved mother, he closes by expressing the hope (this was written in 1894) that:

> Whate'er thou, my fatherland, hearest of me
> Shall add to thy glory—I truly loved thee!

In this magnificent poem are also found the much-quoted lines, addressed to Iceland, "Your antiquity and sagas dwell in my heart," as indeed they did, without exaggeration.

With his native tongue, he had brought to the new land his knowledge of the history of Iceland and its sagas, which he had enshrined in his memory in his youth and which were to bear such a rich fruit in his poetry. He found in the old Icelandic literature and in other Icelandic lore themes for some of his most powerful and original poems, interpreting them in such a fashion that they take on symbolic and universal significance. This is well illustrated in his "Illugadrápa," about Illugi, the faithful and heroic brother of Grettir the Strong, and in "Hergilseyjarbóndinn" (The Farmer at Hergilsey), about the brave protector of Gísli Súrsson. In subject matter these poems are also characteristic; he chose those men and women from ancient days who embody the spirit of heroism and independence, courageously face great odds without flinching, and remain true to their best selves. Moreover, he effectively related his historical themes to his own day. He was of both the past and the present, heeding his own admonition: "Be a friend of the evening sun and a son of the dawn."

Much as he loved his native land and was steeped in its literary tradition, he also struck roots in the soil of his adopted country, Canada, and paid it an affectionate and sincere tribute in such poems as "Minni Alberta" (Toast to Alberta). For public occasions, he provided poems of characteristic vigor and originality.

He has, however, done much more. Always living close to Mother Earth and gifted with great insight, a sensitive ear, and a keen eye, he wrote numerous nature poems rich in colorful detail and profound thought. Here as nowhere else does his fertile and vivid imagination find a striking expression, particularly in his graphic and charming pictures of Alberta, its moods changing with the shifting seasons. His immediate surroundings, in such poems as "Sveitin mín" (My Home District) and "Sumarkvőld í Alberta" (A Summer Evening in

Alberta), and the distant Rockies towering in all their grandeur he portrays with great sweep and magnificence of pictorial quality. "No other Canadian poet in any language presents a comparable picture of Western Canada," declares Watson Kirkconnell.[8]

Stephansson's descriptive and interpretative ability is seen at its best in his cycle of poems, *Á ferð og flugi*, in which he rolls up a series of unforgettable pictures of the prairie and of pioneer life, which he himself had experienced in such a full measure; interwoven with the lifelike and authentic description are striking similes from Old Norse mythology.

His deep human interest and sympathy also find memorable expression in this series of poems and are summed up in the well-known lines in which he says that he harbors a brotherly feeling toward foreign lands, but the soil that shelters the remains of an Icelander tugs at his heartstrings. Naturally, a man so sensitive and whole-souled felt himself linked with strong bonds to his fellow travelers on the pathway of life, not least old friends and neighbors; he was, therefore, deeply moved by their passing and said farewell to many of them in notable memorial poems, such as "Helga-erfi" (Helgi's Memorial), about his friend Helgi Stefánsson, brother of the author Jón Stefánsson (Þorgils Gjallandi). Here the poet's ideal of manliness is forcefully expressed; the poem is, as a matter of fact, a truthful characterization of the author himself. Especially significant is his poem in memory of André Courmont, a French scholar, for whom Iceland had become a second homeland and who had interpreted some of its ancient literature with rare penetration. Such a man, of course, appealed strongly to Stephansson, as did Willard Fiske, the great friend and benefactor of Iceland, to whom he paid glowing tribute in a splendid poem.

Much as Stephansson detested sentimentality, the warmth of his affection for his friends and others whom he admired is unmistakable in his memorials and in other poems about them. Especially tender are his poems about his son Gestur, who died young, and his poem "Kurlý," about a six-year-old curly-headed youngster who became very fond of him while he was working on her father's farm during his first year in Wisconsin.

[8] *Op. cit.*, p. 272.

More general in theme, but penetrating and revealing the poet's philosophy of life, is the poem "Bræðrabýti" (The Brothers' Destiny), symbolically contrasting two brothers. One perishes in the search for gold whose discovery becomes a curse; the second one, a tiller of the soil, is dedicated to fruitful labor for coming generations and exemplifies the poet's teaching: "Not to think in years but ages, not to demand in full at day's end the wages earned." That idealism and progressive spirit are strikingly expressed in the closing lines of this remarkable poem: "The world which the seer visualizes is not his own age, unduly glorified, but a better and happier future."

Such was the poet's vision, which stemmed from his unusual human interest, so deep-rooted that even his nature descriptions and historical poems reflect his reactions to contemporary problems. He was endowed with a deep sense of justice and keen understanding of what constituted true human worth, greatness, and nobility of soul. He had likewise an uncommonly rich sympathy for his fellow man, not least the weak and the downtrodden. In numerous social satires he pours out his condemnation of capitalistic exploitation and the unfair distribution of wealth with its resultant evils, and takes his stand squarely with the laboring class, considering himself at heart a socialist; in his interpretation of his liberal and leftist social views he goes far beyond the level of mere materialism. As a self-dependent pioneer farmer, he remained a thoroughgoing individualist and was too independent in his thinking to join any political group, as he explicitly states in his letters.

His interest and sympathies were world-wide, and frequently he found inspiration, or rather challenge that could not go unanswered, in current events. In "Transvaal," dealing with the Boer War, and one of his greatest poems, he mercilessly flays Great Britain and pleads the cause of the Boers, aligning himself as always with the suffering and the oppressed. He is thus a cosmopolitan of the noblest kind and, therefore, a genuine lover of peace. "The sword cuts all heart bonds" is a fundamental part of his creed. This firm conviction and his abhorrence of war he expressed fearlessly and forcefully in *Vígslóði* (The War Trail), his impassioned reaction to the First World War. In this cycle of poems, especially in the poem "Vopnahlé" (The Truce), he describes and denounces with stark realism the horrors of modern warfare and condemns the leaders on both sides. This outspoken poem is not free from extremes and at the time made the poet very unpopular among his Icelandic countrymen in America, but he lived long enough to regain his former popularity. Most certainly the poem did not in the long run detract from his poetic reputation.

Stephansson was as radical in his religious views as in his attitude toward social problems; he opposed and attacked reaction, narrow-mindedness, and hypocrisy and was in that sense antichurch and anticlerical. At the same time he was sympathetic toward the more liberal movements, such as Unitarianism, and it is, therefore, natural that he wrote a memorial poem on Robert G. Ingersoll. His radical religious views naturally aroused opposition and made him unpopular in some quarters, but he was never one to compromise in his convictions.

On the other hand, in his poem "Eloi lamma sabakhthani" (O Lord, Why Hast Thou Forsaken Me) his love of truth, his profound understanding of the teaching of the Master from Nazareth, and his undying idealism find beautiful and heart-warming expression. In that faith in the future and the ultimate victory of truth and justice, penetratingly revealed in his poem "Kveld" (Evening) and his later great poem "Martius," he lived and labored to the last.

Masculine quality and rugged intellectuality, together with deep though often restrained emotional power, are fundamental characteristics of Stephansson's poetry; but he also possesses the genuine lyric touch in such poems as "Við verkalok" (At Close of Day), light in tone and mellow in mood. Nevertheless, his poems are often, as he himself recognized, roughhewn in form and heavy in style, both because he primarily stresses thought content and originality and because he did not have the leisure to polish them. At the same time, the variety of his verse forms is very great and matches the range of his themes; and his mastery of his native tongue and his wealth of language are amazing. He has been accused of obscurity; assuredly, it demands mental effort to follow his thought, but a serious attempt to do so usually more than repays the trouble.

Stephansson was therefore a pioneer thinker and poet no less than a pioneer farmer. Through the introduction of new words and new verse forms, and the extensive use of new themes, he has enriched the Icelandic language immensely. He was born to the great cultural heritage of the saga land, personified that inheritance in a rare degree, and was endowed by nature with surpassing genius. At the same time, it was his good fortune to live and work in the midst of a civilization richer and more varied than that of his native land. His poetry is the greater for it; it bears the stamp of universality.

He is not only one of the greatest Icelandic poets but also one of the greatest Canadian poets; in fact, Professor Kirkconnell considers him Canada's leading poet; and Professor F. S. Cawley goes so far as to call him "The greatest Poet of the Western World" and categorically states that he considers him "greater than Poe, Whitman, or even Emerson."[9] Both men, it may be added, had read his poems in the original and therefore based their estimates on first-hand information.

At any rate, no one can read Stephansson's poetry thoughtfully and intensively without coming to recognize the greatness of the man as well as of the poet. He is a singular and inspiring example of the fact "that the human spirit in its highest manifestations can rise above material circumstances, can make them fall into their rightful place of unimportant accessories in the thrilling adventure which men call life."[10]

3. Kristinn Stefánsson was born on July 9, 1856, at Egilsá in Skagafjarðarsýsla in northern Iceland. He was among the earliest Icelandic emigrants, one of the large group (some two hundred), that left the northern part of the country for Canada in the spring of 1873. After first settling in Ontario, he moved to Winnipeg in 1881. Here he made his home most of the time until his death on September 26, 1916. A carpenter by trade, he was entirely self-educated, but was widely read in English, American, and Scandinavian literatures.

All his poems (or at any rate those in print) were written in America. The earliest was in *Framfari*, the first Icelandic paper published on the American continent. His first collection of poems, *Vestan hafs* (West of the Ocean), was published in Reykjavík in 1900. It is a small book, but contains some pretty nature poems and many excellent epigrams. However, few of his more notable poems are to be

[9] In his article by that title, *Scandinavian Studies and Notes*, XV (1938), 101.

[10] F. Stanton Cawley, *op. cit.*, p. 105.

found here. He was still to attain greater maturity and undertake larger themes in his later book, *Út um vötn og velli* (From Lake and Prairie; Winnipeg, 1916), published and edited by Rögnvaldur Pétursson and Gísli Jónsson, with a biographical sketch of the poet written by the former. The author himself had prepared many of the poems for publication, but did not live to complete that task. This book contains most of his poems and all of his best ones.

His fine command of his native tongue, his great metrical skill, and his keen powers of observation are here more clearly seen than in his promising earlier poems. His nature descriptions are generally original, vigorous, and rich in pictorial quality and are excellently illustrated in "Vorsins dís" (The Goddess of Spring), in which the personification of spring as a beautiful woman is particularly effective, in "Sumarkvöld við vatnið" (Summer Evening by the Lake), and in "Raddir" (Voices), in which the contemplative element is intimately interwoven with the description. This combination is characteristic of the author, for there is a deep undercurrent of seriousness in many of his poems.

The two elements, the descriptive and the contemplative, are perhaps nowhere more strikingly entwined and expressed than in his poem "Gamla húsið" (The Old House). The weathered and neglected condition of the house, graphically portrayed by the poet, causes him to ponder sadly upon past events and friends associated with the house and calls forth a denunciation of man's greed and materialism. And the denunciation, too, is characteristic of the poet; his interest in social reform can be seen in other impressive and penetrating poems. His satirical darts, such as his scathing indictment of hypocrisy and superficiality in the highly ironical poems "Kurteisi" (Politeness) and "Lygi" (Falsehood), do not miss their mark. His human sympathy is, however, equally evident elsewhere in his poems. The wide spiritual horizon—freedom and progress—is dear to his heart. It is characteristic that he eulogizes such poets as Swinburne, Shelley, Björnson, Ibsen and Þorsteinn Erlingsson, as well as Jón Sigurðsson, the great leader in the Icelandic struggle for independence. They were his men, freedom-loving and fearlessly progressive.

However, much as he admired these and other non-Icelandic poets and much as he may have been influenced by some of them, he was at the same time profoundly Icelandic. He excelled in the traditional quatrain, in both individual verses and longer poems. He pays glowing tribute to such older Icelandic poets of his generation as Steingrímur Thorsteinsson. Kristinn Stefánsson's love of his native land also frequently finds expression in his poetry and, in his poem "Canada," mingles harmoniously with his deep devotion to his adopted country. In short, strongly rooted as he was in the Icelandic soil and literary tradition, his horizon had been widened and his experience greatly enriched by his life in the new and larger world where he spent his mature years.

4. Jón Runólfsson was born at Gilsárteigur in Suður-Múlasýsla in eastern Iceland on September 1, 1856, and grew up in that vicinity. On both sides he came of well-known families. He emigrated to Minneota, Minnesota, in 1879, and four years later moved to Winnipeg. His limited schooling he supplemented with extensive reading in Icelandic and foreign literatures, and he early became a public-school teacher among the Icelandic colonists in Manitoba. This profession he followed throughout most of his life. He visited Iceland in 1903 and 1913, spending almost a year in Reykjavík during his second visit. He died in Manitoba on September 12, 1930.[11]

His original production was not extensive, because of circumstances unfavorable to literary pursuits, rigid self-criticism, and the fact that, according to good authorities, some of his poems were lost in manuscript. Nearly all of those preserved are included in his collection *Þögul leiftur* (Silent Flashes; Winnipeg, 1924); this is a striking title, for these poems are calm in mood and unostentatious, but frequently contain "silent flashes" of genuine poetry. There is in them no roar or rushing waters, but rather the quiet murmur of the flowing mountain springs of his native land. One of his most beautiful poems is "Mig heilla þær hægstrauma lindir" (The Soft-Flowing Springs Enchant Me). This and all his best poems are lyrical and personal, clearly the outburst of an inner urge; the poet's heart beats in them and they mirror his experiences, often bitter, sorrowful, and melancholy.

---

[11] For his life and literary career, see also J. Magnús Bjarnason, "Jón Runólfsson skáld," *Óðinn*, XXV (1929), 23–26; Richard Beck, "Skáldið Jón Runólfsson," *Tímarit Þjóðræknisfélags Íslendinga í Vesturheimi*, XX (1938), 92–100.

"Hillingar á Sahara" (Fata Morgana) is probably his finest poem, concentrated and symbolic not only of the poet's own futile search for happiness but also of the similar fate of all humankind. And he himself, a lonely man in need of understanding, had a deep sympathetic feeling for other stepchildren of fortune. He writes one of his most touching poems about the seaman's wife, alone at home with her children, whose heart fears for her husband out on the stormy ocean. The poet's sympathy extends to the animals and even farther, as he writes a deep-felt poem, "Frostnótt" (Night of Frost), about the leaf bud that the hoarfrost has given the kiss of death, while the flowers and other plants flourish all around. The lyric "Sefýrus" is addressed to his native Iceland, which has not received many greetings more tender or warm-hearted. While his poems are generally serious in theme and melancholy in mood, he occasionally strikes a lighter humorous note very successfully.

He had splendid command of the Icelandic language and verse forms and was painstaking in his selection of both diction and meter. On the whole he also succeeded very well in harmonizing theme and metrical form. He would not have been a successful translator had he not possessed mastery of language, metrical skill, and sensitiveness to beauty. Almost half of his book consists of translations of choice poems and hymns from Scandinavian, English, Canadian, and American literature, always faithfully rendered, often excellently, as "Bergmanden" by Ibsen and "The Dream of Pilate's Wife" by Edwin Markham. But the artistic level of his translations is nowhere uniformly higher than in his renditions from Tennyson, such as "Home They Brought Him" and "Flower in the Crannied Wall," and in "Enoch Arden," his major translation and the fruit of several years, effectively rendered both in language and spirit. It is not unlikely that the great poet laureate influenced Jón Runólfsson to the extent of stimulating his literary taste and sharpening his critical faculty. He also translated several famous hymns, some of them masterfully, such as Cardinal Newman's "Lead, Kindly Light," R. Heber's "From Greenland's Icy Mountains," and N. F. S. Grundtvig's "Paaskemorgen"; the third, combining rich inspiration and eloquence, has not lost any of its ecstasy and sonorousness in the translations. Some of these translations have found their place in the

Icelandic hymnal on both sides of the Atlantic. Considered as a whole, Jón Runólfsson's translations would have sufficed to ensure him a place as a poet of more than ordinary merit.

5. Magnús Markússon was born on November 27, 1858 at Hafsteinsstaðir in Skagafjőrður in northern Iceland and grew up in that neighborhood. He emigrated to America in 1886 and made his home in Winnipeg, where he died on October 20, 1948. He was for years in the Canadian Immigration Service and also engaged in real-estate and insurance business. In his younger days he was a prominent athlete. Like most of his fellow American-Icelandic poets, he was self-educated.[12]

He published two books of poems, *Ljóðmæli* (Poems; Winnipeg, 1907) and *Hljómbrot* (Fragments of Melody; Winnipeg, 1924). In his earlier book there are a number of beautiful and melodious poems, such as his warm tribute to his native Skagafjőrður, as well as a deep-felt homage to his mother. This first collection reveals his principal characteristics: musical quality, lightness of touch, smoothness, and fluency. His metrical skill was unusual and his sense of form never failed him; versemaking obviously came very naturally to him. These qualities also mark his second book, in such lyrics as "Bjőrkin" (The Birch), "Harpan mín" (My Harp), and "Ljóðdísin" (The Goddess of Poetry). In both volumes there are many occasional poems in the same lyrical vein.

Elevation of thought and strong moral and religious feeling characterize many of his poems, revealing his deep faith and ingrained idealism. On the other hand, his poetry is neither particularly original nor vigorous. He is Icelandic to the core, spiritually akin to the older Icelandic poets, who have visibly influenced him, not least Matthías Jochumsson.

After the publication of Magnús Markússon's books, a large number of his poems, similar in theme, spirit, and quality, appeared in the American-Icelandic weeklies and elsewhere. To a remarkable degree he retained his mental vigor and his poetic faculty in mastery

[12] Concerning his life and literary career, see further Einar P. Jónsson, "Aldursforseti íslenzkra skálda vestan hafs," *Tímarit Þjóðræknisfélags Íslendinga í Vesturheimi*, XXVII (1946), 32–33; Richard Beck, "Magnús Markússon skáld," *Almanak Ó. S. Thorgeirssonar*, LV (1949), 21–27.

of both form and language until his dying day; in fact, some of his last poems are among his best efforts, such as "Kári í Brennu Njáls" (Kári at Njál's Burning) and "Sumardagur 1945" (A Summer Day 1945). The subject matter of these two poems—an Icelandic historical theme and a nature description—is very characteristic of him.

His many generous poems addressed to his contemporaries were inspired by his warm human interest, and his patriotic poems are eloquent evidence of his filial devotion to the motherland, in which he, though a good Canadian, took great pride and whose welfare was always close to his heart.

6. ÞORSKABÍTUR, pen name for ÞORBJÖRN BJARNARSON, was born at Írafell in the Kjós district in southern Iceland on August 29, 1859, but he lived in Reykholtsdalur in the south almost without interruption until he emigrated to Canada in 1893. After a four-year stay in Winnipeg, he moved to Pembina, North Dakota, where he resided until his death, on February 7, 1933. He was a manual laborer and entirely self-educated, but well and widely read and possessed of great intellectual curiosity and a mind unusually receptive to new ideas.[13]

Only one collection of his poems was published, *Nokkur ljóðmæli* (A Handful of Poems; Winnipeg, 1914), but later many splendid poems, including a long and notable poem on Bólu-Hjálmar, were published in American-Icelandic papers and periodicals.

Þorskabítur was a gifted poet, a skillful master of form and of choice and sonorous language and, at his best, highly eloquent and inspired. His similes are striking; he paints colorful word pictures as sharp as if they were etched in stone, as in his patriotic poems, like "Ísland" (Iceland), the opening poem in the collection, and numerous others in similar vein. The same skill is evident in his eloquent tribute to the beloved Borgarfjörður and in his impressive description of Eiríksjökull, which towers majestically over the region. He was well versed in the history of Iceland and Icelandic lore, and into these nature descriptions he weaves vivid glimpses of historical events that took place in the district.

[13] For further information about his life and literary career, see Richard Beck, "Skáldið Þorbjörn Bjarnarson (Þorskabítur)" *Tímarit Þjóðræknisfélags Íslendinga í Vesturheimi,* XV (1933), 49–65.

The pictorial element and the emotional quality are also seen in his gentle spring poems. Clearly, the poet loves the beauty of nature both on land and sea, and he finds in it both consolation for his tired soul and renewed spiritual strength.

Bitter disappointments and poverty had been his lot, and when he contemplated the similar fate of others about him, his sense of justice and human sympathy found an outlet in forceful social satires. He was, in this sense, spiritually akin to Þorsteinn Erlingsson; both were whole-hearted socialists. On the other hand, in his satirical epigrams containing philosophical observations, Þorskabítur resembles Steingrímur Thorsteinsson, whom he greatly admired. Many of his poems are, as a matter of fact, philosophical and religious in theme. He was just as critical of the shortcomings and the worldliness of the established church as he was of the social order, and he went his own way in religious matters. Conversely, his deep reverence for the Master of Nazareth and his teaching of brotherly love are revealed in the beautiful poem "Fjallræðan" (The Sermon on the Mount) from his later years. Elsewhere in his poems, especially in "Lofsőngur heiðingjans" (The Pagan's Hymn of Praise), also from his later years, his pantheism finds eloquent expression.

Among his numerous and uneven occasional poems, the one on the poet Bólu-Hjálmar is the most impressive and significant—sonorous, fraught with thought, and rich in sympathetic understanding.

Þorskabítur's poems are thoroughly Icelandic in spirit and theme, revealing scarcely any influence from non-Icelandic sources. His spiritual kinship was with the older Icelandic poets, and his love for Iceland and Icelandic cultural values is a fundamental note in his poetry.

7. K. N., pen name for Kristján Níels Júlíus, was born at Akureyri in northern Iceland on April 7, 1860. The son of a blacksmith, he came from families in which the poetic talent had been very common. His father Jón possessed versemaking ability and was the nephew of the well-known versifier Níels "Skáldi," for whom K. N. was named. His mother was a near relative of Jónas Hallgrímsson, the poet. K. N. grew up at Akureyri and in its vicinity in the beautiful district of Eyjafjőrður, which left its mark upon him; fond memories of the haunts of his youth are frequently seen in

his poetry. He emigrated to America in 1878, among the early Icelandic newcomers, and first made his home in Winnipeg. For some years he lived in Duluth, Minnesota, but he spent most of his last fifty years in the Icelandic settlement in Pembina County, North Dakota. This beautiful and historical settlement the poet came to cherish greatly, and he commemorated its fiftieth anniversary in a fine poem done in his characteristically humorous vein.

Both in themes and language, his poetry reflects the environment in which for decades he "moved and had his being." Lifelong he earned his living by manual labor, farm work, and the like, and his poems and verses attest his intimate knowledge of wheat threshing and other agricultural labor. They also reveal his close association with domestic animals; the cows and the cow barn are in particular a favorite theme for humorous and sometimes whimsically philosophical observations. For he had the rare ability of transforming the humblest and apparently most insignificant themes into uniquely humorous verses or into serious or semiserious poetry of universal application. Self-educated beyond the schooling received in rural Iceland, he was widely read in Icelandic literature and also had considerable knowledge of American and English poetry. He never visited his native land after he emigrated, much as he loved it; he would have been a welcome guest, as he enjoyed as great popularity there as among his countrymen in America. He died at his home in North Dakota on October 25, 1936.[14]

K. N.'s versemaking ability very early revealed itself, and his faculty for extemporizing was amazing, according to his intimates. At the time of his death he had for more than half a century entertained his countrymen on both sides of the Atlantic with his strikingly humorous verses. He was not only the greatest and most unusual humorist among the Icelanders in America; he was also without a peer among contemporary poets in the homeland.

A collection of his verses and poems, which previously had been

---

[14] Concerning his life and poetry, see also Jón Helgason, "Vestur-islenzkt alþýðuskáld (Kr. Júlíus)," *Iðunn*, I (1915–16), 177–185; John G. Holme, "Iceland's Younger Choir," *American-Scandinavian Review*, X (1922), 550–553; Sigurður Nordal, "K. N.," *Dvöl*, IV (1936), 346–351; Richard Beck, "Skáldið Kristján N. Júlíus (K. N.)," *Samtíðin*, IV (1937), 10–14, 18–23, V (1938), 20–25.

published in the American-Icelandic weeklies and elsewhere, *Kviðlingar* (Ditties), appeared in Winnipeg in 1920, with a preface by Wilhelm Paulson. A definitive edition of his works, *Kviðlingar og kvæði* (Ditties and Poems; Reykjavík, 1945), was edited with a biographical introduction by Richard Beck and included reminiscences of the poet by the Reverend Haraldur Sigmar, a long-time friend and for years the pastor of the Icelandic congregations in Pembina County.

K. N.'s sparkling and infectious humor consists primarily in an original and versatile play on words. He had an uncanny ability to cast new light on things, not least through brilliant use of anticlimax and the unexpected ending. Local individuals and happenings are largely the targets of his humor, although he occasionally goes farther afield. Generally, his whimsical humorous sallies are good-natured, arousing laughter rather than leaving a lasting sting, and pleasing by their unfailing linguistic skill; but sometimes his swift rapier thrusts are biting in their sarcasm. His fondness for Bacchus was well known and is reflected in many of his verses; Prohibition was a thorn in his side.

His humor had a salutary educational value, because genuine humor, after all, is rooted in a highly developed sense of proportion. By holding the mirror up to people he made them see themselves and life generally in a truer light. In a broader sense his satire was directed at narrow-mindedness, folly and superstition, hypocrisy and superficiality. He was, however, human enough, and one of his most attractive qualities was his delight in making fun of himself on occasion. And underneath his humor and satire runs a deep sympathy and very often profound seriousness. His long journey through life, often hard, had taught him to sympathize with the weak and the unfortunate; and as he said himself he was much more akin to the prodigal son than to the rich man. His fondness for children was exceptional and finds expression in some of his finest verses. Tenderly he shared the sorrows of his friends and commemorated them affectionately in obituary poems. These and other of his longer poems are often noteworthy, or at any rate contain splendid passages.

But as a rule his most characteristic and best efforts are his epigrams and his shorter poems. One is the inimitable "Ævintýri á gőngufőr" (Tale of the Wayside), celebrating one of his frequent jousts with Bacchus; for a time the poet had to bite the dust, but finally emerged victorious, or as he himself puts it (in Dr. G. J. Gíslason's translation):

At last my feet grew stronger, my eyes began to see,
And Satan lost a sheep he would'st devour;
And thus it has been proven on Lazarus and me,
That life surpasses death in strength and power.[15]

While the poet had deep roots in the Icelandic cultural soil and literary tradition, his kinship with the unschooled poets being especially close, he was also the product of his American environment, both in his themes from daily life and in his use of American words and phrases from everyday speech, which add local color and a new humorous twist to the subject matter. He, therefore, not only introduced novel themes and a different brand of humor into Icelandic literature, but through his verses and poems threw light on many aspects of the life and the culture of the Icelanders in America, especially during their pioneer years.

8. Jónas A. Sigurðsson was born at Litla Ásgeirsá in Húnavatnssýsla in northern Iceland, on May 6, 1865. After growing up in a home atmosphere of culture and literary interest and studying privately under a neighboring clergyman, he attended the Agricultural School at Ólafsdalur, graduating in 1886. The next year he emigrated to America and, after spending some years in North Dakota, studied theology at a Lutheran Seminary in Chicago. He received his degree in 1893 and was ordained the same summer. Thereafter he served Icelandic congregations in North Dakota, Saskatchewan, and Manitoba, except between 1901 and 1918, when he was primarily engaged in public work of various kinds in Seattle, Washington. He died in Winnipeg on May 10, 1933. In the course of his long pastoral career among his countrymen in the United States and Canada, he played a very prominent part both in church and secular affairs, among other things serving repeatedly as president of Þjóðræknisfélag Íslendinga í Vesturheimi (The Icelandic National League in America).

His poems and hymns, original and translated, had for years

[15] Richard Beck, *Icelandic Lyrics* (1930), p. 235.

appeared regularly in various Icelandic and American-Icelandic publications, but not until 1946 did they appear in book form, when an extensive selection, *Ljóðmæli* (Winnipeg), was published posthumously, edited by Richard Beck, with a biographical introduction by the Reverend K. K. Ólafsson.

Jónas Sigurðsson was endowed with great metrical skill and, at his best, reaches heights of commensurate inspiration. His poems are vigorous in diction and style, reflecting his unusual command of the Icelandic language, and many of them are characterized by a manly and thoroughly Norse spirit. The poet found inspiration in the Icelandic sagas and other Scandinavian lore, and frequently draws on them for both references and themes. In fact, fervent national feeling—love of his native tongue, Icelandic history, the country and the nation—is one of the fundamental elements in his poetry.

This characteristic is eloquently revealed in his numerous patriotic poems, such as his elaborate tribute to his native land read at Þingvellir in June 1930, at the millennial celebration of the Icelandic Althing, where the poet appeared as the representative of his countrymen in America. His national spirit also permeates the many and forceful exhortations in which he calls upon his countrymen in the New World to preserve their Icelandic national and cultural values. Naturally, the national note is also strong in his poems on subjects from the sagas and folklore, containing many splendid passages and characterizations. Akin to these is his poem "Hálfur-Máni" (Half Moon), one of his more impressive poems, on an Indian theme.

Among his nature poems, "Mt. Rainier" has the greatest sweep. Others, like "Vorblær" (Breath of Spring) and "Fyrir dag" (Before Dawn), have a lighter, lyrical touch. So also do his sincerely felt and appealing personal poems like "Vögguljóð" (Cradle Song), "Ljósálfurinn minn" (My Fairy of Light), about his daughter, and not least his lilting patriotic poem "Nú er sóley í varpanum heima" (Buttercups Are Blooming at Home), in which his love of country finds charming expression.

In some of his nature poems, like "Hafræna" (Sea Breeze), there is an undertone of deep contemplation. That sober chord is, naturally, dominant in his numerous memorial poems about Icelandic friends and cultural leaders on both sides of the Atlantic, whom he eulogizes with affection and eloquence. His many sacred poems and hymns, original and translated, reveal his strong religious feeling, abiding faith, and burning interest in the cause of the church and Christianity. The social satire in some of his poems, especially in his epigrams, often hits the mark and is evidence of his reformatory spirit.

Besides several hymns, he translated a number of secular poems into Icelandic; among his major translations are his renditions of "Thanatopsis" by W. C. Bryant and "Oriana" by Tennyson. They are faithfully and fluently translated, especially the latter, which calls for great metrical skill. His translations show his wide acquaintance with English and American literature, not least with the principal poets of the last century.

9. Sigurður Júlíus Jóhannesson was born at Lækur in the Ölfus district in southern Iceland on January 9, 1868, but grew up at Svarfhóll in Borgarfjörður in the south. After graduating from the College of Iceland in 1897, he attended the Medical School in Iceland until he emigrated to America in 1899. He worked his way through college and received his degree in medicine both from Jenner Medical College, where he had served as an instructor, and from the National Medical University in Chicago in 1907. After having served as a country doctor in various Icelandic communities in Canada, he moved to Winnipeg permanently in 1920. Besides his medical practice, he has played a many-sided and prominent part in American-Icelandic cultural life; for instance, he served as secretary of The Icelandic National League, and engaged in journalism and other literary work.[16]

Journalism has, as a matter of fact, been one of his major interests. Before he left Iceland, he had been the principal founder and the first editor of the juvenile paper *Æskan*, published by the Grand Lodge of the Icelandic Good Templars, and had also edited the paper *Dagskrá* (1898–1899). In America he has been the editor of *Dagskrá II* (1901–1903), *Lögberg* (1914–1917), and *Voröld* (1918–1921). As he possesses wide human interest and deep social awareness, together

[16] For further information about his life and literary work, see Jón Ólafsson, "Sigurður Júlíus Jóhannesson," *Óðinn*, VI (1910), 5–6; Richard Beck, "Sigurður Júlíus Jóhannesson skáld," *Almanak Ó. S. Thorgeirssonar*, LIV (1948), 21–28.

with a fluent and vivid style, he has proved an effective journalist no less than a gifted poet. His numerous newspaper contributions always reveal his freedom-loving and progressive spirit and his radical social views.

His contribution in the field of juvenile literature has been particularly conspicuous. In both *Lögberg* and *Voröld* he had special children's sections, consisting largely of his own writings in prose and verse, and he also edited, with great success, the juvenile paper *Baldursbrá* (1934–1940) for The Icelandic National League. He has an unusual ability for writing on the child's level in a simple and attractive style and on happily selected themes. His children's stories, originally appearing in *Æskan,* were published in book form in Reykjavík in 1930, and in the same year there appeared a collection of fifty of his children's poems.

Many of his early poems were written in Iceland and were included in his first book, *Sögur og kvæði* (Stories and Poems; two vols.; Winnipeg, 1900–1903). Here are well-written and deep-felt poems, such as "Sőgunarkarlinn" (The Sawyer), "Halta Finna" (Lame Finna), and "Guðsríki" (God's Kingdom), that reveal an unmistakable lyric gift and a noble view of life. Clearly the poet has a keen eye for the injustices of the social order, and his rich human sympathy is a strong strain in most of these poems. Touching is his description of Lame Finna, who has been forced to become a vagrant. His picture of the itinerant sawyer is equally graphic and sympathetic, although painted in stronger and sharper colors.

Sigurður J. Jóhannesson's poetic gift is, however, seen in a much truer light in his second book, *Kvistir* (Twigs; Reykjavík, 1910). Here are numerous poems characterized by splendid craftsmanship and poetic beauty, such as "Mús í gildru" (An Entrapped Mouse), "Jólahugsun" (Christmas Thought), and "Í leiðslu" (Entranced). Many of his epigrams are also excellent in both thought and emotional quality. In two characteristic stanzas ("Stőkur") he sums up his philosophy of life: to bring happiness to his fellow men, to be a guide to those who may have gone astray, and to stimulate love of humanity in the hearts of men. Such is the general undercurrent in these poems—a warm and deep sympathy with men and all living creatures.

The poet generally finds his themes in the life around him. Since he is deeply moved by contemporary social evils, his poems often take the form of merciless satires attacking injustice and oppression in any form. He is a fervent revolutionary and reformer; he was one of the founders in 1901 of the Jafnaðarmannafélag (Socialist Society) in Winnipeg. His reformatory zeal is seen in many of these poems, for instance, in the excellent "Hvar er verk til að vinna?" (Where Is Work to Be Done?), an eloquent and impassioned challenge to progressive action. The same attitude is no less forcefully revealed in his stirring poems, original and translated, in the interest of the Temperance cause, which he has championed among his countrymen with great fervor, for many years as a leading and influential member of the Icelandic Good Templars. He has always been the fearless spokesman of the downtrodden and unfortunate, rejoicing in the battle for the good and noble.

Besides the original poems revealing his human sympathy, *Kvistir* contains excellent and notable translations, as those of "The Song of the Shirt" by Thomas Hood and Edwin Markham's "The Man with the Hoe."

He has grown much in stature as a poet since the publication of *Kvistir*. Numerous splendid poems, excellent in both literary style and penetration, have appeared in American-Icelandic papers and periodicals. A number are inspirational and general in theme and as a rule are lyric in quality. His occasional poems are likewise always fluent and noble in thought, often most successful, as he has the rare faculty of knowing what appeals most to the heart of man. His many poems addressed to individual contemporaries reveal his generous spirit and warm humanity.

During the past three decades, he has contributed a very large number of excellent translations, especially from English and American poets, to American-Icelandic publications. He is an uncommonly fluent translator and has the knack of giving his renditions an Icelandic flavor in mood and language, which well bespeaks his fine mastery of his native tongue.

His poetic talent is, therefore, both rich and many-sided, and his production in that field is very extensive. He has published several prose translations in book form, and an enormous number of various kinds of articles have appeared in American-Icelandic publications. All these he has done in addition to his own editorial work.

Sigurður J. Jóhannesson is an idealist and a humanitarian with world-wide interests, and he abhors shallow and narrow nationalism. But although he is a cosmopolitan and has spent most of his mature years abroad, his poems and articles reveal his deep attachment ot his native land and nation, illustrated in numerous warm-hearted patriotic poems. He wants his countrymen, on both sides of the Atlantic, to preserve and fructify their dearly bought and precious cultural heritage, and he expects much of his national group, because he has strong faith in the inherent abilities of the Icelandic national character.

10. Gísli Jónsson was born at Hárekssta̋ðir in Jőkuldalur in eastern Iceland on February 9, 1876, and comes of a fine farm family. He graduated from the school at Mőðruvellir in 1896, emigrated to Canada in 1903, and has since resided in Winnipeg. His wife, Guðrún H. Finnsdóttir (1884–1946), was a gifted and well-known short-story writer, and has, therefore, been included among the prose writers.

A printer by trade, Gísli Jónsson has for years been manager of a printing establishment in Winnipeg. He has in many ways taken an active part in American-Icelandic cultural work and among other things served for years as secretary of The Icelandic National League. Furthermore, he was a tenor singer of note and has contributed much to the musical life of the community. Together with the Reverend Rőgnvaldur Pétursson, he was founder of the periodical *Heimir* and in 1940 succeeded Pétursson as editor of *Tímarit Þjóðræknis-félags Íslendinga í Vesturheimi*, the annual publication of The Icelandic National League, to which he has contributed both articles and poems.

His only volume of poetry, *Farfuglar* (Birds of Passage), appeared in Winnipeg in 1919. The opening poem, or rather cycle of poems, "Útilegumaðurinn" (The Outlaw), tells "the old story," as the poet puts it, of a young couple who are prevented from marrying because of class distinction, but prefer exile in the mountains to parting. The account centers around the hero of the story and records the highlights in his eventful life, which ends on a tragic note, after the loss of his beloved and later the accidental death of a cherished son. The poem recounts the story vividly and sympathetically, in smooth-flowing meter varying with the changing theme. Many of the descriptive passages are especially successful, such as the first poem, which sets the stage effectively.

In addition the book contains occasional, nature, and personal poems, generally in good taste and lyrical in quality, frequently with a contemplative strain. The poet's human interest and his idealism are seen directly in such poems as "Samherjar" (Allies).

Among the most attractive poems in the book are the tender lullaby "Góða nótt," (Good Night), addressed to a son temporarily left behind in Iceland, and "Móðurmálið" (The Mother Tongue), a splendid tribute to the Icelandic language, which has become widely sung to the beautiful music by Sveinbjörn Sveinbjörnsson, the noted Icelandic composer. The poet's appreciation of the Icelandic cultural heritage and his love of his native land are expressed here and in patriotic poems like "Ísland" (Iceland), rich in pictorial quality. Elsewhere he has paid Canada, his adopted country, tribute in verse, characterized by the same qualities of sincerity and graphic description.

The book also includes a number of translations from the works of Scandinavian, German, English, and American poets, an indication of the translator's wide reading and literary interest. The translations, generally both accurately and smoothly rendered, include Goethe's "Erlkönig" and Kipling's "If," as well as several from the works of the Canadian poetess E. Pauline Johnson.

Since the publication of his book, Gísli Jónsson has contributed a number of poems to American-Icelandic publications, especially *Tímarit Þjóðræknisfélags Íslendinga* (Annual of The Icelandic National League). These include a group of song lyrics, original and translated, as well as three of his most notable poems. "Fardagar" (Moving Days) is a sincerely felt and concentrated poem, in which the contrast between old age and youth, the meeting of the generations at the crossroad of life, is portrayed with effective symbolism. "Áning" (Resting on the Road), written on the occasion of the poet's sixtieth birthday and in a mellow mood, surveys the road he has traveled; a well-constructed poem with sustained emotional quality, it reveals his manly outlook upon life. "Iðunnarkviða" (Ode to Iðunn), an eloquent and inspired tribute to poetry, is written in the sonorous *hrynhenda* form of Skaldic fame.

11. GUTTORMUR J. GUTTORMSSON occupies a very prominent and in many respects a very unusual position among American-Icelandic writers. He has the distinction of being the only major Icelandic poet on this continent—writing in the Icelandic language—who was born on North American soil. The son of Icelandic pioneers from the eastern part of the country, he was born November 21 (not December 5 or 15 as has been held), 1878, at Icelandic River (now Riverton), Manitoba, and grew up in that frontier community. His family background and career have been sketched in the account of the prose writers; suffice it to add that his mother possessed considerable versemaking ability and that poems of hers were printed in the first Icelandic papers in America, *Framfari* and *Leifur*.[17]

Orphaned at the age of sixteen, he was thrown on his own; his schooling having of necessity been very limited, he was compelled to earn his living by manual labor. After trying his hand at many means of livelihood, he succeeded in 1911 in buying his parental farm at Riverton, where he has since made his home, wresting his living from the soil to provide for a large family.

His achievements in the realm of letters are, therefore, particularly remarkable. No doubt, his circumstances have in a degree thwarted his intellectual development; at the same time they have been a fruitful challenge to him. Besides a volume of one-act plays, he has published the following volumes of poetry: *Jón Austfirðingur* (John from the East Fjords; Winnipeg, 1909), *Bóndadóttir* (The Farmer's Daughter; Winnipeg, 1920); and *Gaman og alvara* (Jest and Earnest; Winnipeg, 1930), which includes new poems as well as the bulk of his earlier work. Between 1930 and 1940 he published a number of new and significant poems. Although, as is only to be expected, his

[17] For further information about his life and literary career, see Jón Jónsson frá Sleðbrjót, "Guttormur J. Guttormsson skáld í Nýja Íslandi," *Óðinn*, XIV (1918), 17–18; Lárus Sigurbjörnsson, "Guttormur J. Guttormsson: Tíu leikrit," *Lögrétta*, XXX (1935), 37–42; Watson Kirkconnell, "A Skald in Canada," *Transactions of the Royal Society of Canada*, XXXIII (1939), 107–121; Richard Beck, *Guttormur J. Guttormsson skáld* (Winnipeg, 1949).

large poetic production is somewhat uneven in excellence, his books amply reveal his rich and original poetic gift and robust intellect. Indicative of the reputation that he enjoys in Iceland is the fact that in 1939 he was invited by the Icelandic government to visit the land of his ancestors as the guest of the nation.

Guttormsson has made up for his lack of schooling by very extensive reading. He is not only steeped in the time-honored Icelandic literary tradition, past and present, but is likewise widely read in European and American literature. As a poet he is thoroughly modern in his outlook upon life and his approach to his themes.

An Icelander by racial origin and cultural background, he is no less a genuine Canadian. This fact is written large in his poetry. He is as conscious of his obligation to the land of his birth as he is of his debt to the country of his forebears. Notably in *Jón Austfirðingur*, he has interpreted the life of the Icelandic pioneers in Manitoba, in poems noted for their graphic description, deep insight, and sympathy. Nowhere has he, however, erected to the pioneers a more lasting literary monument than in his inspired poem "Sandy Bar," named after a pioneer settlement and graveyard on the west shore of Lake Winnipeg, not far from Riverton; in this noble tribute, penetrating thought, understanding, and mastery of form go hand in hand. With equal vividness and sympathy he portrays in his poem "Indíánahátíðin" (Indian Festival), the life of the North American Indian as he had seen it during his youth in New Iceland; the poem is, therefore, thoroughly authentic and unique in Icelandic literature.

Many of his other most significant and original poems are also directly based on his personal experience. In "Býflugnaræktin" (The Care of the Bees), as Professor Watson Kirkconnell has effectively expressed it, the poet "uses a familiar episode of bee-keeping to adumbrate the spiritual tragedy of his own life."[18] Through his penetrating portrayal, Guttormsson's tragedy takes on a universal application. This strikingly original and effective poem is representative of the symbolic quality of Guttormsson's poems. Symbolism had become increasingly important, although among his earlier work it is found in such an excellent poem as "Sál hússins" (The Soul of the

---

[18] *Canadian Overtones* (Winnipeg, 1935), p. 14.

House), in which he uses the old symbol of the fire on the hearth for the soul of the house.

His poetry is also rich in original and colorful nature descriptions. Striking similes are a characteristic element in such poems as "Haustsőngur" (Autumn Song), "Desemberkvőld" (December Evening) and "Vetrarkvőld" (Winter Night). One of his most poetic nature descriptions is found in a charming lyric of only four short stanzas, in which the personification of an Indian girl as Indian Summer is brilliantly and consistently carried out.

Elsewhere in his nature poems the lyric quality and the light touch are the outstanding features. That is especially true of his beautiful lyric "Góða nótt" (Good Night), which also clearly reveals the fundamental note in his philosophy of life and the surging undercurrent of his poetry—his profound sympathy with the oppressed, with those whose "luckless steering wrecks their ships." He is their champion and defender and gives vent to his radical and humanitarian views in social satires bitterly assailing the injustice, greed, and inequalities of the social order. In "Bőlvun lőgmálsins" (The Curse of the Law), the grain speculators who grow fat on the sweat and the toil of the farmer are the subjects of the poet's merciless flaying. "Vatnið" (The Lake) is in a similar vein, with its picture of the lake, smooth and lovely on the surface, but hiding in its depths a furious battle between the small fishes and the pike that swallows them in large numbers. This poem excellently illustrates how well the poet uses symbolism in his satires. He also uses the epigram effectively as a vehicle for his satire and irony, as well as for his more good-natured humor. His use of the quatrain here and in many of his excellent nature descriptions, often in a very intricate form, carries on brilliantly the literary tradition of his Icelandic forebears.

His metrical skill is seen to good advantage in his easy handling of such intricate meters, and he uses some verse forms of his own invention, which are even more elaborate, with no less dexterity. His verse forms range from rigid Skaldic meters, heavy-moving hexameters, and intricately rhymed quatrains to forms of the lightest and most musical kind. His diction is equally rich and varied, revealing an amazing mastery of the Icelandic tongue, eloquent evidence of his knowledge of Icelandic lore, history, and literature. He has also, of course, drawn rich spiritual nourishment from English and other non-Icelandic literatures, which he has read extensively.

Not only has Guttormsson made a lasting name for himself in the realm of Icelandic poetry; his one-act dramas are also a significant contribution to Icelandic literature and have been dealt with among the prose writings.

Guttormur J. Guttormsson combines in an unusual degree a fruitful appreciation of the Icelandic cultural heritage and affection for Iceland with a deep filial devotion to Canada, the land of his birth, having eulogized both with equal warmth in his poems. In his penetrating poem "Íslendingafljót" (Icelandic River) he has masterfully interpreted the relationship between the Icelanders on both sides of the Atlantic; the birch trees joining their branches across the river become to him a symbol of the brotherly handclasp that he is desirous of having for all time bridge the ocean separating them.

He has said that the Norse spirit in Icelandic literature most attracts him, the manly spirit and the vigor, which is in full harmony with his character and outlook upon life and is revealed in his poetry. Like his admired friend and fellow poet-farmer, Stephan G. Stephansson, he has succeeded in overcoming adverse circumstances by making them a source of poetic inspiration and spiritual strength. And with his authentic and penetrating portrayal of Icelandic pioneer life in Canada and of the Canadian scene, he has enriched Icelandic literature with new themes clothed in an original and often highly poetic garb.

12. His older brother, Vigfús Guttormsson (b. 1874), came from Iceland with his parents when he was less than a year old. Self-educated, he has been a farmer and merchant at Lundar, Manitoba. His poetry has for many years appeared in the American-Icelandic papers. It is lyrical and light in touch, especially his nature poems, and reflects his musical ability and interest, which also is expressed in various ways in his contributions to local community life.

13. Þorsteinn Þ. Þorsteinsson was born November 11, 1879, at Uppsalir in Eyjafjörður in northern Iceland. He came to Canada in 1901 and resides in Winnipeg. He is the most versatile of the American-Icelandic poets, with short stories, essays, and sketches of great merit to his credit, as well as his extensive and significant

writings on American-Icelandic history. These prose works, as well as his career, have therefore been dealt with in the account of the prose writers.

He has published two collections of poetry, *þættir* (Strands; Winnipeg, 1918) and *Heimhugi* (Home Thoughts; Winnipeg, 1921). All his best poems are characterized by intellectual vigor and virile language; he is original in treatment of his themes, choice of diction, and verse forms, often inventing his meters and harmonizing them well with his themes. He may, therefore, be said to possess great metrical skill, although his rhythm sometimes is on the heavy side and the thought content sometimes outweighs the form.

He has written many noteworthy sonnets, concentrated in thought, such as "Áfram" (Onward), a resounding challenge to head straight for "vision's highest mountains" and let nothing deter one. In other sonnets, equally excellent, he has paid tribute to his favorites, Walt Whitman and Stephan G. Stephansson.

Many of his poems are also characterized by deep emotional power as well as intellectual quality. His independent and radical views, rooted in his love of freedom and truth and his human sympathy, find expression in forceful social satires. In that respect he appears to have been influenced, or at any rate stimulated, by Þorsteinn Erlingsson, but he is no slavish imitator. In an elaborate spring poem, "Vorsőngur" (Spring Song), exalted and ecstatic in tone, the social satire is impressively interwoven with the vivid nature description and exhortation to fruitful living.

He also has a genuine lyric touch in such poems as "Dőgg" (Dew) and "Hljómdísin" (The Goddess of Melody), and not least in his heartfelt and lyrical "Til Íslands á nýári" (To Iceland at New Year), in which his deep love of country is beautifully expressed. He is steeped in Icelandic literature and is an ardent and outspoken champion of the Norse spirit and Icelandic cultural values. There is nothing superficial about the title of his second collection of poems, *Heimhugi*; it strikes at the very heart of his poetry.

Considered as a whole, the poems in his two books are of an unusually even literary quality. They reflect his good taste, stimulated by his wide reading not only in Icelandic but also in foreign literature. Among his most striking poems are "Leikmærin" (The

Actress) and "Sőngmærin" (The Songstress), in which the rhythmical and the pictorial qualities blend effectively. Many of his nature and other descriptive poems are also excellent.

Since the appearance of his later collection he has published a large number of well-wrought and significant poems, many of which were included in his periodical *Saga* (1925–1930). Three of these will be specially considered.

"Á Þingvelli 1930" (At Thingvellir 1930) commemorates the millennial of the Icelandic Althing; it is a cycle of poems, rich in thought and descriptive quality, with a fitting undertone of genuine patriotic feeling. "Askur Yggdrasils" (Yggdrasil's Ash) is inspired by the famed World Tree of Old Norse mythology, which the poet not only describes with sweeping imagination, but which strikes from his anvil illuminating observations of life and poetic similes. "Signýjarfórnin" (Signý's Sacrifice) is based on the well-known story of Sigýn and Loki in the *Poetic Edda*; the poet develops his arresting theme into a striking symbol of the spirit of self-sacrifice. (As the title indicates he uses the young form of the name, "Signý.")

Other later poems, such as the magnificent tribute to Vilhjálmur Stefánsson, the explorer, have appeared in the American-Icelandic weeklies. They have also published a number of his memorial poems on outstanding Icelandic pioneers in America; these poems are written with rich sympathy and understanding from his vast knowledge of the history of the Icelanders in America. Deeply rooted as he is in his native soil and the Icelandic literary tradition, he has with equal sincerity expressed his appreciation of Canada in both a beautiful sonnet and his longer poems on the subject.

14. Einar Páll Jónsson was born at Hárekssta∂ir in Jőkuldalur in eastern Iceland on August 11, 1880, and is a half-brother of Gísli Jónsson. He attended the College of Iceland, 1902–1905, but has supplemented his schooling with extensive reading, not least in the field of literature. During his early years in Reykjavík, he took an active interest in public and political affairs and also engaged in journalism and other literary work. He emigrated to Canada in 1913, where journalism became his lifework. He became assistant editor of the weekly, *Lőgberg*, in 1917, and since 1927 (almost without interruption) has been its editor-in-chief; of late he has been the sole

editor. He is musically inclined, has served as an organist, and has even tried his hand at musical composition. In many ways he has played an important part in the cultural life of his countrymen in Winnipeg and the New World generally.[19]

Considering his manifold duties as an editor, it is surprising how rich in literary merit many of his editorials are, not least those dealing with cultural matters, such as literature and art, the Icelandic cultural heritage, ideals, and philosophy of life. They reveal his wide interests, love of liberty, and firm belief in international co-operation.

He has, however, made his greatest contribution with his poems, which possess uniformly high literary quality. His first book, *Öræfaljóð* (Songs of the Wilderness; Winnipeg, 1915), contains many fine poems, personal and lyric in quality, characterized by simplicity, naturalness, and sure taste in language and form. Here also are some splendid epigrams. Since the publication of his first book, he has gained greatly in concentration and penetration and has achieved a firmer mastery of form, retaining at the same time his characteristic good taste and lyric touch.

He often finds for his thoughts and feelings a symbolic expression in attractive pictures from nature, as in "Haf" (Ocean), a lyrical and colorful description of the ocean in all its enchantment, and "Brim" (Surf), penetrating in thought and firmly wrought. Other poems are pure nature descriptions, like "Upprisa vorsins" (The Resurrection of Spring), in which poetic similes and fertile imagination go together. Incidentally, this poem won second prize in an extensive poetry contest sponsored by the Manitoba branch of the Canadian Authors' Association in 1938. His autumn poem "Sumarlok" (The Close of Summer) is, however, even more striking in its pictorial quality and symbolism. And "the undying faith in summer," to paraphrase one of the closing lines, is an expression of the deepest and the most fundamental strain in the poet's view of life. This idealism, which makes him hear the heartbeats of spring in the winter storms, is revealed in his vigorous poem "Vetur" (Winter), imbued with manly spirit.

Elsewhere in his poems Einar P. Jónsson paints vivid and realistic

[19] Concerning his life and literary career, see further Richard Beck, "Einar Páll Jónsson skáld," *Eimreiðin*, XLVIII (1942), 211–222.

pictures from life, as in "Jarðyrkjumaður" (The Tiller of the Soil), which is especially penetrating and rich in sympathy with those who till the soil. His faith in the victorious power of fruitful living—idealism of the truest kind—is written large in such poems as "Þjónn ljóssins" (The Servant of Light), a hymn of praise to the fearless pioneer, and in "Draumur" (The Dream), beautifully expressing how all great achievements first have their being in the dreams of the idealist.

His numerous and excellent poems about Iceland and the Icelandic cultural heritage constitute a large and significant part of Einar P. Jónsson's poetry. They breathe his deep-rooted love of Iceland and the Icelandic people and interpret with poetic sensitiveness the close kinship between the Icelander and his native soil. An example is his splendid poem "Móðir í austri" (Mother in the East). The challenge to his countrymen in America to preserve the Icelandic cultural heritage burns like a bright flame. With his poetry, journalistic work, and other activities, he has richly contributed to that preservation. He has also written splendid poems eulogizing those who, faithful to their rich heritage, have added luster to the name of Iceland with their accomplishments in America. Characteristic and impressive are his tributes to such Icelandic cultural leaders as Einar Benediktsson, the poet, and Einar Jónsson, the sculptor. Among his obituary pieces, the memorial poems about the poets Matthías Jochumsson and K. N. are especially noteworthy, vividly bringing out the widely different characteristics of each.

All things considered, Einar P. Jónsson's rich poetic gift nowhere finds a fuller flowering than in his touching poem "Við leiði móður minnar" (At My Mother's Grave), in which penetration in thought and polished verse form blend masterfully with an undertone of deep sadness and longing. His poetic sensitiveness and mastery of language are also seen in his several successful translations, notably in excellent renditions of "Vestigia" by Bliss Carman and "Woodrow Wilson" by Worrell Kirkwood.

15. Jónas Stefánsson frá Kaldbak was born on March 31, 1882, at Kaldbakur in Suður-Þingeyjarsýsla in northern Iceland. He graduated from the Agricultural School at Hólar in 1902, emigrated to Canada in 1913, and has for years been a farmer at Mikley (Big

Island), Manitoba. Wide awake intellectually, he is a man of extensive reading.

His poems, which had often appeared in the American-Icelandic weeklies, were published in collected form as *Ljóðmæli* (Poems; Víðir, Manitoba, 1939). Although they are uneven in quality and far from being faultless in craftsmanship, they reveal a strong and genuine lyric vein, and the warm emotional undercurrent frequently finds an outlet in poetic and beautiful form.

The poet is a sensitive soul and a fervent idealist, whose revolutionary and reformatory spirit is fanned into flame when he contemplates how the weak and the defenseless are trampled underfoot and how badly truth and brotherly love fare in the world. This feeling finds expression in social satires such as "Jól" (Christmas), with great force in "Borgin brennur" (The City is Burning), and not least in the scathingly ironical "Lofgerð dalsins" (In Praise of the Dollar). Nor is it accidental that Jónas Stefánsson has a keen eye for social evils and a deep sympathy with those whose life has been a stormy journey. He has himself shared that fate in no small measure, and he writes one of his finest poems, "Eg ann þér" (You Are a Man after My Own Heart), as a glowing tribute to the man who courageously braves the cold blast raging about him.

Some of his best verse is found, however, in his lyric poems, when he lays aside his battle dress and rests his soul in Nature's refreshing fountains of beauty in such poems as "Nótt" (Night). Akin in theme and spirit and perhaps the most beautiful poem in the collection is "Októberfífillinn" (The October Dandelion), hauntingly melancholy and strikingly symbolic of the life of man. The poet's love of his native Iceland, which he cannot forget, is beautifully expressed in "Óður útlagans" (The Exile's Song). Although his occasional poems contain some splendid passages, they are as a whole inferior to his poems personal and general in theme. On the other hand, many of his epigrams hit the mark very well.

Since the publication of this collection, he, like his fellow American-Icelandic poets, has contributed many and varied poems to the Winnipeg Icelandic weeklies.

16. Páll S. Pálsson was born in Reykjavík, Iceland, on September 17, 1882, but grew up at Norður-Reykir in Borgarfjőrður

in the south. He is widely read and largely self-educated. In 1897 he emigrated to Canada and has since made his home in Winnipeg, where he has taken an active part in the work of Icelandic cultural organizations. He is a gifted actor and has been prominently identified with the efforts on the part of his national group in the field of play production. He had long been known, especially in the New World, for his poems published in American-Icelandic papers and periodicals, when a selection of his production appeared in collected form, *Norður-Reykir* (Winnipeg, 1936), with a preface by the Reverend Rőgnvaldur Pétursson.

As the earliest poem in the book was written when he was fifteen, his literary interest must have awakened very early; his poems indicate that writing of verse comes very easily to him. Generally, his poems are well written and lyrical, revealing sensitiveness and love of beauty. Especially attractive and light in touch are his nature poems, such as "Vormorgun" (Spring Morning), "Sólaruppkoma" (Sunrise), "Nótt" (Night), and not least "Haustnótt" (Autumn Night), in which the autumn mood is very well reproduced.

In a different tone, less lyrical and more striking and vigorous, are "Tréð á Fljótsbakkanum" (The Tree on the River Bank), "Í Surtshelli" (In Surt's cave), and "Holskeflan" (The Wave), symbolic, rich in thought, and concentrated in form. The impact made upon the poet by current events and his deep human interest are also seen in these three as in others of his poems. His sympathy is all for the unfortunate and suffering, as revealed in "Eintal Flóttamannsins" (The Refugee's Soliloquy) and "Týndi sonurinn" (The Prodigal Son). Direct social satire is not, however, much in evidence in his poems. Glimpses of humor brighten some of them.

"Jólanótt" (Christmas Eve) and "Íslenzki smaladrengurinn" (The Icelandic Shepherd Boy) are splendid poems, the former for its pictorial and contemplative quality, the latter as a vivid picture from the poet's youth in rural Iceland. The memories from those days are a recurrent strain in many of these poems; the descriptive passages likewise often stem from that source. The very title of the book, *Norður-Reykir*, the name of his childhood home in Iceland, shows how strong are the bonds that link him to the haunts of his youth and the native soil. In "Sumarnótt á Signýjarstőðum" (A Summer

Night at Signýjarstaðir), his beloved Borgarfjörður, in its scenic glory, is vividly pictured in the embrace of a still summer night. Since the appearance of his book, the author has contributed a number of poems of merit to American-Icelandic publications, including some splendid memorial poems.

17. Nor is he the only one in his family who has made a name for himself with his poetry. His brother KRISTJÁN PÁLSSON (1886–1947), who emigrated to Canada in 1897 and resided in Selkirk, Manitoba, a self-educated man, had contributed a large number of splendidly wrought poems, generally very lyrical in quality, to American-Icelandic publications. His versatility as a poet may be indicated by pointing out that he wrote personal poems, nature descriptions, occasional poems of various kind, religious and historical poems, and humorous and satirical verses with equal facility.

Illustrative of his major efforts is his historical poem "Skjöldurinn" (The Shield) about the widely known episode in the *Egils saga Skallagrímssonar* when Einar skálaglamm, the skald, presented his friend and fellow poet Egill with an magnificent shield, forcing him, in accordance with prevailing custom, to repay with an elaborate poem. Kristján Pálsson has retold and interpreted the episode well and vividly, with his characteristic mastery of form. His poetic gift will appear in its true light when his poems, scattered in papers and periodicals, are collected and published in book form.

Finally, it may be mentioned that the third brother, JÓNAS PÁLSSON (1875–1947), who emigrated to Canada in 1900 and became a noted musician in Winnipeg and elsewhere, also wrote lyric poetry of merit.

18. JAKOBÍNA JOHNSON was born at Hólmavað in Suður-Þingeyjarsýsla, in northern Iceland, on October 24, 1883, the daughter of the poet Sigurbjörn Jóhannsson. With her family she emigrated to Canada in 1889, settling in the Argyle district in Manitoba, where she grew up. After graduating from the Winnipeg Normal School, she was for some years a public-school teacher in Manitoba. Shortly after her marriage to Ísak Jónsson, brother of the poets Gísli and Einar P. Jónsson, she moved to Seattle, Washington, where she has since resided. The mother of seven children, with the resultant household duties, she has found time for much writing, has been active in cultural and literary societies, and has lectured extensively

on Iceland and Icelandic literature and culture. In 1935 she visited Iceland as the special guest of the Young People's League and other groups, traveled extensively through the country, of course, visited her childhood home, and everywhere received a warm welcome. As might be expected, the visit inspired her to write a number of beautiful poems on her impressions and her reactions to the land of her birth.[21]

Her poems had for years appeared regularly in American-Icelandic publications, before the publication of a selection, *Kertaljós* (Candle Light, 1939). These poems are rich in beauty and characterized by genuine lyric quality and literary artistry. The natural, mellow, and flowing language is most remarkable when it is remembered that the poetess left Iceland as a mere child.

The collection contains a number of poems revealing her deep-rooted love of Iceland and the Icelandic cultural heritage, not least the sagas and the old poets, as seen in "Íslendingur sőgufróði" (The Learned Icelander) and "Fornmenn" (Men of Old). Iceland itself is uniquely portrayed in her poem "Íslenzk őrnefni" (Icelandic Place Names), in which the names of places and natural phenomena are dexterously interwoven to form an enchanting metrical picture.

Then there are the beautiful nature poems, like "Vor" (Spring) and "Spőrfuglinn" (The Sparrow). Her deep-felt and feminine mother poems, such as "Gestur í vőggu" (A Guest in the Cradle) and "Vőgguljóð" (Cradle Song), are instinct with mother love and mother joy; her deep attachment to her home is appealingly expressed in "Hugsað á heimleið" (Thoughts When Homeward Bound). It may be added that she excels particularly in tenderly felt children's poems.

Poems in Icelandic folklore strain form, as it were, a prelude to the concluding group in the collection, the ones from the memorable visit to the old homeland, and centering around fond memories from that visit. These poems are especially charming in their warmth of feeling and melodious form. In "Harpan" (The Harp) the poetess expresses her indebtedness to the past, the old Icelandic literary heritage, which is so much a part of her, although her poetic gift has also been fructified and inspired by other sources. Characteristic

---

[20] Concerning her visit, career, and poetry, see further Friðrik A. Friðriksson, "Skáldkonan Jakobína Johnson," *Lesbók Morgunblaðsins*, X (1935), 2–3; Sveinn Sigurðsson, "Góður gestur," *Eimreiðin*, XLI (1935), 257–260.

of her noble view of life and idealism, the closing lines of the book express her faith in the ultimate victory of goodness in the world.

Jakobína Johnson has done far more than write many excellent and uncommonly beautiful poems. She has translated into English a large number of choice poems by leading Icelandic poets, generally with rare sensitiveness and mastery of form. These have appeared in various American literary magazines, and a considerable number of them are included in the collections *Icelandic Lyrics* (1930) and *Icelandic Poems and Stories* (New York, 1943), edited by Richard Beck. She has also successfully translated into English the following notable Icelandic dramas: *Lénharður fógeti* (Governor Lenhard) by Einar H. Kvaran, *Galdra-Loftur* (Loft's Wish) by Jóhann Sigurjónsson, and *Nýársnóttin* (New Year's Eve) by Indriði Einarsson. With her translations she has, therefore, extended the range of Icelandic literature, just as she has, on the other hand, enriched Icelandic literature with her original poems rich in pictures from the forest-clad hills and mountains in her impressive scenic surroundings on the Pacific Coast.

19. Of the many other American-Icelandic poets and versifiers who have published their work in book form the following deserve at least brief consideration.

Sigurður J. Jóhannesson (1850–1933), who came from western Iceland to Canada in 1892, published several collections of poems, including *Nokkur ljóðmæli forn og ný* (Some Poems Old and New; Winnipeg, 1915). Traditional in theme, largely occasional, nature, and patriotic poems, they frequently have a deep contemplative strain. His later work is often lighter in touch than his earlier efforts. "Heimspeki áttræðs manns" (The Philosophy of an Octogenarian) is sonorous in rhythm and reveals his independent Icelandic spirit, which poverty and other adverse circumstances could not break, his idealism, and his deep roots in his native soil.

Sigfús B. Benedictsson (b. 1865), a long-time resident of Manitoba, has from time to time published and edited several papers and other publications, some of which are mentioned in the account of the prose writers. He has also been a productive writer of verse and has to his credit one collection of poetry, *Ljóðmæli* (Poems; Winnipeg, 1905), more notable, however, for the author's radical and progressive ideas, which he has always championed fearlessly, than for craftsmanship and general poetic quality. Since its publication, he has, however, contributed to American-Icelandic papers and other publications many poems, original and translated, of much better lyric and literary quality.

BJARNI ÞORSTEINSSON (1868–1943), a photographer by profession, who emigrated from eastern Iceland to Canada in 1903 and resided for a long time in Selkirk, Manitoba, had contributed numerous original and translated poems to the American-Icelandic papers. Under the title *Kvæði* (Poems; Winnipeg, 1948) a selected edition of his work was published with an introduction by Gísli Jónsson. Although neither very original nor vigorous, the best of these poems, such as the nature descriptions, reveal a true lyric strain, as in the fine sonnet "Haust" (Autumn). The contemplative element is the outstanding characteristic of the deeply felt and well-constructed poem "Í grafreitnum" (In the Graveyard). The historical poems are also worthy of special note, as are the translations from the poetry of Robert W. Service.

There are a number of other American-Icelandic poets, who have for years been contributing poems of literary merit to American-Icelandic publications, but who had not up to 1940 published their poems in book form. Among these, listing them chronologically, are the following:

JÓN JÓNATANSSON (b. 1876) came from northern Iceland and is a long-time resident in Winnipeg. A barber by trade, he is self-educated. He is a great-grandson of the Reverend Jón Þorláksson, the noted poet and translator, and has, among other things, written nature and occasional poems showing considerable mastery of form and individuality in thought and language. Some of his best efforts are found among his memorial poems, which often contain splendid characterizations.

SVEINN E. BJÖRNSSON (b. 1885) came from eastern Iceland to Canada at the age of nineteen, graduated in medicine from the University of Manitoba in 1916, and has been a practicing physician in Arborg, Manitoba. His production is extensive and varied, consisting of nature, patriotic, and satirical poems, occasional poetry of all kinds, and translations from English poetry, all of which evidence his wide interests and mastery of form. He has some splendid original poems to his credit, and his renditions of Keats's "Ode to a Nightingale" and Shelley's "The Cloud" are commendable efforts in that field.

PÁLL GUÐMUNDSSON (b. 1887) emigrated from northern Iceland to Canada in 1913 and is a house painter in Winnipeg. He attended the high school at Akureyri for two years, but is otherwise self-educated. He has written a number of personal, general, patriotic, and nature poems, uniformly characterized by fine taste in the handling of diction and verse forms and by genuine lyric quality. His two poems, "Á sléttunni" (On the Prairie) and "Til Íslands" (To Iceland), included in the collection *Vestan um haf* (Reykjavík, 1930), are good examples of his tasteful craftsmanship and emotional quality. A collected edition of his poems would, as in the case of Kristján Pálsson, show his splendid poetic talent in full light.

It is clear that the Icelanders did not lose their appreciation of poetry or their ability to write verse when they migrated to the shores of the New World. In fact, the new environment and conditions under which they have lived have, as might be expected, challenged them to literary expression. The list of American-Icelanders who have published their poems in book form could be made much more extensive were this a bibliographical and not a literary survey. And a great number of other versifiers have contributed enormous quantities of verse to the American-Icelandic papers. Whatever else may be said about this vast production, it bears witness to the ingrained literary and cultural interest which has been, generally speaking, cultivated under conditions hostile to intellectual and literary pursuits. The most gifted of these poets have also written poetry of genuine and lasting literary value. However, since most of these Icelandic poets have lived and labored in Canada, let a Canadian scholar and poet sum up their achievement: "It is the glory of the Icelandic settlers that in their first generation among us they have created a poetry, based on Canada and their experience of it, that is worthy of challenging comparison with the best that three centuries have produced in their foster-country."[21]

---

[21] Watson Kirkconnell, *Canadian Overtones* (Winnipeg, 1935), p. 15.

20. Some of those American-Icelanders who came to America as children and others born on American or Canadian soil have, as one would expect, tried their hand at writing poetry in English. Thus CHRISTOPHER JOHNSTON (d. 1927), an Icelander by birth, contributed a number of delicately wrought lyrics to Canadian and American papers and also translated a number of Icelandic poems into English. LAURA GOODMAN SALVERSON, the novelist, born in Winnipeg of Icelandic parentage in 1890, was, however, the first one in the Icelandic group to publish a collection of original poems in the English language, *Wayside Gleams* (Toronto, 1925), containing poems in lyric vein and of considerable literary value. HELEN SWINBURNE (b. 1892), daughter of Iceland's noted pioneer composer Sveinbjőrn Sveinbjőrnsson and a Scotch mother, for years a resident of Saskatchewan, has contributed to Canadian papers and other publications a number of genuinely felt and well-wrought lyrics. Still others could be mentioned who have written individual poems of merit in the English language. Therefore, in a limited way the prophecy made by the American-Icelandic journalist John G. Holme back in 1922 has begun to find realization:

> In the United States and Canada there must be between thirty and forty thousand persons of Icelandic birth and descent. They are successful farmers, merchants, lawyers, physicians, teachers, etc., but thus far they have not picked up in the Western World the tools of their ancestors. They have not begun to create. Was the gift lost in the process of transplanting, or has not the second generation caught the genius of the English language? I believe there are to-day some tow-headed youngsters, whose grandparents emigrated from the saga island, running around on Saskatchewan or Minnesota farms, who inside of fifteen or twenty years will be piping some interesting lays in the language of this land.[22]

The voices of that generation are gradually letting themselves be heard, and although so far rather faint and lacking in robust and distinctive quality, it is to be hoped that they will in the future swell into a chorus of might and magnificence worthy of the old and rich Icelandic literary tradition.

Besides Jakobína Johnson and Christopher Johnston, several

[22] *American-Scandinavian Review*, X (1922), p. 553.

American-Icelanders have successfully translated Icelandic poetry into English, among whom the most productive and noteworthy are: Guðmundur J. Gíslason (1877–1934), Runólfur Félsted (1879–1921), Vilhjálmur Stefánsson (b. 1879), Páll Bjarnason (b. 1882), and Skúli Johnson (b. 1888). All of them have also written poetry in English. Just as the American-Icelandic poets have enriched Icelandic poetry with new themes based on their experience in America and with translations into the Icelandic, these translators have, with their renditions of Icelandic poems into English, extended the realm of Icelandic literature by making excellent selections accessible to English readers. Thus, in both directions, the American-Icelandic poets have been ambassadors of literary and cultural values, bridgebuilders between Europe and the Western World.

Index of Authors and Historical Persons

EXTRACTS FROM THE WILL OF THE LATE

WILLARD FISKE

——"I give and bequeath to the Cornell University at Ithaca, New York, all my books relating to Icelandic and the old Scandinavian literature and history. . . ."

——"I give and bequeath to the said Cornell University . . . the sum of Five Thousand (5000) Dollars, to have and to hold forever, in trust, nevertheless, to receive the income thereof, and to use and expend the said income for the purposes of the publication of an annual volume relating to Iceland and the said Icelandic Collection in the library of the said University."

In pursuance of these provisions the following volumes of ISLANDICA have been issued:

I. Bibliography of the Icelandic Sagas, by Halldór Hermannsson. 1908.

II. The Northmen in America (982–c. 1500), by Halldór Hermannsson. 1909.

III. Bibliography of the Sagas of the Kings of Norway and related Sagas and Tales, by Halldór Hermannsson. 1910.

IV. The Ancient Laws of Norway and Iceland, by Halldór Hermannsson. 1911.

V. Bibliography of the Mythical-Heroic Sagas, by Halldór Hermannsson. 1912.

VI. Icelandic Authors of to-day, with an Appendix giving a list of works dealing with Modern Icelandic Literature, by Halldór Hermannsson. 1913.

VII. The Story of Griselda in Iceland. Edited by Halldór Hermansson. 1914.

VIII. An Icelandic Satire (Lof Lýginnar), by Þorleifur Halldórsson. Edited by Halldór Hermannsson. 1915.

IX. Icelandic Books of the Sixteenth Century, by Halldór Hermannsson. 1916.

X. Annalium in Islandia farrago and De mirabilibus Islandiæ, by Bishop Gísli Oddsson. Edited by Halldór Hermannsson. 1917.

XI. The Periodical Literature of Iceland down to the year 1874. A historical sketch by Halldór Hermannsson. 1918.

XII. Modern Icelandic. An essay by Halldór Hermannsson. 1919.

XIII. Bibliography of the Eddas, by Halldór Hermannsson. 1920.

XIV. Icelandic Books of the Seventeenth Century, by Halldór Hermannsson. 1922.

XV. Jón Guðmundsson and his Natural History of Iceland, by Halldór Hermannsson. 1924.

XVI. Eggert Ólafsson. A biographical sketch by Halldór Hermannsson. 1925.

XVII. Two Cartographers: Guðbrandur Thorláksson and Thórður Thorláksson, by Halldór Hermannsson. 1926.

XVIII. Sir Joseph Banks and Iceland, by Halldór Hermannsson. 1928.

XIX. Icelandic Manuscripts, by Halldór Hermannsson. 1929.

XX. The Book of the Icelanders (Íslendingabók), by Ari Thorgilsson. Edited and translated with an introductory essay and notes, by Halldór Hermannsson. 1930.

XXI. The Cartography of Iceland, by Halldór Hermannsson. 1931.

XXII. Sæmund Sigfússon and the Oddaverjar, by Halldór Hermannsson. 1932.

XXIII. Old Icelandic Literature. A bibliographical essay by Halldór Hermannsson. 1933.

XXIV. The Sagas of Icelanders (Íslendinga sögur). A supplement to Bibliography of the Icelandic Sagas and Minor Tales. By Halldór Hermannsson. 1935.

XXV. The Problem of Wineland. By Halldór Hermannsson. 1936.

XXVI. The Sagas of the Kings and the Mythical-Heroic Sagas. Two bibliographical supplements by Halldór Hermannsson. 1937.

XXVII. The Icelandic Physiologus. Facsimile edition with an introduction by Halldór Hermannsson. 1938.

XXVIII. Illuminated Manuscripts of the Jónsbók, by Halldór Hermannsson. 1940.

XXIX. Bibliographical Notes, by Halldór Hermannsson. 1942.

XXX. The Vinland Sagas. Ed. with an introduction, variants and notes, by Halldór Hermannsson. 1944.

XXXI. The Saga of Thorgils and Haflidi. Ed. with an introduction and notes, by Halldór Hermannsson. 1945.

XXXII and XXXIII. History of Icelandic Prose Writers: 1800–1940, by Stefán Einarsson. 1948.

There have also been issued:

CATALOGUE of the Icelandic Collection bequeathed by Willard Fiske. Compiled by Halldór Hermannsson. Ithaca, N. Y. 1914. 4° pp. viii, 755.

——Additions 1913–26. Ithaca, N. Y., 1927. 4° pp. vii, 284.

——Additions 1927–42. 1943. 4° pp. vii, 295.

CATALOGUE of Runic Literature forming a part of the Icelandic Collection bequeathed by Willard Fiske. Compiled by Halldór Hermannsson. Oxford, Oxford University Press. 1917 4° pp. viii, (2), 106, 1 pl.